Asian Management Systems

The interest generated by the post-war "economic miracle" of the East and Southeast Asian countries has so far largely centred on Japanese management systems. This perhaps over-zealous interest on the part of the West in Japanese management styles has led to some deep-rooted misunderstandings of other kinds of Asian management systems.

This is the first volume to look at four major Asian management systems: Japanese, mainland Chinese, Overseas Chinese and Korean, on a comparative basis. All the main aspects of each system are looked at in detail, including cultural and historical influences, evolving operational environments, organizational structures, managerial processes and competitive strategies. Special areas of focus include the creation and management of successful joint ventures in China, a comparative study of trading systems in China and Japan, and a look at negotiating with Chinese and Japanese business partners.

Min Chen shows how, though sharing some common cultural traditions, each system has a unique competitive edge and range of problems. Providing a dynamic blend of theoretical concepts and practical guidelines, as well as questions for discussion and references for further reading, this book is a vital resource for both international business executives and students of international business and management.

Min Chen is Assistant Professor at the American Graduate School of International Management in Arizona.

D1359585

Asian Management Systems

Chinese, Japanese and Korean Styles of Business

Min Chen

INTERNATIONAL THOMSON BUSINESS PRESS
I (T) P An International Thomson Publishing Company

London • Bonn • Boston • Johannesburg • Madrid • Melbourne • Mexico City • New York • Paris
Singapore • Tokyo • Toronto • Albany, NY • Belmont, CA • Cincinnati, OH • Detroit, MI

Asian Management Systems

Copyright ©1995 Min Chen

 A division of International Thomson Publishing Inc.
The ITP logo is a trademark under licence

British Library Cataloguing-in-Publication Data
A catalogue record for this book is available from the British Library

First published by Routledge 1995
Reprinted by Routledge 1995
Reprinted by International Thomson Business Press 1996, 1997, 1998 and 1999

Typeset by Michael Mepham, Frome, Somerset
Printed in Croatia

ISBN 1-86152-500-1

International Thomson Business Press
Berkshire House
168–173 High Holborn
London WC1V 7AA
UK

http://www.itbp.com

Contents

Figures

Tables

Preface

The spectacular rise of the Asia–Pacific economies, led by Japan in the 1950s and followed first by the four Asian tigers in the 1960s, then major ASEAN members in the 1970s, and finally by China and Vietnam in the 1980s and 1990s, has given rise to countless volumes in the West, which have tried to understand and interpret the driving forces of this post-Second World War economic miracle. Much has been attributed to the influence of Confucianism as a major source of East Asian cultural traits, such as strong work ethic, high family values, pragmatism, thriftiness, and heavy government involvement. Another often-mentioned reason was the Cold War system in which the United States, based on strategic considerations, not only provided economic and military support but also opened its enormous market to many of these thriving Asia–Pacific economies.

Nevertheless, these economic miracles would not have been possible without the numerous Asian companies themselves, whose efforts and competitiveness have provided a major stimulus for the continued high rate of economic growth. For a long time, most of the literature on Asian management has largely focused on the Japanese management system, though an increasing number of publications have recently dealt with Overseas Chinese businesses in East and Southeast Asia, and the Korean and mainland Chinese management systems. All four major Asian management systems have been influenced to varying degrees by Confucianism and have developed under very different social and historical environments. I have brought attention to these issues to compare the similarities and differences, so as to better understand the unique competitive advantages and disadvantages of each management system. Since the indigenous Southeast Asian companies have very different cultural values, with strong Indian and Islamic influences, they have not been included in this book.

This book is written for international executives and business school students who have interest in doing business in Asia. It is intended to educate the readers on various aspects of the four major Asian management systems, ranging from their cultural and historical sources, evolving operational environments, the outstanding features of their organizational structures and managerial processes, to their competitive strategies. Special topics also include negotiating with Chinese and Japanese business partners, comparing the trading systems of China and Japan, understanding the Japanese distribution maze, and creating and managing successful joint ventures in China. An understanding of the material in this book will provide the readers with a comprehensive knowledge of the competitive advantages and disadvantages of companies in these four major Asian management systems.

The book is divided into four parts: the first part explains the conceptual framework of the book and introduces readers to major theoretical models as well as describing relevant cultural and traditional influences. The second part concentrates on the two major Chinese management systems: Procapitalist Overseas Chinese management and the rapidly changing management system in mainland China. The third part covers a comparative study of Japanese and Korean management systems, which share many similarities but are also significantly different from each other in many ways. The fourth part offers general guidance for readers wanting to understand how to cope with different management systems. A detailed explanation of the book's general layout can be found in the Introduction.

While written in plain language that suits the needs of practical business professionals and business school graduate students, this book also serves the needs of business academics interested in both teaching and further study of Asian management systems. Brief reference notes are provided throughout the text. Suggestions for further reading are listed at the end of each chapter, as are user-friendly summaries and questions for classroom discussion. All monetary figures are in United States dollars, unless otherwise noted.

Writing any book is a long-term commitment and involves time-consuming effort. The successful completion of a book depends on the support and generosity of many people. This book is certainly not an exception. I am deeply indebted to a number of individuals who helped to bring this book to completion. Dr. David A. Ricks, Vice-President of Academic Affairs at the American Graduate School of International Management (AGSIM), Dr. Llewellyn D. Howell, AGSIM's International Studies Department Chair, Dr. Martin H. Sours and Dr. Glenn Fong, professors of AGSIM International Studies Department, and Dr. John E. Walsh Jr., professor in the School of Business, Washington University in St. Louis. All deserve sincere thanks for encouraging me along the way.

Prof. Chen Qi-jie of the Shanghai University of Finance and Economics deserves earnest thanks for his contribution to Chapter 8. Leon T. Liem, a graduate student at AGSIM, spent considerable time in helping edit the book. His sincere efforts and the time he spent on the project are much appreciated. Also, a debt is owed to Ms Linda H. Liao for her inspiring input and help. Thanks are also due to the students of my International

Competitiveness and Asian Management classes, whose opinions and comments in class provided me with many useful insights into the subject matter.

I also wish to thank my parents and my family for their consistent encouragement and support. Without their understanding this book could not have been completed.

Three chapters in this book have been previously published in slightly different forms. I am grateful to the journals concerned for their permission to use material in Chapter 3 from "Sun Tzu's strategic thinking and contemporary business," *Business Horizons* 37(2) (March/April 1994), pp. 42–48; in Chapter 17 from "Understanding Chinese and Japanese negotiating styles," *The International Executive* 35(2) (March/April 1993), pp. 147–160; and in Chapter 20 from "Unlocking joint venture potential in China," *The International Executive* 36(2) (March/April 1994), pp. 189–202.

I hope that this book will be of some value to international business managers in the West as well as in Asia for better understanding different Asian management styles, competitive strategies and ways of doing business. Such an understanding is crucial for the success of business goals in Asia. Not only do Western business managers need to understand their Asian counterparts, but Asian managers also need to understand each other.

Min Chen,
Thunderbird,
American Graduate School of
International Management,
Glendale, Arizona, USA.

Introduction

This book is a comparative study of Confucian Asian management systems. The reason that the word "Confucian" is applied here is because all the four Asian management systems that the book will cover, i.e. the mainland Chinese, Overseas Chinese, Japanese and South Korean, have been heavily influenced by the Confucian tradition (Oh 1983). The book will examine the influence of Confucianism, ancient strategic thinking and other East Asian traditions upon the development of the four Asian systems of management and business strategies, analyzing their comparative strengths and environments. Special topics include managing joint ventures, cross-cultural negotiations and comparative trade systems. Finally, the book will discuss the general differences among the four major Asian management systems. Also, brief discussions will be made on general differences between the East and West, the most likely areas of convergence, and the examples that can be learned from the East.

The purpose of this introduction is threefold: to define comparative management and explain why comparative management is important, to describe the four Asian management systems and their importance in comparative management studies, and finally to discuss the broad layout of the book that proceeds from a general theoretical framework to a practical guide for coping with East Asian management challenges.

COMPARATIVE MANAGEMENT

Comparative management, broadly defined, analyzes the similarities and differences between various management and business systems from one country or different countries. These comparisons can be made on large versus small organizations, manufacturing versus service industries, profit versus nonprofit organizations, successful versus unsuccessful companies, and one management system versus another. Defined more narrowly, comparative management refers to the comparisons of organizations and general aspects of management from different countries and cultures (Nath 1988: 1). According to Robinson (1978), there are three basic approaches to comparative management. The universalist approach argues that few major differences exist among managers from different social and cultural backgrounds and that management theories and practices can be easily transferred from one culture to another. This approach stresses the overall similarities among cultures rather than differences. The economic cluster approach, however, contends that the economic similarities and differences among nations, or among groups of nations, constitute the most important basis for management tasks. In contrast to the first two, the cultural cluster approach puts an emphasis on how attitudinal and behavioral differences among cultures determine management tasks.

While each of the three approaches may contribute to the understanding of multinational management process from a different angle, the cultural cluster approach seems to have gained increasing interest. The growing activities of multinational corporations have increased the need to understand how an organization can best manage its employees from different cultural backgrounds, how it should deal with business firms from very different cultural and social backgrounds, and how a strategic alliance is properly made and maintained between firms from different cultural and social backgrounds. According to Ronen, "the goal of comparative management is . . . to design the most effective organizational strategy and structure possible and make the most effective use of human resources in different cultures. Organizations must understand how and why cultures take the forms they do because the organization must function in these different cultures. No organization can function effectively without understanding all aspects of its environment" (Ronen 1986: 20).

What, then, are the major differences between comparative management and international business? Simply put, comparative management focuses on studying the similarities and the differences among management systems of different countries while international business is primarily interested in the study of issues and problems that involve the management of multinational corporations. Thus, comparative management is not primarily concerned with the specific issues arising from transnational business activities (Robock and Simmonds 1983: 4–5). For example, the question of political risks in multinational corporations – the protection of intellectual property, trade barriers, and geographical environment – is normally not among the top priorities in comparative management studies. Nevertheless, comparative management and international business are also interrelated and overlapping. Therefore, an international executive can learn a great deal from comparative management studies.

According to Nath (1988: 2–4), there are several major reasons for studying comparative management. To begin with, humankind is living in a more interdependent world and this interrelationship has become increasingly important for doing business today. A large portion of international business is conducted by multinational corporations that maintain operations in various countries with distinct management systems. Therefore, managers of these corporations and those dealing internationally in non-multinational corporations should be aware of these political and economic systems, cultures, and business norms and practices. Even managers of companies solely focused on domestic markets are under increasing pressure to think globally. As many American corporations and industries have learned from losses in the domestic market share to international competitors, foreign competition can challenge an industry or a corporation in its own backyard. Today no industry or company is totally immune from foreign competition; all managers must think and plan in a global context.

Next, the comparative approach is unavoidable. To acquire a better understanding, people assess and measure many things in reference to others. The comparative approach is universally applicable. It is not merely limited to management studies but has been used in such disciplines as politics, economics, sociology, law, education, literature and religion. In fact, almost all disciplines can benefit from a comparative approach. The study of comparative management can expand the knowledge base by widening the range of variables over which a particular management or organizational issue can be understood. Various cultures can be organized along a continuum of variables, on which a certain culture represents only a limited range. A well-selected set of cultures can significantly extend the range.

Last but not least, the study of different management systems can improve the understanding of one's own culture, helping to develop sensitivity toward and an appreciation of diversity in transnational exchanges. This is essential to a successful business encounter with people of other cultures. It also helps an international manager appreciate his or her own culture and environment. People tend to take for granted the role of their own culture and environment in shaping management systems. According to ancient Chinese philosophy, "One cannot know the true face of the *Lu* Mountain simply because one is inside it." In fact, when the study of management is restricted to the United States, the role of culture or environment often fails to receive due attention. Comparative management scholars regard culture and environment as crucial factors in the study of management systems. Perhaps, the best way to understand the strength and weakness of the American management system is through a comparison with other systems.

It is obvious that the study of comparative management is important for international business managers and students. Nevertheless, comparative management is still not a required course in many American business schools, even those focusing on international business. As the increasingly interdependent world requires managers to think and plan in terms of global competition, comparative management will gain in importance. The study of comparative management can help develop the international thinking and skills demanded by the globalization of business.

ASIAN MANAGEMENT SYSTEMS AND THEIR IMPORTANCE

As is already well known, the economies of East Asia and Southeast Asia, including those of Japan, China, Taiwan, South Korea (hereafter referred to as 'Korea'), Hong Kong and the ASEAN countries, have recently been some of the most dynamic in the world. This has resulted not only from their general political and economic policies but also as a benefit from the competitive activities of their business organizations. There are four major management systems in the region: Japanese, mainland Chinese, Overseas Chinese, and Korean. Except for state-owned mainland Chinese organizations, the other three management systems have proved to be very competitive in their own respective ways. The mainland Chinese business organizations are currently undergoing radical changes, with some of them having already emerged in the international business world as powerful competitors.

In the words of Gordon Redding, a professor at the Business School of the University of Hong Kong, "the world now has five major 'cuisines' – three of them Asian – for business and economic success" (Redding 1992: 50–52). The Asian cultures have kept a unique tradition of holding an organization together as a dynamic group, which suits the hierarchy-sensitive and collectivist norms of Asian culture. This tradition is responsible for the division of the capitalist world into two camps – collectivist capitalism and individualist capitalism. While pure forms of these two types of capitalism are rare in the real world, they do have some major ideological differences, which will be discussed in detail in Chapter 1. The two typical forms of successful Western organizations, according to Redding, are the Western multinational and the Western state-influenced firms. The three most successful Asian management systems are the Japanese, Korean and the Overseas Chinese.

The large business groups, the *keiretsu*, are the dominant forces in the Japanese economy, embodying typical features of the Japanese management system and organizations. They grew out of earlier family-dominated *zaibatsu* and are now dominated by professionals. Very large and sophisticated, these groups maintain their uniqueness in global competition. Closely interlocked, self-financed, and extensively networked, they have proved to be fiercely competitive and adopt long-term market-share strategies.

The *chaebols* have led Korea's revival from a war-devastated, agriculture-dominated economy into one of the most dynamic economies of the four tigers. Like the *keiretsu*, they are extremely large and sophisticated. They have maintained close relationships with the Korean government and have been heavily dependent on government finance. Also, like the Japanese, the *chaebols* have expanded very rapidly in the world market and produce major international brands. Despite their pronounced success, these groups are still dominated by founding family members and seem to be even more closely-knit and competitive in spirit than their Japanese counterparts.

The Chinese family business is the kind of organization adopted by the Overseas Chinese in their vigorous entrepreneurial pursuit of wealth. These organizations, commonly dominated by one owner, tend to have simple structures and limited capacities. They thrive in relatively non-complex industries such as property, trading, and simple manufacturing, where they have successfully carved their niche. The Chinese, known for their hard-working ethic, maintain close family ties and through networking dynamics have prospered in the booming economies of Taiwan, Hong Kong, Singapore and other major ASEAN countries. Their competitive edge lies in their ability to forge a sophisticated network and maintain a high degree of flexibility, which allows them to transcend the limits of small size.

All three management systems have benefitted from Confucian influence, though each has developed a unique system based on their respective historical and social development. Although business organizations of mainland China have not been included as one of the most competitive, the rapid economic development and radical economic reform that is taking place in China is reshaping many of its inefficient state-owned enterprises and creating a whole generation of new corporations, which are leading China into the world market. An understanding of the comparative advantages of these Confucian Asian management systems will not only help Western businesses to compete but also contribute to the development and reform of Western management systems. In today's borderless business world, multinational corporations must be able to develop a sophisticated and truly international management system to cope with the challenge of multinational operations.

THE GENERAL LAYOUT OF THE BOOK

Part I gives the *conceptual framework*, introducing readers to the major models of studying comparative management, the major cultural differences between the East and West thinking, and the influences of classical thinking. Chapter 1 introduces general concepts of comparative management and major schools of thought in the study of comparative management. The general trends of comparative management are also covered, which will give readers a better idea of where existing scholars currently stand on comparative management. Major differences in management philosophies between the East and West are discussed in Chapter 2. It helps readers understand why Asians have quite different management systems and philosophies. This is followed by a detailed discussion on traditional East Asian strategic philosophies, which are best embodied in Sun Tzu's *Art of War*, which has been widely regarded as the most important doctrine of East Asian classical thinking and has significant influence on Asian strategists, such as Japan's Miyamoto Musashi, the author of *A Book of Five Rings*. This strategic masterpiece has had considerable influence on many executives from the Confucian Asian management systems. Finally, key values of Confucian ethics and the dynamics of *guanxi* (connection) and the major differences between the Chinese and Japanese in building up their connection networks are analyzed. *Guanxi* is the key to understanding the dynamics of interpersonal relationships among the Chinese. Since personal relationships are very important for business in Asia, a knowledge of *guanxi* and the distinctions between the Chinese and Japanese in building up their connection networks is useful.

Part II concentrates on two major Chinese management systems: the procapitalist Overseas Chinese management and the rapidly changing management system in mainland China. It first defines the Overseas Chinese and traces the historical evolution of the general environment in which these Overseas Chinese have been operating. The thrust is to explain how the overall operational environment of the Overseas Chinese in Southeast Asia has contributed to their unique approaches to management and competitive business strategies. Next, it focuses on the most typical Overseas Chinese business organization, the family enterprise, including its structure and management process. This is followed by discussions on the competitive business strategies of Chinese companies in ASEAN and their comparative advantages and disadvantages. Then, the mainland Chinese business environment, characterized by state ownership and state domination, is reviewed, as it has had the most significant influence on the development of Chinese State Enterprises. This is followed by a detailed analysis of the basic patterns of state enterprise management in mainland China and the reform of these state enterprises since 1979. Finally, a comparative study is conducted to help readers understand the similarities and differences in management between the Overseas Chinese and mainland Chinese as well as their future trends.

Part III covers a comparative study of Japanese and Korean management systems, which share many similarities despite some obvious differences. Chapter 11 draws attention to the fact that close government contact and business relationships have played a significant role in the development of big business and their strategies in both Japan and Korea. The following chapter is a comparative study of large business conglomerates in Japan (*keiretsu*) and Korea (*chaebol*), focusing on comparisons of their business organizational structures. Many of these *chaebols* have developed in the model of Japanese *zaibatsu*, which were the large Japanese conglomerates before the end of the Second World War. A comparative study of the two will bring out their similarities and differences. Core values of Japanese management and competitive strategies of *kaisha* are discussed in Chapters 13 and 14. Discussions include the social environment in which these core values were developed, the advantages and disadvantages of these core management values and the trends of development in the 1990s. Chapter 15 provides a detailed analysis of Korean management values and business strategies. Finally, a comparative study of Japanese and Korean management is discussed.

Part IV offers some guidance for readers wanting to understand how to cope with different management systems. By this point of the book, readers will already have general ideas about various Confucian Asian management systems and their business comparative advantages. Within the framework of the previous chapters, readers should have no difficulty in understanding the technical areas discussed in the final chapter. The final part begins with a discussion on how to negotiate with the Chinese and Japanese in a comparative way, as these two negotiation styles are quite different from each other, even though they share some outstanding similarities, while the Korean style seems to be somewhere in the middle. Next, Chapter 18 provides a comparison of Japanese *sogo shosha* and the large Chinese foreign trade corporations, as *sogo shosha* seem to be a proper model for the large Chinese foreign trade corporations to follow in reforming themselves. Chapter 19 provides an introduction to the Japanese distribution system, which has been widely regarded in the West as a major barrier to Western access to the Japanese market. Finally, Chapter 20 is devoted to understanding how to establish and manage joint ventures in China, because joint ventures have become the most popular form of foreign investment in the country.

At the end of the book, there is a brief summary of overall similarities and differences between the Asian management systems and a general comparison between the Asian and Western management systems. By noting the differences, readers should better understand the comparative advantages and disadvantages of Asian management systems. Other issues, such as a convergence of the Western and Eastern systems and what can be learned from Asian management systems will also be discussed.

The book is intended for international managers as well as business school students, but general readers will also find it of interest to them. There is a continually growing interest among Western managers and business school students in knowing about Asian management systems because they have together created the most dynamic economic growth in the post-Second World War world. In Dan Waters's words, "an economy is only as efficient as the firms of which it is composed, and a company is only as effective as the personnel and business methods it employs" (Waters 1991: xv–xvi). The aim of this book is to convey the message that Western managers and business school students can indeed obtain some useful inspiration and insights by acquainting themselves with these Asian management systems. The book is written in a plain and straightforward style. Selected references and notes are provided for those who are interested in pursuing further studies after reading the book.

QUESTIONS FOR DISCUSSION

1 What is the broad and narrow definition of comparative management?
2 What are the three basic approaches to comparative management?
3 What is the goal of comparative management?
4 What are the major reasons for studying comparative management?
5 How many major Confucian management systems are there in Asia and what is the significance of studying them?

FURTHER READING

Oh, Tai K. *et al.* (1983) "A Comparative Study of the Influence of Confucianism on Japanese, Korean, and Chinese Management Practices," *Proceedings of the Academy of International Business, Asia–Pacific Dimensions of International Business* (December 18–22), Honolulu, Hawaii.

Nath, Raghu (1988) "Comparative Management," in Raghu Nath (ed.), *Comparative Management: A Regional View*, Cambridge, Mass.: Ballinger Publishing Company, pp. 1–21.

Redding, Gordon (1992) "Capitalist Cooking Lessons," *Asian Business* (November): 50–52.

Robinson, R.D. (1978) *International Business Management – A Guide to Decision Making* (2nd edn), Hinsdale, Ill.: Dryden.

Robock, R. and K. Simmonds (1983) *International Business and Multinational Enterprises*, New York: Praeger.

Ronen, Simcha (1986) *Comparative and Multinational Management*, New York: John Wiley & Sons.

Waters, Dan (1991) *21st Century Management: Keeping Ahead of the Japanese and Chinese*, Singapore: Prentice-Hall.

Part I

Conceptual framework

Chapter 1

Major comparative management models

INTRODUCTION

Management and organization scholars have historically looked for universal laws. For a long period, they had either ignored the roles of culture and environment or used them superficially. Comparative management scholars were the first ones to identify the importance of culture and environment in the study of management systems. Comparative management represents a shift away from the traditional focus on a universal organization and management toward seeking patterns of relationships in various settings. Comparative management study did not appear until the 1950s and was not accepted as a distinctive discipline until 1960. Since then, many attempts have been made to develop a conceptual framework for the explanation of managerial similarities and differences across cultures. Although it is still a young discipline, there is already a considerable body of literature with diverse concepts and methodology. Major thrusts in the comparative management literature can be generally classified into four categories: the economic development model, the environmental model, the behavioral model, and the open systems model. This chapter will review these four models and their related development. On this basis, a working model is built for the benefit of following chapters.

FOUR MAJOR MODELS OF COMPARATIVE MANAGEMENT

Economic development model

This model, first developed during the 1950s, is best represented by the work of Harbison and Myers (1959), who traced the initial large-scale projects of industrialization in developed countries and raised the notion that managerial beliefs reflect a country's level of industrial development. This is essentially a macro model, concentrating on the examination of trends in management rather than managerial practices at the micro level. They hypothesize that there is a universal logic behind the process of industrialization of all nations, which develops through four stages: from an agrarian-feudalistic society, to an industrial-democratic system. Harbison and Myers suggest that for each of the four stages of economic development, there is a corresponding management system.

As gaps in the level of industrial development gradually narrow, managerial philosophies and practices are expected to become more similar. All management systems will eventually resemble the participatory and democratic theory Y management. In the final analysis, this model is not very much different from the traditional universalist management school that argues for the eventual applicability of a certain management system to all organizations from different cultures and societies. However, postwar development has witnessed a growing gap between the developed and developing nations. Even if gaps should disappear in the distant future, a commonly accepted management system may still have various versions, as has already been proved in the case of the Japanese management system. Therefore, it should be recognized that culture and environment will have a strong impact on managerial behavior as well as on managerial and organizational effectiveness for at least a significant period. Despite their universalist conclusion, Harbison and Myers did encourage management scholars to engage in detailed studies on selected aspects of a few industrial nations. Their pioneering research justified the need for comparative management and heralded the emergence of the field.

Environmental Model

Farmer and Richman (1965) have also developed a macro model (Figure 1.1) that considers culture as an important variable influencing managerial effectiveness. A number of external constraints, such as legal–political, economic, socio-cultural and educational, are identified as having an impact on the management process. Whereas Harbison and Myer's research concentrates on the economic factors in the environment, Farmer and Richman conceptualize environmental factors in a much broader context. They argue that the traditional universalist studies have been conducted in a "black box," and exclude environmental factors. These studies are valid when the external environment is the same for all companies, but are not adequate in explaining the differences in the environment because the transnational environment varies so extensively.

If a few cultural factors are carefully selected and systematically analyzed, their influences on managerial effectiveness may be identified. Therefore, the model can be relevant also at micro level by improving a business organization's awareness of the cultural impacts on the performance of individual employees and groups. For a multinational corporation, such awareness can help avert unrealistic expectations on culturally different local employees or shape an appropriate strategy to overcome cultural constraints.

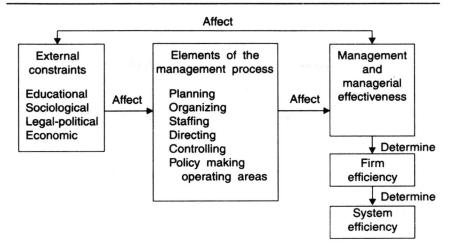

Figure 1.1 Farmer and Richman model
Source: Farmer and Richman, 1965, p. 35.

Although Farmer and Richman's model represents a major step forward in comparative management, it suffers from two major defects. One is that the model fails to consider the impacts of industrialization on several environmental variables, such as political–legal, economic, and technological. It is basically a static model in a dynamic environment. Another problem is its overemphasis on external factors to the complete negligence of internal organizational dynamics. The corporations are viewed as passively adapting to external variables. In spite of these problems, Farmer and Richman's work has provided a useful conceptual framework for understanding the impact of environment on the management process.

The Behavioral Model

Toward the end of the 1960s, the behavioral model began to gain popularity among comparative management scholars who tried to explain behavioral patterns of individuals and groups in organizational contexts. This is basically a micro model. The basic premise to this model is that management practices and effectiveness depend on cultural variables such as attitudes, beliefs, value systems, need hierarchies, etc. Behavioral research has had the tradition of employing empirical methodology. Representatives in this school include S.M. Davis, G.V. Barrett and B.M. Bass.

Unlike the first two macro models, this school espouses operationalized cultural variables and divides them into three different categories (Davis 1971, Barrett and Bass 1970): (1) national character contours, which are related to specific organizational behavioral variables; (2) attitudes and perceptions of managers regarding key management concepts and activities; (3) prevalent beliefs, need hierarchies and value systems in a given society.

Obviously, attitudes, beliefs, value systems, hierarchies, and managerial practices vary in different nations and cultures. Even within the same nation and culture, subcultural groups (such as ethnic groups, dialect groups and occupational groups), have clear differences in the aforementioned aspects. When management practices are transferred from one culture to another these differences should be considered.

The behavioral model, while clearly making up for the shortcomings of the first two models to some extent, has several problems of its own. One major drawback has been that while culture has not been explicitly defined in many studies, the differences found have been attributed to culture. These differences may be caused by other environmental factors such as political and/or economic conditions, or market geographical location and technology. Another major drawback has been that the measurement of organizational effectiveness has been overlooked. Finally, most of the research instruments have been developed in the United States and validated without regard for their impact on different cultures.

Open Systems Model

This school was developed in the 1970s, with the pioneering work of Negandhi and Prasad (1971), who argued that if environmental and cultural factors were the main determinants of management practices, the management practices of two comparable business enterprises in the same culture should be similar to each other. However, reality presents a different scenario. Two American retail chains – Montgomery Ward and Sears-Roebuck – are compared to illustrate that, while both are in the same market and environment, they have applied different managerial practices.

Negandhi and Prasad conclude that the management process is dependent not only on external environmental constraints and culture but also on management philosophy. Management philosophy is defined as management's attitudes toward and beliefs regarding governments, community, consumers, distributors, suppliers, employees, and stockholders. Under the premise that management philosophy is not necessarily a product of a given culture and environment, they have provided a model of open systems, in which managerial philosophy has considerable influence on the management process and effectiveness.

Their model (Figure 1.2) also hypothesizes that environmental factors directly influence not only management practices but also management and organizational effectiveness. Within this context, three kinds of environments – organizational, task, and societal – are identified. The

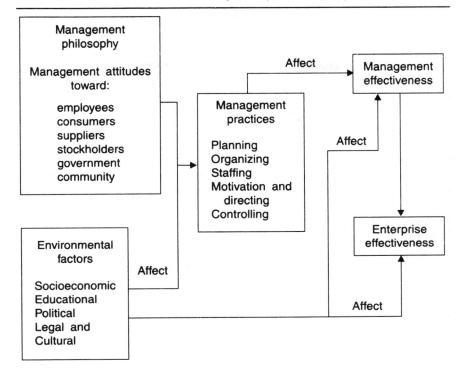

Figure 1.2 Negandhi and Prasad model
Source: Negandhi and Prasad, 1971, p. 23.

organizational environment involves organizational climate, size, human and capital resources and technological variables. This kind of environment is believed to be under the control of managers. Second, environment covers task agents such as governments, communities, consumers, distributors, suppliers, employees, and stockholders. Cross-cultural studies have been conducted to illustrate how this environment influences organizational patterns and effectiveness. The societal environment resembles the macro environment as identified by Farmer and Richman.

Negandhi and Prasad's model seems to be the most comprehensive of the four, but does not go without criticism. Although it includes culture as a variable, the model does not recognize the importance of culture as much as it does managerial philosophy. In Negandhi and Prasad's research (1971), American subsidiaries in Argentina, Brazil, Uruguay, India, and the Philippines, are examined along with local companies. A close relationship is identified between management philosophy and management practice. Managers in the American subsidiaries tend to delegate more power than managers in the locally owned companies. The managerial style and effectiveness of U.S. subsidiaries are not much different from the local companies, which have developed a compatible management philosophy. The research may have truly established the importance of managerial philosophy, but any successful managerial philosophy cannot go against the cultural environment in which a corporation operates. Therefore, the role of culture cannot be ignored. In a sense, the model of Farmer and Richman and that of Negandhi and Prasad complement each other with their relative importance varying from country to country.

A major development related to the open systems model is the contingency model (Lawrence and Lorsch 1969), which describes the nature of the relationship between organization and environment. The basic premise of the contingency model is that the management system should be compatible with the nature of people, the nature of the task, and the nature of the environment. If the tasks are routine and the technology used is established, if the people are basically dependent, and if the environment is stable and certain, then theory X style of management is suitable. However, if the nature of the task is non-routine, the technology is rapidly changing, the environment is unstable and uncertain, and the people are well educated and independent, the proper management philosophy is participatory theory Y management. Once again, the contingency model fails to give adequate attention to the role of culture and environment.

ROLE OF CULTURE IN COMPARATIVE MANAGEMENT

Although scholars of comparative management had long acknowledged the influence of environment, their universalist tendency prevented a systematic application of cultural concepts in explaining management behavior. During the 1960s, a large number of works were published to define the role of culture in comparative management, but the quality and methodology of most of these studies were far from being mature. The concept of culture itself was defined in so many different ways that it was difficult to reach a consensus. Much of the cross-cultural research resembled cross-national studies, which compared not only cultures but also political–legal to socioeconomic, as well as educational to technological dimensions.

More recently, some interesting progress has been made in cross-cultural and comparative management study. Hofstede (1980b: 42–63), for example, has operationalized *culture* into four dimensions: the power distance dimension, the uncertainty avoidance dimension, the individualism dimension, and the masculinity dimension. By applying the concept of these four dimensions, he examines major Western management theories to see if they are universally applicable. He suggests that while the principles of leadership, motivation, and decision-making may be applicable almost everywhere, their success or failure depends heavily on ways in which managers adapt to the local culture and work situation.

Along this line of argument, Adler has compared leadership theories, motivation and decision-making (1991: 146–178). Having examined two kinds of leadership theories, McGregor's "Theory X" on one side, her "Theory Y," Likert's "System 4" management, and Blake and Mouton's "Managerial Grid" on the other, Adler concludes that participatory management models, which are widely encouraged by American theorists and managers, are not appropriate for many cultures. Employees in high power distance cultures (like Japan and China), for example, expect managers to lead and are less comfortable with the delegation of discretionary decisions than those from low power distance cultures such as the United States.

A similar situation is found in motivation theories, including Maslow's Need Hierarchy, McClelland's Three Motives, Herzberg's Two Factor Theory, and Vroom's Expectancy Theory. Adler argues that in countries with high uncertainty avoidance (like Japan and China), security motivates employees more strongly than does self-actualization. She also finds that people in countries with high need for achievement or a high masculinity dimension have a relatively high need to produce and feel more comfortable with risk, and are less concerned with avoiding uncertainty. While appreciating the logic of the expectancy theory, Adler points out that culture makes a difference in terms of the types of rewards that motivate a given group of employees and the amount of control that people believe they have over their environment. While Americans see success as contingent upon their own efforts, Hong Kong Chinese tend to balance their own efforts with an element of "joss" or luck in their business dealings. A promotion in Japan as a reward for hard work may be detrimental to the employee's performance, as the highly cherished harmony between the promoted person and his/her colleagues may be disturbed.

As for decision-making, Adler has made similar distinctions. In each of the five basic steps of decision-making (i.e. problem recognition, information search, construction of alternatives, choice, and implementation) she has identified major cultural differences. Concerning problem recognition, situation-accepting managers tend to accept fate or God's will as a significant variable in managing production, whereas problem-solving managers are more likely to believe in their own efforts. American managers (problem-solvers) may identify a problem long before their East Asian counterparts (problem-accepting people) would choose to recognize it. In terms of information search, sensers (Westerners) mainly use their five senses to gather information and facts about a situation and are more deductive; intuitive people (Asians) more often use ideas from the past and future for their data gathering. As for constructing alternatives, future-orientated cultures (typically Western cultures) tend to create more "new" alternatives, whereas past-oriented cultures (typically Asian cultures) often search for a historical precedent. The questions about who makes the decision, how quick the decision is made, the types of decisions and how the decision is implemented all involve cultural differences.

Kelley and Worthley (1981: 164–173) believe that cross-cultural studies are different from cross-national studies. In order to isolate culture, and measure its role in the management process, they took samples of Japanese, Japanese-American, and Caucasian-American managers from Hawaii. While their research emphasizes the importance of culture in the formation of managerial attitudes, the statistical result also shows the significance of national differences arising out of the differences in legal–political systems. Although the use of the second and third generation Japanese-Americans as samples may be questionable in terms of their cultural distinction from other Americans, their research has lent credence to the significance of clearly defining culture.

Child (1981: 303–356) studies the role of culture in a different way by comparing organizational research across cultures. He finds that one group of well-known researchers consistently draw the conclusion that management systems are growing in similarity, while another group of well-known researchers repeatedly conclude that these systems are maintaining their differences. Child's own conclusion is that macro-level variables such as the structure and technology of the organizations themselves become more and more similar while micro-level variables, i.e. the behavior of people, continue to retain their cultural identity. One implication of his conclusion is that organizations from two cultures may look more similar from the outside, but people within them behave differently.

In spite of these advances in defining and operationalizing culture and its influence on organizational behavior, most of the research in the field of comparative management still suffers from ambiguity with regard to the boundary and role of culture. The argument about the appropriate role of culture in comparative management studies continues into the 1990s. More systematic effort is needed in order to achieve breakthroughs in this field.

THE ISSUE ON MANAGEMENT TRANSFER

Comparative management is not only interested in finding similarities and differences among various management systems, but also in identifying the aspect of managerial philosophies, values, attitudes, and practices that has some universal applicability and can be transferred to other systems. As mentioned earlier, the scholastic balance in the field of comparative management has traditionally leaned toward a universalist view, which argues that efficient management is largely based on universal principles, practices, and techniques that can be transferred to any culture.

With all the progress in cross-cultural and comparative management studies, many scholars still hold on to the universalist view of management in the United States. To some extent this reflects the tendency of American parochialism in the field of management studies. Most of the world's management schools are in the United States, where the majority of management professors and researchers are trained and pursue their research. After reviewing over 11,000 articles published in 24 management journals between 1971 and 1980, Adler (1991: 12) found that about 80 percent were studies of the United States conducted by Americans. Fewer than 5 percent of these articles described the behavior of people in organizations by applying the concept of culture. Fewer than 1 percent focused on the interaction of people from two or more cultures in the workplace. This situation is beginning to change as businesses rapidly transcend national boundaries.

Cross-cultural management transfer involves not only the technical dimension of management implied in general principles, concepts, and theories, but also a behavioral dimension of management, found in the actual performance of managerial functions. While the technical dimension may not be compromised due to impacts from cultural differences, the impact of the behavioral dimension is culturally evident. Therefore, a management transfer is not complete until the knowledge of the transferred management, when applied, succeeds in bringing forth effective organizational behavior compatible with a given cultural and environmental context.

The dynamics of cultural influence on the behavioral dimension are clearly represented by Adler's chart of cycle. As shown in Figure 1.3, individuals express culture through the values they hold about life and the world around them. The values then influence their attitudes about the form of behavior considered most appropriate under given situations. The

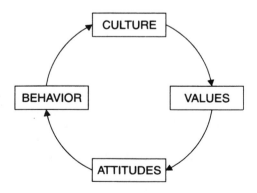

Figure 1.3 Influence of culture on behavior
Source: Adler, 1991, p. 16. Reproduced with the permission of South-Western College Publishing. Copyright 1991 by South-Western College Publishing. All rights reserved.

attitudes in turn provide the basis for daily behavior by generating the norms of behavior to be applied to a specific culture. Finally, the continually changing pattern of behavior affects the society's culture. A new cycle begins.

A random sampling of the research papers presented at the Academy of Management conferences for the mid-1980s and of the papers published in major journals in the field showed that serious methodological problems remained in most of the research. In assessing the literature of comparative management studies, Richard Peterson (1986: 5–10), Chairman of the Academy of Management's International Management Division, has given a long list of the shortcomings, including:

1 Ethnocentrism: this is the tradition of assuming that companies in other countries should adhere to the Western industrial model.
2 Lack of theoretical foundation: theoretical oɪ conceptual models are often not well tested against a broader framework.
3 Confusion on cultural variance: researchers tend to overlook the similarities across nations on the one hand while ignoring variances within a culture (nation) on the other.
4 Dependence on a single research method: there is an inclination to be dependent on one method of acquiring information, i.e. questionnaires; other methods, such as interviews, behavioral scenarios and participant observation, are underutilized.
5 Reliance on the study of one nation: researchers tend to examine the situation in one country without relating their findings to those of other countries.
6 Over-concentration on certain areas: there is a myriad of studies on a few Western countries and Japan, but very limited number of studies elsewhere. This is especially true of the tigers of East Asia, where distinct management styles have been developing.

CONCEPTUAL MODEL FOR COMPARING MANAGEMENT SYSTEMS

The review of various models in the field of comparative management has made it apparent that a model, which combines the advantages of the previous models, and is also manageable, is needed. As discussed earlier, Negandhi and Prasad have developed the most comprehensive model, which combines macro- and micro-oriented models. It seems to be a good base model on which the new model can be built (Negandhi and Prasad, 1971: 23). While their model is still susceptible to various criticisms, their method of concentrating on only a few controllable variables simplifies the research in understanding dynamic relationships between environmental and other related factors and the management process. This research also makes it easier to examine the transferability of the behavioral dimension of management across cultures.

To build a basic and manageable model, the author also takes advantage of Parson's concepts (1956: 62–85), which divide management practices into three distinctive layers: managing technical core activities, managing the social systems in an organization, and managing external relationships. The technical core activities of organizations, including planning and supervising, are influenced by technical variables like market conditions, size, and managerial policy. The social system in an organization refers to interpersonal relationships and is more affected by socio-cultural variables. External relationships are heavily influenced by the political–legal and economic environment. The definition of culture is based on that of Hofstede (1980a: 25), who sees culture as "the collective programming of the mind which distinguishes the members of one human group from another . . . [and] the interactive aggregate of common characteristics that influences a human group's response to its environment."

One major dimension that the author feels necessary to add to Negandhi and Prasad's model is that of competitive strategies. This is a fairly young field, with most of the important developments occurring in the 1970s and 1980s. A major contribution to this field is the notion that strategy is developed to achieve a fit between the organization and its environments. Chandler (1979) finds that structure tends to follow strategy in successful organizations. More recently, this concept has been applied to the study of the entire management system.

Regarding the environmental dimensions of Negandhi and Prasad's model, the author would like to draw special attention to the role of industrial policy. Two management scholars, Reich and Magaziner (1982: 74–81), have pioneered the work in this field by noting the role of industrial policy to Japanese competitive advantages. They call for the development of an explicit industrial policy for the United States. Their argument is that as Japan and other nations have explicitly developed their industrial policies, the United States should follow suit in order to maintain its competitiveness in a borderless world. Another scholar, Ouchi, in his book, entitled *The M-Form Society* (1984), argues that there are elaborate institutional arrangements in Japan which bring together government, industrial organizations, financial institutions, and labor to develop industrial strategy and that such integrated planning at the societal level accounts largely for Japan's success. It is obvious from these studies that industrial policy has tremendous impact on management systems and organizations, especially in the Asian context.

The model shown in Figure 1.4 is the one that the author used in developing the main themes of this book.

It is based on a triangular framework, with three interrelated but distinctive focuses: organization, strategy, and environment. It is the author's

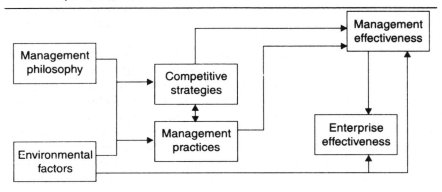

Figure 1.4 Adapted comparative model

belief that these three combined focuses will help us understand (1) the major differences among the Asian management systems, (2) the major trend of development in the Asian management systems, (3) the major differences between the East and West management systems, (4) the transferability of West and East management values and styles, and (5) the manageability of encounters between West and East management systems.

SUMMARY/CONCLUSION

This chapter has reviewed four major models of comparative management: the economic development model, the environment model, the behavioral model, and the open systems model. The open systems model seems to be the most comprehensive, in which the organizational systems are considered a part of the larger societal environment with which they continuously interact. The discussion on the role of culture has not only indicated tremendous potential for further research but also hinted at the problems of ambiguity. The issue of management transfer is explored. Major problems in comparative management are reviewed. Finally, a comprehensive model for understanding the competitive edge of differing management systems is built, which will be used to guide the discussion on various management systems in the following chapters. The new model is built on the basis of the open system model by absorbing some elements of Parson's basic concept on management practices, Chandler's ideas on the importance of strategies, Ouchi's M-form society and Reich and Magaziner's emphasis on the significance of industrial policy toward management systems.

QUESTIONS FOR DISCUSSION

1 What are the four basic models of comparative management and their main points of argument?
2 What do you think is the role of culture in comparative management?
3 What are your thoughts concerning Hofstede's four dimensions?
4 Do you agree with the criticism that comparative management studies have been dominated by American ideas?
5 What do you think of the new model created in this chapter in terms of comparative management studies?

FURTHER READING

Adler, N. (1991) *International Dimensions of Organizational Behavior* (2nd edn.), Boston: PWS-Kent Publishing Co.

Barrett, G.V. and B.M. Bass (1970) "Comparative Surveys of Managerial Attitudes and Behavior,", in J. Boddewyn (ed.), *Comparative Management: Teaching, Researching and Training*, New York: New York University Press, pp. 179–207.

Chandler, Jr., A.D. (1979) *The Visible Hand: The Management Revolution in American Business*, Cambridge, Mass.: Belknap Press.

Child, J. (1981) "Culture, Contingency and Capitalism in the Cross National Study of Organizations," in L.L. Cummings and B.M. Staw (eds), *Research in Organizational Behavior* (Vol. 3), Greenwich, Conn.: JAI Press, pp. 303–356.

Davis, S.M. (1971) *Comparative Management: Cultural and Organizational Perspectives*, Englewood Cliffs, N.J.: Prentice-Hall.

Farmer, R.N. and B.M. Richman (1965) *Comparative Management and Economic Progress*, Homewood, Ill.: Irwin.

Haire, M., E.E. Ghiselli, and L.W. Porter (1966) *Managerial Thinking: An International Study*, New York: Wiley.

Harbison, F. and C. Myers (1959) *Management in the Industrial World: An International Study*, New York: McGraw-Hill.

Hofstede, G. (1980a) *Culture's Consequences: International Differences in Work Related Values*, Beverly Hills: Sage.

—— (1980b) "Motivation, Leadership and Organization: Do American Theories Apply Abroad?," *Organization Dynamics*, 9: 42–63.

Kelley, L. and R. Worthley (1981) "The Role of Culture in Comparative Management: A Cross-Cultural Perspective," *Academy of Management Journal*, 24(1): 164–173.

Lawrence, P.R. and J.W. Lorsch (1969) *Organization and Environment,* Homewood, Ill.: Irwin.

Nath, R. (1986) "Role of Culture in Cross-Cultural and Organizational Research," in S. Mailick (ed.), *Advances in International Comparative Management,* New York: Anchor Press/Doubleday, pp. 392–416.

Negandhi, A.R. and S.B. Prasad (1971) *Comparative Management,* New York: Appleton-Century-Crofts.

Ouchi, W.G. (1984) *The M-Form Society: How American Team Work Can Recapture the Competitive Edge,* Reading, Mass.: Addison-Wesley.

Parsons, T. (1956) "Suggestions for Sociological Approach to the Theory of Organizations," *Administrative Science Quarterly* (June): 62–85.

Peterson, R.B. (1986) "Future Directions in Comparative Management Research: Where We Have Been and Where We Should Be Going," International Management Newsletter (Fall): 5–10.

Reich, R. and I. Magaziner (1982) "Why the U.S. Needs an Industrial Policy," *Harvard Business Review,* 60(1): 74–81.

Chapter 2

Understanding national competitiveness
East–West comparisons

INTRODUCTION

National culture and tradition have had a significant impact on the development and performance of organizational culture. By the early 1980s, Asian businesses had already proved to be fiercely competitive with their Western counterparts. By late 1980, Japan controlled 40 percent of the world's financial assets and became the largest creditor with a net foreign investment of $248 billion. Moreover, the United States sank to the status of the world's largest debtor, and the European countries were under similar competitive pressures from Asia (McCord 1991: 4). The Asian model of economic development is represented by export expansion, governmental involvement, high-saving rates, free-marketing, equal income distribution, etc., and continues to attract increasing attention from all over the world.

Many scholars point out that the economic progress of East Asian nations has benefitted from the Confucian ethic. Some of these scholars have even envisioned "the post-Confucian Challenge to the West," by emphasizing the increasing importance of East Asian culture and industrial power (Macfarquer 1980: 7). These scholars suggest that Confucian ethics have a number of positive influences, including the leadership of government, consensus formation, an emphasis on education, the work ethic, the East Asian entrepreneurial spirit, and the East Asian management style. There are mainly two schools in the West studying the relationship between national cultures and traditions on the one hand, and national competitiveness on the other. One school is focused on the study of the relationship between religion and the economic behavioral pattern and the other on the role of ideology in national competitiveness.

MAX WEBER'S STUDY OF THE PROTESTANT ETHIC AND THE RISE OF CAPITALISM

Weberian thesis

Max Weber (Gerth 1968 and Andreski 1983) is among the earliest scholars who focused on studying the relationship between religion and economic behavioral patterns. His thesis suggested a connection between the rise of capitalism in the West and the Protestant ethic. He argued that if one examines a person closely, one will find that a connection exists between the person's religious beliefs and his behavior in the economic domain. This does not mean that this person will consciously apply his religious beliefs or values to his economic activities. Instead, he tends to unconsciously translate values from his religious beliefs into variables that inspire his economic behavior. It does not mean that his mind is compartmentalized into separate religious and economic sectors with one clearly having more influence than the other. However, the religious values that a person strongly believes in may naturally spread into other aspects of his life.

Another German philosopher and sociologist, Jurgen Habermas (Tu 1984: 67–69), made a major contribution in developing the Weberian thesis. Habermas proposed two conceptual processes in defining what one holds as a central value with regard to the world. The first, theocentric, affirms God and the unity of man with God, while the other, the cosmocentric, emphasizes the unity of man with the universe (see Tables 2.1, 2.2, 2.3). From the Weberian point of view, most religious traditions reject the world. Some of these traditions, such as the Judeo-Christian, are theocentric. Others, such as Buddhism and Hinduism, are cosmocentric. Although he did not study any world-affirming theocentric tradition, Weber did explore a fourth tradition, world-affirming cosmocentrism, i.e. the Confucian tradition. According to Weber's analysis, Confucianism affirms the real world and the unity of man with the universe; it is not orientated toward a transcendent extrinsic view of the world.

Weber held that the Protestant ethic cultivates a specific type of personality that relinquishes all intermediaries between God and himself. A

Table 2.1 Contents of religious world view

| | Conceptual strategies: | |
Evaluation of the world	Theocentric	Cosmocentric
World abnegation	Judaism Christianity	Hinduism Buddhism
World affirmation	–	Confucianism Greek philosophy

Table 2.2 World attitudes

	Methods for pursuit of highest good	
Evaluation of the world	*Active: asceticism/ vita activa*	*Passive: mysticism/ vita contemplativa*
World abnegation	Mastery of the world	Flight from the world
World affirmation	Adaptation to the world	Theoretical grasp of the world

Table 2.3 Rationalization potential

	Degree of rationalization:		
Dimension of rationalization	*Higher (Occident)*	*Lower (Orient)*	
Ethical	Mastery of the world: e.g. Christianity	Flight from the world: e.g. Hinduism	Redemptory religions
Cognitive	Theoretical grasp of the world: e.g. Greek philosophy	Adaptation to the world: e.g. Confucianism	Cosmological/ metaphysical world views

Source: Tu 1984, pp. 67–68.

Protestant relates from the secret inner center of his heart directly to God, which separates him from his fellow people. This relationship promotes a sense of dignity of the individual, thus bringing forth an individualism that is commensurate with the rational organization of labor. Therefore, a Protestant is someone who believes in his individual efforts and tries to master or transform his environment in the way he deems right, while nourishing a strong work ethic. For Weber, if one wants to understand the driving force of capitalist development in Europe and North America, one must understand the Protestant ethic. He compared the Protestant ethic to "a true prophecy" which "creates and systematically orients conduct toward one internal measure or value. In the face of this, the world is viewed as a material to be fashioned ethically according to the norm." Rockefeller and Carnegie were typical examples of economic Protestants.

With this characterization of the Protestant ethic in mind, Weber then turned his attention to the Confucian ethic. In contrast to the transformative thinking inherent in the Protestant ethic, Weber found that the Confucian ethic tended to exhort people to accept or adjust to their environment. All that the Confucian ethic teaches is how a man should relate to society in a harmonious way. Therefore, he is developed to be accommodating to his environment. He should be able to follow a whole set of social formalities. He is least actualized for material success, since the Confucian ethic describes a good gentleman as someone devoted to virtue and a petty man as someone devoted to profits. He can be a bureaucrat, poet, amateur painter, and scholar at the same time, but he is not an aggressive and competitive entrepreneur.

Weber's study had a far-reaching influence. By the 1960s, many scholars in the United States still used his concept to study the relationship between Confucian ethics and modernization. Most of them, with only a few exceptions, were convinced that the Confucian ethic was fundamentally at odds with modernization for a number of reasons. To begin with, the Confucian ethic does not advocate individualism, which is the single major driving force for the restructuring of the environment inherent in the Protestant ethic. Confucian gentlemen are too group-orientated and too dependent on guidance. Moreover, the Confucian scholar attaches too much importance to the cultivation of a well-rounded personality for the best adaptation to his environment, instead of an aggressive personality greatly interested in and capable of mastering the world and conquering nature. A well-adjusted person may be good at cultivating a harmonious relationship with people around him, but is not likely to become a competitive businessman. Last, it is argued that Confucian gentlemen are too focused on wisdom according to its traditional definition. This is the type of knowledge transferred from one generation to the other through experiential comprehension, rather than through an accumulation of knowledge.

New approaches

The basis for the Weberian thesis began to shake as East Asian nations, especially Japan, began to emerge in the 1970s. The same set of values blamed for the lack of capitalist development in East Asia began to be used to explain why a particular kind of entrepreneurial spirit prevalent in East Asia had been so successful in developing a competitive edge against the West. For Professor Tu Wei-ming (1984: 80–88) of Harvard University, the spirit of capitalism that Weber identified with the characteristics of individualism, mastery over the world, *laissez-faire* economy and market mechanism, and the quest for specialized knowledge all represent a type of capitalism. This one type has proved useful in the formation of capital in the West. Other styles may also exist and can be very dynamic, as has been shown by East Asian success.

He suggests a comparative approach in examining how these different types are related. The Protestant ethic views the individual as an isolated entity and as a force reshaping society, while the Confucian ethic regards the self as the center of relationships, thereby leading to a new kind of entrepreneurial spirit and managerial style. The self is dignified in a network of human relationships. This forms a sharp contrast to the notion of the individual as an isolated entity who should sever all roots and ties in order to promote independence. The self is a relationship center, realizing its dignity by taking advantage of human interaction.

The difference between the Protestant and Confucian ethics also lies in their perception of rights and obligations. The Protestant ethic is highly rights-conscious and is keenly aware of one's rights within a given legal framework, knowing full-well where one's self-interests lie should a defense be necessary. If he cannot recognize his own self-interests, how can he be considered a rational being? The Confucian ethic has a strong sense of duty-consciousness. A Confucian gentleman should first and foremost know his social responsibilities and duties. He should be a group man, willing to cooperate with people surrounding him. He is not encouraged to ask "What are my rights?" As an integral element to the community, he should refrain from openly displaying his egotistical drive because such behavior will bring disdain and criticism from others in the community.

Tu examines social manifestations of these two kinds of consciousness, one of which is social ritual. Western culture is basically a low ritual context while the Asian is a high ritual context. In a low ritual society, normative ritual behavior is relatively underdeveloped. What is viewed as correct social behavior tends to be ambiguous on many occasions. Although this vagueness is expected to generate a high level of tolerance, the lack of standardized behavior also causes a dilemma in that one is rarely completely certain of the behavioral boundaries. Each new interaction entails a certain degree of new rituals and certain new patterns of behavior. On the one hand, this low ritual environment is relaxed and comfortable and relatively tolerant of diverse behavioral patterns. On the other hand, it is difficult for people living in such an environment to cultivate lasting and solid relationships, especially when the society becomes increasingly mobile.

In a high ritual environment, much of the human interaction follows a pattern accepted by the society. The members of society, having been brought up under this pattern since birth, do not necessarily realize how heavily their behavior follows a pattern. But, when a foreigner is present, the pattern becomes distinctive. It is difficult for a foreigner to assimilate into the society because as soon as he walks into the environment, his clothing, his way of walking, and his gestures all show that he is unfamiliar with the accepted codes. Learning how to behave properly and how to interact with the native members can be time-consuming. However, once he knows the rituals he becomes a member of the society and no longer feels uneasy. Both high or low ritual environments have positive and negative sides, depending on how these are viewed; they are also closely associated with the two types of ethics discussed earlier.

Another social manifestation related to the nature of the community examined by Tu is the adversary system vs. the fiduciary community. The United States exemplifies the adversary system, while Japan represents the fiduciary community. The adversary system, designed to guarantee and protect the rights of the individual, recognizes and supports self-interest and the competitiveness of individuals. Since the rule of law is assigned high moral value, the adversary system is highly legalistic. Therefore, human interaction tends to be modeled after the adjudication system and the bargaining of conflicting interests. The important role that lawyers play in American society can be understood from this perspective. On the contrary, a fiduciary community emphasizes a commitment to shareable values in society and a basic trust, as the word "fiduciary" suggests. A fiduciary society is often developed on the basis of single ethnic experience and sharing particular ritual forms as well as a long history of socialization. Economic systems also reflect some of these contrasts. In the adversary system, *laissez-faire* and free market competition are highly respected; under a fiduciary system, the leadership and intervention of the government is essential.

In brief, the Confucian ethic cultivates a different kind of capitalism emphasizing the self as a center of relationships, the sense of personal discipline, personal cultivation, and as a consensus formation and co-operation. A high priority is placed on education and rituals; also, the fiduciary concept and governmental leadership are highly valued. The managerial ethos comprises a ritual of learning a set of patterns for doing things and packaged know-how. In the Confucian ethic there is also a transformative potential. For Tu, when an Asian begins to shift his focus from traditional Confucian learning to the maximization of profit he can unleash tremendous energy. He will not only tap into his own inner energy but also will try to collectively mobilize his closest relatives and trusted friends. This collective strength is the comparative advantage of an East Asian society in competing with the West. However, he fails to explain why Confucian ethic, long identified as a conservative force preventing scientific and business development throughout most of Chinese history, became a probusiness ethic in the 1970s.

IDEOLOGY AND NATIONAL COMPETITIVENESS

George C. Lodge and Ezra F. Vogel (1987) studied the role of ideology in national competitiveness. To provide a framework for understanding this role they raised this hypothesis: each nation has an ideology, perhaps several. An ideology is a set of beliefs and assumptions about values that a nation holds to justify and legitimize the purposes and actions of its institutions. A nation is successful when its ideology is both coherent and adaptable, allowing it to define and reach its goals, and when there is a minimum gap between the prevailing ideology and the actual practice of a country's institutions.

The concept of ideology and its components

Ideology is defined by Lodge and Vogel (1987: 2–3) as the collection of ideas that a community uses to make "values" explicit in some "relevant context." The term "values" in this definition means universal, timeless, and noncontroversial notions that all communities in the world have revered, such as justice, survival, economy, self-respect, and self-fulfillment. The phrase "relevant context" refers to the assemblage of events, facts, phenomena, insights, and institutions that influence the community from within and from without. Ideology links the two together, endowing values with institutional vitality.

"Economy," for example, is a value in which everyone desires more benefits than costs, but what constitutes a benefit and what constitutes a cost vary with respect to the related contextual evolution. Although the value "economy" remains, ideology changes. Lodge and Vogel used the case of the push toward an ecologically sound environment. There was an increasing pressure for clean air and water. At first, business resisted the growing costs incurred by governmental environmental regulations, arguing that by its traditional ideology the marketplace was the appropriate mechanism for fixing costs. With the passage of time, the ecological costs of pollution became increasingly obvious to the community, and businesses realized the need to accept the shift in their traditional ideology.

A great variety of contextual factors mold ideology and are affected by it. These factors are both internal and external to the community. Internal factors include economic performance (growth, recession, productivity, income distribution, levels of income, employment rates, and inflation), religions (Confucianism, Buddhism, Christianity), geography and demography, and political parties. External factors include wars, foreign occupation, colonialism, missionaries, resource dependencies, immigration, and multinational corporations.

According to Lodge and Vogel, the context not only includes physical and economic elements, but also accepts notions about the nature of matter, spirit, and feeling. While this domain was once the territory of priests and poets, scientists have taken over the bulk of it over the course of the last three hundred years. One dilemma is that scientific discovery has continually modified what humankind originally interpreted to be irrefutable laws of nature. Sir Isaac Newton discovered that physical reality could be understood in terms of particles. Albert Einstein later concluded that only by understanding the relationship among particles in time and space could one fully explain reality. Now ecologists, microbiologists, geneticists, and other scientists are making new discoveries that suggest reality is still very different from what humankind has come to accept. As one group of scientists continues to delve into the dark tunnels of specialization, another group is increasingly interested in studying reality based on the concept of whole entities rather than separate pieces. These changing perceptions are bringing forth technological and institutional changes that have broad implications for prevailing ideologies.

The relationship between ideology and practice normally adheres to a fairly standard pattern for a period of time, during which institutional practice coincides with the prevailing ideology for some time. Afterwards, developments in the real world may induce or force the institutions to change their practices accordingly. At that point, practice begins to deviate from ideology. As time passes, institutional practice becomes so different from what ideology preached that old notions are only talked about and no longer practiced. Ideological schizophrenia takes place: the new practice may generate a new ideology for its own justification, but loyalty to the old hampers its acceptance. A legitimacy gap develops between institutional practice and ideology. As it widens, leaders of a given community are under increasing pressure in two directions: one group of people tries to pull the institutions back into line with the traditional ideology, while another group will push for a new ideology to justify the new practice.

Ideology is very important to managers as it justifies their role and power. When they function in accordance with a prevailing ideology they are entitled to their authority. But as the environment changes, managers are often compelled to adjust accordingly, thereby deviating from the old ideology and, as a result, they lose their legitimacy in the eyes of those who cling to it. They are under growing pressure to either go back to the old ideology or establish a new one to justify their practices. Other managers may simply resist the pressure to change under the weight of the old ideology and, thereby, become increasingly inefficient. Their authority will be undermined because their old pattern can no longer suit the needs of the new context.

Lodge and Vogel (1987: 95) identified five components to ideology: the first is the relationship between humankind and society, the individual and the group, and the means of self-respect and fulfillment; the second is the institutional guarantees of those relationships (ex. property rights); the third is the means of controlling the production of goods and services; the fourth is the role of the state; and the fifth is the prevailing perception of reality and nature, such as the role of science and education.

They classified existing ideologies into various combinations of two ideal types, "individualism" and "communitarianism." Individualism implies an atomistic notion of society, in which the individual is the ultimate source of value. The interests of the community are elucidated and satisfied via self-interested competition among many, especially small, entrepreneurs. In contrast, communitarianism holds a more organic view that the community is more than just the total of the individuals living in it and requires a definition of its own needs and priorities. In the purest form, these two types can be regarded as end points on an ideological continuum between which various mixtures are formed. By analyzing advantages and disadvantages of these two types, Lodge and Vogel tried to bring out choices available to managers of different national systems.

Individualism

According to Lodge and Vogel (1987: 10–14), there are five basic elements of individualism:

1 Individualism. It is the atomistic conception that regards the community as merely the total of its individuals. Fulfillment depends on the lonely struggle of an individual within which only the fittest survive. Those who can't survive are naturally deemed unfit. Closely associated with individualism is the idea of *equal opportunity*, and the notion of the *contract*, which are used to bind individuals together as employers and employees and as buyers and sellers. In the political arena, an interest group develops pluralism to determine the priorities and the direction of society.
2 Property rights. The rights of the individual are of the utmost importance. The best guarantee of these rights is the protection of property rights. In other words, the individual should be assured of freedom from the ravenous powers of the state.
3 Competition to meet consumer need. Adam Smith most vigorously forwarded the notion that capitalism will thrive if individual entrepreneurs can compete to satisfy individual consumer needs in an open market. The concept of free market competition is reflected in traditional U.S. antitrust law and practice. According to this notion, a good society arises automatically from marketplace competition; the more heated the competition, the better the society.
4 Limited state. The least government is considered the best government. Advocates of individualism are not only concerned about the size of government but also about its role; they resist any attempt to build an omnipotent government. American governmental institutions, for instance, are kept separate and held in constant check and balance despite the painstaking efforts required. The government should get out of the way and allow individuals to be free. According to the typical notion of individualism, a strong government is inherently illegitimate, while a legitimate government should be weak.
5 Scientific specialization. This notion corresponds to the general notion of individualism, placing parts in front of the whole. According to the notion, if the parts are taken care of by specialists, the whole will take care of itself. Subsequently, the thrusts of scientific research should be divided into a number of "disciplines," separated from one another by concepts, language, and modes of abstraction. To pursue these

disciplines, scholars at universities and research institutions are expected to be specialized in a narrow field, concentrating on specific topics
while disregarding any connection between their separate fields.

Looking back at the development of human history, Lodge and Vogel
found that this individualist ideology represented a fundamental but also
dignified deviation from the communitarian norm. It facilitated radical
deviations from tradition, contributed to the industrial revolution and
rapid development in 19th century Europe and North America. In the 20th
century, however, this individualist concept has been consistently challenged by various developments, such as economic depressions, wars, new
political and economic systems, increased population growth and density,
the polarization of the society, as well as ecological deterioration.

The practices of small enterprises, for example, may remain consistent
with the terms of individualist ideology, but the managers of large corporations in the West are compelled to depart from the norm. According to the
notion of individualism, many Western governmental institutions and
large corporations undoubtedly lack legitimacy and authority. The gap
between the dominant ideology and institutional behavior has caused
many organizational problems in the West. In spite of growing pressure to
moderate individualism, the five components of the individualist ideology
continue to sustain a great vitality throughout the West. More important,
what Lodge and Vogel did not emphasize was the growing influence of
individualism in other parts of the world, including traditionally communitarian East Asia.

Communitarianism

Lodge and Vogel also divided communitarianism into five elements (1987:
14–23):

1 Communitarianism. The community is more than the total of the individuals in it and is not atomistic. The community as a whole has
   identifiable needs that go beyond the needs of its individual members.
   Individual fulfillment depends on an identity with a community, where
   the individual is involved as a member in an organic social process. If
   the community – country, enterprise, etc. – is well organized, its members will be closely related to it and be able to use their abilities
   thoroughly. If the community is poorly organized, people will feel
   frustrated and alienated. There are two factors: The first is *equality of
   result or hierarchy*. Government guarantees and protects those being left
   behind. Self-respect and individual fulfillment are derived from accepting one's place in a social structure, which may be determined in a
   variety of ways. Places within social structures may be defined by God,
   by the king, or by a rigorous examination system, as in Japan, Confucian

China and Korea. The second is *consensus*, which is used instead of the contract to regulate the relationships between individuals. Social consensus may be imposed autocratically by authority or through democratic discussions. The decision-making process in many Japanese firms, characterized as *ringi seido*, is a typical example.

2 High duty-consciousness. In contrast to the tendency in an individualist society to overlook the importance of duties by overemphasizing the sacredness of rights, duties-conscious societies tend to place more importance on social duties than on individual rights. The logic at work is that if a community wants to guarantee rights it must expect duties to go along with these rights. Once the goals of a community are established, it is the duty of each of its members to strive hard for those goals. Very often, the interests of a community take priority over individual interests. The extreme form of Western individualism has been recently identified as a major source of its competitive deterioration, while communitarian values are seen as a major strength contributing to Asian competitiveness.

3 Community need. The needs of the community for safety, energy, clean air and water, competitive exports, jobs, etc., are becoming more important than the need to satisfy individual consumers' wants. As a result, the mechanisms of determining community need should be appropriately established. Priorities should be identified, as the community cannot possibly meet all its needs at once. Business activities should be harmonized with the community needs in the following four ways: prescribed marketplace competition, governmental regulations of business, partnership between government and business, and the corporate charter. The communitarians may also encourage the marketplace to be a means of guiding and pushing business activities toward the fulfillment of community needs, though its needs should not solely be determined by the whims of the marketplace.

4 Powerful state. The state in a communitarian society not only plays the role of defining community needs but is also responsible for their fulfillment. Naturally, the state is expected to plan and coordinate economic activities. The state should be capable of making the difficult tradeoffs between various interests and needs on the basis of satisfying the needs of the community. There is a wide range of forms of the state under the conception of communitarianism. In some countries, government may be democratic and benevolent, while in others it is autocratic and ruthless. Some are more centralized while others can be federalist. The Asian communitarian states seem to be more probusiness than the non-interventionist Western states. As their conception of the purpose of business is closely linked to an identified community need, these Asian states can concentrate their limited resources on the most important industries and ask their people to make sacrifices in order to compensate

for temporary economic downturns, or to catch up with more advanced nations in the shortest possible time.

5 Holism and interdependence. The narrowly defined scientific specialization is replaced by the awareness of the interrelatedness of different things. Earth, ocean, ecology, population growth, economic development, wars, natural disasters, etc. – all these are interrelated. Harmony between human development and the demands of nature has become a fundamental requirement for survival. An organic whole approach is designed to cope with the complicated phenomena of the real world. To solve the Third World debt crisis, for example, requires an understanding of the problems of the world trade system, under which debtor nations are unable to generate sufficient capital to pay their debts.

Related research

In a similar vein, Lester Thurow (1992), Dean of MIT's Sloan School of management, conducted a detailed research on the relationship between ideology and global competition. For Thurow, Anglo-Saxon firms are profit maximizers (individualist); Japanese and German business firms (communitarian) focus on "strategic conquest." Americans believe in "consumer economics" while the Japanese adhere to "producer economics." The Americans doggedly adhere to the principle of a free "market" economy, whereas the Germans and the Japanese practice the "social market" economy. These major differences have serious consequences for business competitiveness. Communitarian ideology allows companies to form powerful alliances, like the Japanese *keiretsu*, generating closer government–business relationships, and contributing to a higher degree of mutual commitment between employees and employers.

He traced the differences back into the early development of capitalism. In the 19th-century formative years of British capitalism, Great Britain was the originator of the Industrial Revolution and the most powerful nation. The same logic was found in American development. Both the Germans and the Japanese were under great pressure to catch up with the most advanced powers. Therefore, their governments felt pressed for economic development and got heavily involved. Under such circumstances, government and industry had to work together in the design of national development strategies for survival. Naturally, the line between public and private sectors became blurred and business firms tended to be organized along military lines. The success story of the German and Japanese economies has shown that communitarianism seems to generate a higher level of competitiveness. In the end, he used a metaphor to illustrate his point. American football, with its frequent time outs, unlimited substitutions, and lots of huddles, is a much slower game in comparison with the more regulated standard football (soccer), in which both cooperative and competitive elements are emphasized.

SUMMARY/CONCLUSION

This chapter introduced two major schools of study in the West concerning the relationship of traditional culture on the one hand and national competitiveness on the other. In the first school there are basically two different ideas: the first is introduced by Max Weber who argues that Confucianism is responsible for the lack of development in Asia, because Confucianism did not provide the incentives that Protestantism provided to produce dynamic entrepreneurs. The other group, contrary to his ideas, argues that Confucianism can make people dynamic entrepreneurs but in a different way. Their argument is based on the great success experienced by the Asian economies following the end of the Second World War. The second school is represented by Professors Lodge and Vogel who emphasize the role of ideology in national competitiveness. They divide ideologies into two categories, individualism and communitarianism. Having analyzed the comparative advantages of these two ideologies, they conclude that communitarianism in today's world is more dynamic than individualism in promoting national competitiveness.

As we have seen, the two schools represent very different approaches and focuses in studying the impact of Confucianism on the development of East Asia. The former treats Confucianism as a sort of religion and compares it with Protestantism. The latter, however, links Confucianism closely with Oriental ideology and studies the impact of different ideologies on the development of human societies. In spite of these differences, the two schools do share some commonalities: both of them recognize that the major difference between the West and the East lies in their different emphases on communitarianism and individualism, they support communitarianism and criticize individualism, and they agree that the West has to introduce more elements of communitarianism. Neither one, however, has addressed the emerging trend in the East in which individualism has been changing many of the traditional communitarian values. Also, they have not explained how Confucianism, a conservative and largely anti-mercantilist ideology that has been blamed by many for the lack of capitalist development in Asia (Fairbank *et al.* 1989: 436), has transformed itself into a probusiness ideology. In addition, religion and ideology constitute only one aspect of competitiveness. Many other factors should also be considered. In spite of these problems, the two schools do provide a useful conceptual framework in which competitive edges of management and organizations can be examined and understood.

QUESTIONS FOR DISCUSSION

1 What is the main argument of Weber on Protestantism versus Confucianism in the development of capitalism?
2 What are the comparative advantages of Confucianism according to Tu?
3 What is the concept "ideology" and what are the five basic elements of ideology?
4 Can you identify five basic elements of individualism and communitarianism?
5 What do you personally think is the major contribution of oriental ideology to the economic miracle of East Asia?

FURTHER READING

Andreski, Stanislav (ed.) (1983) *Max Weber on Capitalism, Bureaucracy, and Religion*, London: Allen & Unwin.
Collins, Randall (1986) *Weberian Sociological Theory*, Cambridge: Cambridge University Press.
Dallmayr, Fred R. and Thomas A. McCarthy (eds) (1977) *Understanding and Social Inquiry*, South Bend, Ind.: University of Notre Dame Press.
Fairbank, John K., *et al.* (1989) *East Asia: Tradition and Transformation* (revised edn), Boston: Houghton Mifflin.
Gerth, Hans H. (trans. and ed.) (1968) *Max Weber on The Religion of China*, New York: The Free Press.
Lodge, George C. and Ezra F. Vogel (1987) *Ideology and National Competitiveness*, Boston: Harvard Business School Press.
McCord, William (1991) *The Dawn of the Pacific Century: Implications for Three Worlds of Development*, New Brunswick, N.J.: Transaction Publishers.
Macfarquer, Roderick (1980) "The Post-Confucian Threat to the West," *The Economist* (8 February): 7.
Thurow, Lester (1992) *Head to Head: Coming Economic Battle Among Japan, Europe and America*, New York: Morrow.
Tu, Wei-ming (1984) *Confucian Ethics Today – The Singapore Challenge*, Singapore: Federal Publications.

Chapter 3

Sun Tzu's strategic thinking and contemporary business

INTRODUCTION

The Chinese expression, "*Shang Chang Ru Zhan Chang*," is translated to mean, "The marketplace is a battlefield." This is how Asian people view success or failure in the business world. From the Asian perspective, the success or failure of a family business directly influences the survival and well-being of the family. The success or failure of a nation's economy affects the survival and well-being of a nation. Therefore, many of them truly treat business competition as life-and-death warfare. Many Western business people, for example, have observed that the Japanese conduct business as if they were waging a war, using the term "waging business" to describe the intensity of Japanese competitive strategies. Since the marketplace, in the eyes of Asians, is a battlefield, military strategy is held to be very useful in guiding business activities. Many Asian business leaders have attached great importance to the classical Chinese military strategies. Many of the principles behind these strategies are even commonly applied to daily-life settings.

MILITARY STRATEGIES AND BUSINESS COMPETITIONS

In Chinese, the word military strategy consists of two parts: *Bing* (meaning "soldier") and *Fa* (meaning "doctrine"), which together can also be translated to mean "the art of war." The golden era in the development of classical Chinese military strategy was the few hundred years between the beginning of the Spring–Autumn period and the end of the Warring States period in Chinese history (772–221 BC). Many of the classic strategies were written during this period, as this was a time of constant warfare and also of the famous "hundred flowers blooming" and "hundred schools debating." Many of the greatest Chinese philosophers, such as Confucius, Mencius, Lao Tzu, Chuang Tzu, and Han Fei Tzu lived during this period. Their philosophic thinking left an indelible imprint on classical Chinese military strategy.

The Sun Tzu Bing-Fa, allegedly written by the master Sun Tzu in the fourth century BC, is the most complete and reputable book of military strategy that has survived to date. It is still difficult to determine the biography of the author, who was supposedly a subject of Kingdom Qi and a contemporary of Confucius. At about 512 BC, he traveled to Kingdom Wu and was appointed general. In the ensuing thirty years, he won numerous wars and eventually helped Wu achieve a sort of hegemony by replacing the traditional hegemon, Kingdom Jin. It was at this point that he came to be regarded as a genius of military strategy (Griffith 1971: 1–12).

Sun Tzu's *The Art of War* has been regarded as the most influential classical strategic thinking in East Asia. Together with Confucianism and other classical Chinese thinking, Sun Tzu's strategic thinking was introduced to Korea and Japan and had significant influence on their native strategists, such as Japan's Miyamoto Musashi. Throughout history, it was a required textbook for the military academies in the three countries. In the era of post-Second World War economic development, the Japanese have systematically studied and applied Sun Tzu's strategic thinking to their management and business strategy-making. Sun Tzu's book is often used in the training seminars of Japanese companies (Li Shi-zun *et al.* 1986: 17–18).

Like other philosophical and strategic texts, Sun Tzu's strategies were heavily influenced by Taoist thinking, which emphasizes the interrelatedness and relativity of everything in the world (Lao Tzu 1990). As one quotation of Taoist thought goes,

The Way (tao) gives birth to the one.
One gives birth to two.
Two gives birth to three.
And three gives birth to the myriad things.
The myriad things bear *yin* and embrace *yang*.
By combining these forces, harmony is created.

Tao not only deals with the truth of Oneness, but also the propensity for change of the Oneness. All things in the world originate at one source; they are different but also interrelated. They change constantly in accordance with the laws of nature. There is essentially no difference between goodness and evil, between ease and difficulty, between high and low, and between long and short. Contrasting motivating factors influencing human behavior, such as love versus hatred, arise from the same place, just like two sides of the same coin. One can turn love into hatred and hatred into love, as they are not essentially different and depend on the circumstances. The same logic is applied to courage versus fear, generosity versus miserliness, as well as extrovert versus introvert, etc. (Chu 1991: 14).

The famous story of "Top Horse, Middle Horse, and Weak Horse" in the Warring States Period (476–221 BC) exemplifies the advantages of the Taoist dialectic. Sun Bin was a master strategist, who served General Tian of the Kingdom Qi. General Tian had raced horses with the princes of Qi as a hobby and often wagered large sums of money. One day, General Tian came up to Sun for advice on an upcoming horse race, which seemed to be at a draw. As the usual practice went, the contest consisted of three races. The traditional strategy for victory was to pit the best, middle, and worst horses against similar horses of one's rival. Sun Bin advised General Tian to race his worst horse against his rival's best horse, to pit his best horse against his rival's middle horse, and finally to use his middle horse to compete against his rival's worst horse. General Tian followed Sun's advice and after one loss and two wins, was declared the final winner of the contest. As a good strategist, Sun Bin saw the larger picture and understood that the goal was to win the contest, not each race.

The story clearly illustrates the Taoist concept of interrelatedness and relativity according to which there is no absolute good or bad thing in the world. Everything is relative to everything else. One should always use one's strong points in competing against weak points in others. The story of the Liangxiang company shows how ancient strategic thinking has influenced the Chinese in commercial dealings. On the whole, the Liangxiang company's computers are no match for Japanese, American, or even Taiwanese computers. But they have adopted a strategy of selling their medium-range computer in the bottom-of-the-range international market, as the costs of their medium-range computers are still low enough to allow them to remain competitive in the bottom-of-the-range market (*The Economist* 1991, p. 41).

There is obviously some compatibility between enterprise competitions and military warfare. First of all, both enterprises and armies strive for a favorable position by defeating their competitors while defending themselves. Second, both competitions and wars are confrontational activities. Third, both organizations must be well organized and managed. Fourth, both require strategies and tactics. Fifth, the leadership of both an army and an enterprise has an important influence on the shaping of success. Sixth, they both need high quality and committed people. Finally, they both thrive on information. But there is a fundamental difference between business and war: the former is an act of construction, the latter an act of destruction. The two are diametrical in nature.

With this in mind, we would be able to expand on those aspects of business that more closely resemble war – namely, business competition and competitiveness. Where business and war overlap, the comparison is sound, the strategies interchangeable.

THE PRINCIPLES OF STRATEGIES

According to the opening statement of Sun Tzu's work: "War is a matter of vital importance to the state; a matter of life and death, the road either to survival or to ruin. Hence, it is imperative that it be thoroughly studied." (Note that all the translations of Sun Tzu's work are quoted from Wu 1990.) This statement enunciates the importance of one aspect of Sun Tzu's principle of strategies, i.e. that of prudence and the need for good planning. Before a decision to wage war is made, one must engage in detailed planning. This is manifested in many parts of his writings, such as:

> With careful and detailed planning, one can win; with careless and less detailed planning, one cannot win. How much less chance of victory has one who does not plan at all! From the way planning is done beforehand, one can predict victory or defeat.

The same is true for business competition, which concerns the survival or death of the company and the fate of the people dependent upon it. Therefore, careful strategic planning is very important.

Sun Tzu also emphasized first and foremost the importance of avoiding bloody conflicts as much as possible. Therefore, the highest form of victory is to conquer by strategy. To win a battle by actually fighting is not the best strategy. To conquer the enemy without having to resort to war is the highest, most admirable form of generalship. The next best form of generalship is to conquer the enemy via alliance, by borrowing strengths from one's allies. This is followed by the strategy of conquering the enemy by fighting on open ground, where one can attack and withdraw easily. The worst form of generalship is to conquer the enemy by besieging walled cities, which is bound to be the most costly of endeavors. As Sun Tzu said:

> For this reason, to win a hundred victories in a hundred battles is not the culmination of skills. To subdue the enemy without fighting is the supreme excellence.

In order to achieve this goal, one has to grasp the total picture of the situation:

> Know your enemy, know yourself, and you can fight a hundred battles with no danger of defeat. When you are ignorant of the enemy but know yourself, your chances of winning and losing are equal. If you don't know both your enemy and yourself, you are bound to perish in all battles . . . know the terrain, know the weather, and your victory will be complete.

Sun Tzu further described the necessity of appraising several basic elements, which include: moral influence of the ruler, ability of the general, the conditions of climate and terrain, comparative strengths of troops, the implementation of laws and rules, training of officers and soldiers, and the use of rewards and punishments.

MORAL INFLUENCE

By moral influence, Sun Tzu meant the way in which the people are able to be in good accord with their ruler, for whom they are willing to fight through all the pitfalls involved in war. If the ruler is wise, he must first acquire the moral support of his subjects, without which he will not be able to win. In order to achieve this, the ruler should take care of the interests of his subjects, exercising benevolent rule and treating them as his own family members.

In the context of a war, this moral influence refers to the principle of "fighting as one man," (*tong-xin*), by which Sun Tzu meant that generals and soldiers share the same goals and difficulties (Min 1989: 16). He wrote that:

> Troops directed by a skillful general are comparable to the Shuai Ran. The Shuai Ran is a snake found in Mount Heng. Strike at its head, and you will be attacked by its tail; strike at its tail, and you will be attacked by its head; strike at its middle, and you will be attacked by both its head and its tail. . . . The principle of military administration is to achieve a uniform level of courage.

To achieve this goal, Sun Tzu emphasized one important principle: i.e. if a general treats his soldiers as his own beloved sons, they will stand by him until death. Many Chinese generals paid attention to this advice. Qi Ji-guang, a general in the Ming Dynasty once said, "although soldiers are not very smart, they are most easily moved." As the majority of soldiers were peasants, they could be easily motivated by a little care from their generals. The famous general Yue Fei of the Song Dynasty, for example, personally prepared medicine for his soldiers.

In an extremely competitive business world, a manager should try as much as he can to set up a common corporate goal to be shared by all employees, so that all in the company come to view themselves as members of the group crossing the river in the same boat. They would more likely consider company affairs as their own and be willing to make personal sacrifices when needed. Only in this way can the company survive fierce competition and make full use of its competitive advantage. As Sun Tzu said, "He whose ranks are united in purpose will win."

THE ABILITY OF GENERALS

A good general, according to Sun Tzu, should possess five important qualities, which are wisdom (*zhi*), sincerity (*cheng*), benevolence (*ren*), courage (*yong*), and strictness (*yan*). By wisdom, he meant the ability to observe changing circumstances and to act accordingly. This quality mainly refers to the ability to discern and judge situations. Sincerity concerns the ability to win the complete trust of subordinates in terms of fairness and trust. By benevolence, what is meant is deep love for his soldiers, the ability to sympathize with their problems and have a true concern for their well-being. Courage requires a general to be brave and decisive, and able to gain victory by taking advantage of opportunities without hesitation. Finally, a strict general is able to implement discipline and mete out punishment so that his troops dare not violate his commands or rules.

Having explained the positive qualities of a general, Sun Tzu also listed five common negative qualities that a general should discard to avert disaster. These five negative qualities are as follows:

> If reckless, he can be killed; if cowardly, he can be captured; if quick-tempered, he can easily be provoked; if sensitive to honor, he can easily be insulted; if overly compassionate to the people, he can easily be harassed.

These desirable and undesirable qualities of generalship can be used to measure corporate leadership. A corporation is not unlike an army in terms of its organization. A powerful and efficient leader is indispensable to the success of a corporation. The five positive qualities of Sun Tzu's generalship are those also needed by chief executive officers (CEOs), whereas the five negative qualities should be avoided by any CEO. A good CEO should be expected to have the following combinations of qualities.

First, he should have broad knowledge and be capable of identifying business trends and opportunities. Second, he should be able to establish mutual trust between management and employees. He must be able to delegate power, while knowing how to tolerate unavoidable mistakes of his subordinates. Third, he should be a benevolent leader, who understands the problems of his subordinates and cares about their well-being. However, he should not be exceedingly compassionate, so much so that he could be easily harassed. Fourth, he should not be afraid of making risky decisions, but at the same time he must not make hasty or reckless decisions. Finally, a good CEO should be able to combine strict discipline with his own example and mete out punishment decisively and fairly.

On the whole, Sun Tzu emphasizes the basic qualities and cultivations of a military leader, i.e. his generalship rather than his military and technical background. According to Sun Tzu, "it is the business of a general to be quiet and thus ensure depth in deliberation; and to be impartial and upright, and thus keep good management." These kinds of requirements contrast commonly accepted standards on the ability of enterprise leaders in the West, which emphasize specialized and outward abilities, such as in manufacturing, management, finance, marketing and creativity. For many Chinese, the technical backgrounds of a candidate can always be improved through training, while the qualities of generalship are not easy to acquire. That is why they say that "it is easier to acquire a large troop with thousands of soldiers than a good general."

CLIMATE AND TERRAIN

By climate, Sun Tzu meant the changing seasons, weather, temperatures, days and hours. Although climatic conditions represent the uncontrollable aspect of military strategies, a good general knows how to use these uncontrollable components to his advantage. He would choose the right time to fight and turn bad weather to the disadvantage of his enemy. The Russian general Kuznetzov, for example, defeated Napoleon's troops with the help of a severe Russian winter. General Zhou Yu of the Chinese Three Kingdoms Period, one night borrowed the east wind to burn down his rival Cao Cao's camp. In business, a CEO also has to grapple with climatic conditions, such as the "economic climate" and the "business climate," which include:

- Political situations, such as stability, ethnic conflicts, wars, etc.
- Economic cycles like booms, recessions, stagnation, etc.
- Investment climate, such as government policies, regulations, incentives, the state of technology, the protection of intellectual property, changes in market structure, etc.
- Other related social and cultural factors, like changes in demography and in consumer attitudes.

(Wee 1991: 23)

To be competitive, a company has to be able to capitalize on the various changes in the economic and business environment and make its strategies accordingly. As in military situations, a company must realize that these environmental variables are basically beyond its control. It can neither command the fluctuations of economic or business environments, nor can it dramatically affect social or cultural norms. A general must know how to fight within the constraints of climatic conditions, and a CEO of a company also has to adapt his strategies for environmental constraints. On the other hand, a good general or CEO knows how to choose the best time and turn these conditions to his advantage. An import substitution policy, for example, may hamper market entrance but at the same time provide opportunities for investment, which can result in access to the closed market.

Terrain refers to the area for military operation, which can be classified as accessible (both we and the enemy can traverse with equal ease), entangling (easy to reach, but difficult to exit), temporizing (equally disadvantageous for both the enemy and ourselves to enter), precipitous and constricted (advantageous for whichever side occupies it first), and distant. It is the highest responsibility of a general to inquire into these various terrains with the utmost care, as these conditions will determine the chances of life and death in battle.

Here, it should be noted that the word "terrain" has two dimensions: the geographical features of the battlefield and the chosen ground for fighting. The geographical features of the battlefield are largely the uncontrollable variables. Once an army is engaged in a battle on specific terrain, it will have to face the consequences incurred as a result of the terrain. Although the terrain is hard to change, a good general can decide where to fight, i.e. he can choose the battleground most favorable to his army and least favorable to his enemy. Again, as with climatic conditions, one can make a choice and turn the uncontrollable into controllable.

The same logic is also applicable in the business context, where a company has to deal with physical and infrastructural variables such as the location of its business operation. The variables include:

- the supplies of industrial and raw materials as well as abundant cheap or high-quality labor.
- infrastructural characteristics, like transportation systems, telecommunications, water and power supplies, etc.
- access to domestic and international market.

(Wee 1991: 25)

Once again, these uncontrollable variables can be turned into controllable ones, if one chooses the best location according to one's needs. If, for example, one needs to tap cheap labor, one should move operations to a developing country. The mass migration of Taiwan's sunset industries to mainland China is a case in point.

In sum, to cope with different climate and terrain, one should, first of all, understand the general picture. As Sun said, "if one knows the place and time of the coming battle, his troops can march a thousand *li* and fight on the field." Although climate and terrain are virtually unalterable, one can make a wise choice. And to cope with ever-changing situations one should maintain a high degree of mobility and flexibility. This is the principle of "coping with change by adapting quickly." For example, the tastes and priorities of consumers change with the change in the economic situation. In an economic downturn, they tend to choose the most price-competitive goods, while in an economic boom many may shift their attention to designs and styles. Enterprises should change their competition strategies accordingly. Sun Tzu said:

Of the five elements, none is ever predominant; of the four seasons, none lasts forever; of the days, some are longer and others short, and of the moon, it sometimes waxes and sometimes wanes. Hence, there are neither fixed postures nor constant tactics in warfare. He who can modify his tactics in accordance with the enemy situation and thereby succeeds in winning may be said to be divine.

STRENGTHS

Strength, for Sun Tzu, is a relative concept. There is no absolute superior strength nor inferior strength. It all depends on how one can arrange it. According to Sun Tzu,

> In war, number alone confers no advantage. If one does not advance by force recklessly, and is able to concentrate his military power through a correct assessment of the enemy situation and enjoys full support of his men, that would suffice.

This is the principle of concentrating one's strength on the most needed area. It can be applied to business, too. Sheer size may be an advantage for major enterprises, but it can also lead to an unnecessarily large organization and low efficiency. Medium and small enterprises, though restricted by limited resources, can also compete with major enterprises if they can take full advantage of talents, and maintain high efficiency as well as flexibility, while developing their unique products in a market niche.

For Sun Tzu, a small army may be small in comparison to a large one, but if it knows how to concentrate its small force for various battles it may look large and eliminate the big armies one by one:

> When outnumbering the enemy ten to one, encircle him; when five times his strength, attack him; when double his strength, engage him; when evenly matched, be capable of dividing him; when slightly weaker to the enemy, be capable of defending oneself; when greatly inferior to the enemy, elude him. For no matter how obstinate a small force is, it will succumb to a larger and superior force.

Another way to enhance one's own strength is to resort to deception, so as to confuse the perception of one's enemy:

> All warfare is based on deception. Therefore, when able to attack, we must pretend to be unable; when employing our forces, we must seem inactive; when we are near, we must make the enemy believe we are far away; when far away, we must make him believe we are near.

An enterprise should also hide its own real strength so that its competitors do not know its real situation and direction of development. The enterprise can prepare stealthily and launch an attack where its competitors are unprepared and take action when it is unexpected.

A third way is to utilize spies. For Sun Tzu,

> The reason that the enlightened sovereign and the wise general conquer the enemy whenever they move and their achievements surpass those of ordinary men is that they have foreknowledge. This "foreknowledge" cannot be elicited from spirits, nor from gods, nor by analogy with past

events, nor by any deductive calculations. It must be obtained from the men who know the enemy situation.

To be competitive, an enterprise also needs the information of its competitors, such as the development plan of its new products, operational plans and financial situations, etc. In this regard, Silicon Valley has learned some lessons, as many Asian firms, having benefitted from its technologies through all possible channels, have become fierce competitors within a very short time.

Finally, Sun Tzu pointed to the importance of borrowing energy from external factors as a way to enlarge one's strength. For him, a skilled commander sets great store by using a situation to its best advantage:

> He who takes advantage of the situation in fighting uses his men as rolling logs or rocks. It is the nature of logs and rocks to stay stationary on the flat ground, and to roll forward on a slope. If four-cornered, they stop; if round-shaped, they roll. Thus, the energy of troops skillfully commanded is just like the momentum of round rocks quickly tumbling down from a mountain thousands of feet in height.

The same principle can also be applied in a business context, where a company should be able to create a favorable external environment. A trading company, for example, can consolidate its position by securing good relations with suppliers or investing directly in suppliers (Li *et al.* 1986: 82–83).

DOCTRINE AND TRAINING

This element stresses the importance of a whole set of regulations and rules, designation of rank, allocation of responsibilities and organizational structure. According to Sun Tzu,

> If the army is confused and suspicious, the neighboring states will certainly cause trouble. As a saying goes: A confused army predicts victory for the enemy.

One important principle of Sun's organizational ideas is to delegate one's subordinates with necessary power. As he explains as one of the five preconditions for victory, "He whose generals are able and not interfered with by the sovereign will win." This is the principle of "not using the suspectable at all and using the trustworthy with full confidence" (Li and Ma 1991: 344–345). He advised a good balance between an authoritarian leader and unorganized decentralization, as either of the extremes is harmful to an organization. In a highly competitive environment, corporate managers should have sufficient power so that they can coordinate their strategies and tactics based on the changing environment. CEOs should have confidence in their subordinates and delegate them with enough power to carry out their assignments.

For Sun Tzu, training is very important to assure organizational efficiency. If soldiers do not know how to follow signals, they cannot act correctly. In a business context, companies with well-trained employees can be managed with great efficiency. Successful business organizations all over the world have good on-the-job training programs.

DISCIPLINE

According to Sun Tzu, a good army always has stringent discipline, which is achieved with the assistance of an efficient reward-and-punishment system. Nevertheless, a good general should know how and when to mete out rewards or punishment. Soldiers must be treated with humanity, but kept under control by iron discipline.

> If troops are punished before they have grown loyal, they will be disobedient. If not obedient, it is difficult to employ them. But if troops have become loyal, but discipline is not enforced, the general can't employ them either.

In addition, orders should be consistently carried out under strict supervision. Otherwise, troops will still be disobedient. Sun Tzu also advised a proper balance of reward and punishment:

> Too frequent rewards indicate the running out of ideas;
> Too frequent punishments indicate dire distress.

The combination of strictness and benevolence is the key to guaranteeing both loyalty and discipline. There are many examples in Chinese history. With tears in his eyes, Premier Kung Ming of the Three Kingdom Period beheaded his most loved general when he disobeyed his orders and lost a battle. In another example, after giving the order that soldiers not trample on crops, Cao Cao cut his own hair to show his determination to instill discipline when his own startled horse ran into the crop field (Guo 1988).

A company that has an effective disciplinary system will be geared toward higher performance and be in a better competitive position. When the employees are well aware of what they will receive, they will perform accordingly. In a sense, strict discipline is a reverse incentive. By introducing the system of "high rewards and severe punishment," the Joint Venture of Fujian-Hitachi TV Ltd of China raised productivity. Top management members were not exempted. The chronic problem of late arrival and early departure was rooted out within a short period and employees became more identified with the company.

SUMMARY/CONCLUSION

This chapter introduced the Taoist influence on classical Chinese strategical thinking as exhibited in Tzu's *Art of War*. The discussions on *Art of War* focus on:

- the major principles of strategies;
- the importance of moral influences;
- the qualities a good general should and should not possess;
- the role of climate and terrain in determining the situation of the battle;
- the strategy of enlarging one's comparative strengths;
- the importance of organization and training;
- the proper usage of discipline which combines severity and benevolence.

In short, Sun Tzu's strategic ideas can contribute to business competitiveness in the following areas. First of all, Sun Tzu emphasizes the importance of moral influence within an organization. In other words, a successful manager should first of all be able to mobilize his own subordinates to work with one heart. Second, Sun Tzu emphasizes the importance of a broadly defined generalship for military leaders as opposed to merely using their technical background. In many Asian businesses, a manager's general qualities are often viewed as much more important than his or her technical qualifications. Third, according to Sun Tzu's views on relativism, there is no absolute superiority and inferiority in competition. The most important thing is to know where one's competitive edge lies, and when, where and how one should be engaged in competition.

QUESTIONS FOR DISCUSSION

1   What is relativism in Taoism and what is its significance to strategical thinking?
2   Who is Sun Tzu and why is his work so important in understanding Asian management styles?
3   Under what circumstances is military thinking not applicable to a business strategy?
4   What option is most preferred by Sun Tzu in a confrontational situation?
5   Why is moral influence so important according to Sun Tzu?

FURTHER READING

Chu, Chin-ning (1991) *The Asian Mind Game*, New York: Rawson Associates.

The Economist (1991) "The Chinese Art of Management," 26 October: 41.

Griffith, Samuel B. (1971) *Sun Tzu: The Art of War*, New York: Oxford University Press.

Guo, Ji-xing (1988) *Three Kingdoms and Management Strategies*, Nanning: Guangxi People's Press.

Lao Tzu (1990) *Tao Te Ching: The Classical Book of Integrity and the Way* (trans. by Victor H. Mair), New York: Bantam Books.

Li, Fe and Ma Hong (1991) *Military Strategies and Enterprise Competitions*, Nanning: Guanxi People's Press.

Li, Shi-zun, *et al.* (1986) *Sun Tzu Art of War and Business Management*, Nanning: Guangxi People's Press.

Min, Jian-shu (1989) "The Competition Model of Sun Tzu Art of War," *The Ancient Management Philosophies and Chinese-Style Management*, Beijing: Economic and Management Press, pp. 11–26.

Musashi, Miyamoto (1974) *A Book of Five Rings* (trans. by Victor Harris) Woodstock, New York: The Overlook Press.

Sun, Haichen (1991) *The Wiles of War: 36 Military Strategies from Ancient China*, Beijing: Foreign Languages Press.

Wee, Chow Hou (1991) *Sun Tzu: War and Management*, New York: Addison-Wesley Publishing Co.

Wu, Jiu-long (ed.) (1990) *Sun Tzu Art of War*, Beijing: Military Science Press.

Chapter 4

Guanxi dynamics and network building

INTRODUCTION

Anyone who has had experience in dealing with the Chinese could hardly fail to observe that Chinese people attach great importance to cultivating, maintaining and developing *guanxi* (connection or relationship). Anyone who has associated with the Chinese at even a minimal level would easily notice the Chinese sensitivity to face and *renqing* (humanized obligation) in their daily life. These traits are shared by the Chinese living not only in mainland China but also by those living in Taiwan, Hong Kong and in other overseas Chinese societies all over the world. Simply put, these three concepts of *guanxi*, face and *renqing* are the keys for understanding Chinese social behavioral patterns and their business dynamics. A Chinese brought up in a Chinese community would have been subtly inculcated with these concepts so much so that he/she would both consciously and unconsciously use them to guide daily activities.

The Chinese societies have experienced tremendous changes in the past few decades. Taiwan, Hong Kong and Singapore have rapidly modernized, while mainland China has been practicing its open door policy for more than a decade. The Chinese living in major ASEAN countries have also been under increasing pressure to change. Nevertheless, these socio-cultural concepts have retained their influence on the social behavior of the Chinese. In the case of mainland China, their influences, particularly that of *guanxi*, seem to have been steadily growing in the past few years, even after Mao and the Chinese communists made several major attempts to eliminate the deep-rooted feudal cultural traditions, notably during the Campaign of Condemning Lin Biao and Confucius in the Cultural Revolution.

This chapter attempts to analyze the dynamics of *guanxi* and network building. First, it defines the three key socio-cultural concepts. Second, it analyzes the five fundamental relationships in traditional Confucian society. Third, it explains the key elements for network building, describes social skills in the establishment and maintenance of personal networks, and analyzes socio-cultural reasons and strategies for *guanxi* avoidance.

The fourth section describes the dynamic interactions between *guanxi* and face. Finally, implications for business and the trend of development will be discussed.

DEFINING *GUANXI*, FACE, *RENQING*

Guanxi

The term refers to special relationships two persons have with each other. It can be best translated as friendship with implications of a continual exchange of favors (Pye 1992: 101). Two people enjoying a *guanxi* relationship can assume that each is consciously committed to the other. They have undertaken to exchange favors in spite of official policies against such practices. *Guanxi* helped many Chinese survive the hardship of deficient supplies during the Maoist period.

Guanxi binds people through the exchange of favors rather than through expressions of sympathy and friendship. The *guanxi* relationship does not have to involve friends, although this is often preferred. The relationship tends to be more utilitarian than emotional. The moral dimension functioning here is that a person who fails to observe a rule of equity and refuses to return favor for favor loses face and looks untrustworthy.

One interesting feature of *guanxi* is that such exchanges of favors tend to benefit the weaker member more. When *guanxi* links two persons of unequal rank or social status, the weaker side usually expects more help than he or she can reciprocate in equal terms. Such unequal exchange reflects the Confucian principle of family cohesion, in which family ties demand mutual assistance (Alston 1989: 28).

Liu Bin-yan (1983), a famous writer and senior reporter of the *People's Daily*, writes:

> In Bin County, it's hard to figure out how people are related. It's as though they carry special switches with them, and if you get involved with one person, you're suddenly involved with a whole network. . . . Complex personal relationships, built of layer upon layer of interlocking connections, formed a dense net. Any Marxist-Leninist principle, any Party plan or policy that came into contact with this net would be struck dead, as if electrocuted. . . . Right and wrong became thoroughly confused, reward and punishment turned upside-down.
>
> (Liu Bin-yan 1983: 53–54)

La (pulling) *guanxi* is the most commonly used strategy by the Chinese in network construction. Pulling *guanxi* means the efforts to establish and build up relationships with others where no previous relationships existed, or where an existing relationship is not close enough to be useful. There are many ways of pulling *guanxi*, involving a wide range of skills and strategies.

Depending on these to manage their daily relations, the Chinese living in mainland China have rightly used a special term, *guanxixue* (relationology) to describe this complicated phenomenon. "Walking through the back door," *zouhoumen*, has become a popular and often essential way to get things done through personal connection networks in mainland China. The influence of *guanxixue* has infiltrated through political, economic, social, cultural and other spheres of life. Hardly any aspect of social life is not touched upon by *guanxi*; whether it is a coupon for an imported product or a place for one's child in a good kindergarten, *guanxi* enables one to get what one needs that would otherwise not be available.

With the further deepening of Deng Xiao-ping's market reform in China, a new term *guanxihu* (specially connected individual or social organization) has become increasingly popular, referring to those individuals or social organizations that have special *guanxi* with each other and would give each other preferential treatment without following market rationality. The social organization is also called *danwei* (work unit). Individuals and *danwei* normally cultivate and maintain a number of *guanxihu* to compensate for their own inherent deficiencies. By so doing, they gradually establish their *guanxiwang* (a web of connection networks). Although *guanxiwang* is not a phenomenon unique to mainland China, it now plays such a significant social role that it is not matched in terms of scope, intensity and pervasiveness by those in other Chinese societies.

Face

The central goal of Confucianism is to achieve social harmony, which depends not only on the maintenance of correct relationships among individuals but also on the protection of an individual's "face" or one's dignity, self-respect, and prestige. If a Chinese loses his or her face, he or she might as well feel, according to tradition, as if he or she had lost eyes, nose, or mouth. Social interactions should be conducted so that nobody's face is lost. Face can also be given, when due respect is paid to someone else (Hofstede and Bond 1988: 8).

Face can be classified into two dimensions – *lian* and *mianzi*. The former is associated with personal behavior whereas the latter is something valuable that can be achieved. A Chinese is socially criticized if he has no *lian* and is deemed as unsuccessful and low in status if he has no *mianzi*. They are often mixed and the Chinese interact with each other to protect, save, add, give, exchange or even borrow "face." *Mianzi* "enters much more into everyday transactions as a form of social currency" (Hu 1944: 45–64; Redding and Ng 1982: 207). In another sense, "face" is a key component in the dynamics of *guanxi*. If one does not have *mianzi*, one has very limited social resources to use in cultivating and developing one's connection network. Therefore, one has to have *mianzi* in order to build one's own network.

Normally, one who holds higher social position or is materially richer has greater *mianzi*. One can also increase one's *mianzi* by dexterously manipulating his relationships with others and tapping into others' social resources.

Renqing

In the Chinese art of relationship management, i.e. the cultivation and development of *guanxi*, *renqing* plays an important role. It should be noticed that *renqing* is not equal to emotional feelings which represent the affective element of human relations. Emotional feelings are more personal than social, whereas *renqing* is more social than personal. In a way, *renqing* can be interpreted as "human feelings," which "covers not only sentiment but also its social expressions such as the offering of congratulations or condolences and the making of gifts on appropriate occasions" (Yang 1957: 292).

Since *renqing* involves social exchanges, there is an inherent obligation for people to keep equity in mind. In this sense, *renqing* is also a kind of favor with the inclusion of a sentimental element. If one fails to follow the rule of equity in exchange of *renqing*, one loses one's face, hurts the feelings of one's friends and looks morally bad, and one's *guanxiwang* (connection network) is in danger. Since the connection network is so important, one is almost obligated to follow the rule of equity, even though one is dealing with one's close friend with whom a strong emotional tie exists. Therefore, *renqing* is best translated as "humanized obligation," which implies that a continued favor exchange with a sentimental touch is involved. *Renqing* is one of the commonly accepted social norms regulating Chinese interpersonal relationships, which is based on the Confucian concept of reciprocity. In a sense, Confucian harmony is maintained through gracious reciprocity of help. Those who do not follow this social norm are condemned to be ignorant of the Confucian concept of behavioral propriety.

It is true that *renqing* is closely related to the Confucian concept of behavioral propriety which stresses the social responsibility of individuals to be aware of and behave according to certain prescribed rules of behavior. If a Chinese is accused of "understanding no *renqing*," it means that he is incapable of managing interpersonal relationships in accordance with the Confucian concept of behavioral propriety. As has been explained earlier, *guanxi* is a kind of social exchange that involves friendly interpersonal relationships with an overture of continued exchange of favors; and the moral principle is the rule of equity. *Renqing* provides the theoretical justification for that moral principle and exhorts people to follow it. Nevertheless, *renqing* only functions in these social exchanges; it has little role in economic exchange, which is strictly dictated by market rationality.

Therefore, *renqing* is an important vehicle in Chinese social exchanges.

There are a number of common expressions related to *renqing*, such as giving somebody a *renqing*, and to owe somebody a *renqing*. In general, *renqing*, like *mianzi*, represents a kind of social capital or resource in interpersonal exchanges. Since *renqing* is so closely intertwined with *guanxi*, the two can be interchangeable on some occasions. The expression "there is hardly any *renqing* between us," for example, can be understood as a statement that "there is hardly any *guanxi* between us." In a sense, to develop *renqing* can be regarded as a precondition for the establishment or maintenance of *guanxi*. The extent of *renqing* that two persons enjoy can clearly indicate the quality of *guanxi* between them. When a Chinese weaves his *guanxiwang*, he automatically weaves his *renqingwang* (web of humanized obligations). In other words, while he enjoys the benefits of his connection network, he also incurs the burden of obligations, which he must take care of in the future.

FIVE BASIC CONFUCIAN RELATIONSHIPS AND *GUANXI*

Since Confucianism is mainly concerned with the question of how to establish a harmonious hierarchical social order in the human-centered world, the individual is not born as an isolated entity. Man can, therefore, be defined as a social being who should interact with others under the guidance of *ren* (benevolence and humaneness). The Chinese character *ren* consists of two components, one illustrating a human being and the other depicting the number two. As this implies, *ren* refers to the way people relate to each other. In other words, man cannot exist alone and must be able to interact with others. *Ren*, as the highest virtue of Confucianism, would be meaningless, if not understood in the context of the social interactions among men.

In short, in the Confucian system, man is a relation-orientated being who has an inherent interest in cultivating his *guanxi*. According to Confucius, there are many kinds of human relationships of which the five cardinal relations are the most fundamental. These five relationships and their appropriate characters are: sincerity between father and son, righteousness between ruler and subjects, distinction or separate functions between husband and wife, order between older brothers and younger brothers, and faithfulness among friends.

These five cardinal relationships are based on differentiated order among individuals. This means that the Confucian concept of these relationships emphasizes the importance of differentiation in social hierarchical order. Hence, Confucius's famous saying goes: "let prince be prince, subject be subject, father be father, son be son." The five fundamental relations can also be classified into predetermined relationships (such as father–son and brother–brother) and voluntarily constructed ones (such as friend–friend relations). This distinction is not absolute: prince–subject and husband–wife can fall into either the first category or the second, but it has significant implication for the role of "self" in social relationships (Hu 1919: 116).

In the first category, the self is underdeveloped, as individual behavior is more or less dictated by fixed status and responsibilities. For thousands of years, it has been drummed into people that relationships, especially those within the family, are very important and the individual *per se* is less important. A Chinese is enmeshed within a network from birth, whether it is the family, the work unit, the government or the Party. Like a collective "womb," with the result that "man, in the sense of man with a strong ego, has never been born in China" (Barme and Minford 1986: 34). In other words, a Chinese is not primarily an individual, rather, he or she is a member of a family. Children should learn to restrain themselves, to overcome their individuality so as to maintain harmony in the family.

While the family in China remains important, the Communist Party has endeavored, since 1949, to build up other groups to which individuals should be committed. In the political sphere, the most important groups are various party organizations. In a broader scope, the organizations that ordinary Chinese attach themselves to are their work units (*danwei*), which are not only responsible for their work-related activities but also control their after-work activities and life, ranging from housing, day-care, and schooling of children to birth-control.

So far, most scholars have observed the Confucian tendency to cultivate a Chinese into a group-oriented and socially dependent being. As discussed earlier, this conclusion is correct in the first category of basic relations, specifically father–son relations. However, the self becomes much more dynamic in the second category. Generally, the first category represents orthodox Confucian relations while the second category allows the self a much more dynamic role.

In building new relationships on a voluntary basis, the self takes initiative and is active. In this case, it is the individual who is capable of defining roles for himself and who is located at the center of the relationships (Fei 1985: 25–26). Simply because of this voluntary nature, the individual is the initiator of social interactions in the non-predetermined cardinal relationships with others beyond the familial environment. The individual is a true and sophisticated architect in relationships.

The dynamic role of the self can be better understood in the interactions between the self and a group, which is a vaguely defined term in Chinese. The Chinese basic social group is *jia* (family), beyond which is *dajia* (big family, i.e. a larger social group that includes nonfamily members); the largest group is called *guojia* (country family, i.e. the state). The self plays a dominant role in defining groups beyond his/her own nuclear family, according to the self's envisioned need. By applying the concept of family to all these different larger groups, the self can conveniently put himself in a favorable position to build his relationships.

The common expression *zi jia ren* (one's own family people), for example, can be used to cover any person one wants to include, ranging from nuclear family members to those who are not even ethnically related. Therefore, the individual can manipulate the concept of *jia* by expanding or contracting his family group. Thus, he has a substantial freedom in regulating his relations with people to his own liking. The family group can be extended to include people from all over the world, as is expressed by *tian xia yi jia* (all the world belongs to one family).

The resiliency of the concept of the group (family and other nonfamily social units) affords a Chinese very useful social and psychological flexibility in constructing his network of kinship or fictive kinship relations. The tendency of the Chinese to address each other by associating "brother" or "sister" with the addressee's surname is a case in point. Often, one can hear a Chinese calling somebody unrelated to them as "Brother Zhang" or "Sister Li." To show due respect or further build up the desired relationship, the order of seniority is clearly expressed, such as "dear big brother Zhou, please forgive your humble little brother Guo for being late." This flexibility gives them a good advantage in building their connection network. They can also easily take away the endearing terms when the relationships are no longer good.

In short, the five fundamental relationships and the prescribed ways of handling these relationships have made *guanxi* a very complicated phenomenon. On top of the complexity is the distinction between the first category of relationships and the second. The dual role of the self as both a passive follower of predetermined relationships and the initiator of a voluntarily constructed relationship makes the picture even more complicated. By comparing the Chinese social system with Western ones, Liang Su-ming (Liang 1974: 95) attempted to address these complexities. He classifies Chinese society as neither individual-based nor society-based, but rather relation-based. In a relation-based social system, Liang writes that the focus is not laid on any specific individual, but on the special nature of the relations between individuals who associate with each other.

Regarding the complexity and importance of *guanxi* in Chinese society, Fox Butterfield (1983), a former *New York Times* journalist to Beijing, has made the following incisive observations:

> *Guanxi* provides the lubricant for Chinese to get through life. In a society which for millennia had no public law as we know it in the West to enforce impartial justice, people depended on their *guanxi*, their personal relationships, particularly their contacts with those in power, to get things done. It was a form of social investment. Developing, cultivating, and expanding one's *guanxi* became a common preoccupation. The

advent of the Communists has not fundamentally changed that. As a result, the Chinese have turned the art of personal relations into a carefully calculated science. There are even people who live entirely on their *guanxi*.

(Butterfield 1983: 80)

Guanxi plays an extremely important role in the Chinese business world. As most of the Chinese family businesses are small and managed by core family members, they are heavily dependent on business opportunities and credit lines provided by their *guanxi* network. No company in the Chinese family business world can go far unless it has good and extensive *guanxi* network. To make his *guanxi* work for him, a Chinese businessman honors his obligations, tries to be loyal to his friends, does favors and maintains a reputation for fairness. He would try very hard to maintain the image of a person who can be fully relied upon and will always reciprocate. *Guanxi* binds millions of small Chinese firms into a big web, within which they excel in competing with Western firms (Montagu-Pollock 1991: 21–22; Kao 1993).

GUANXI NETWORK BUILDING AND *GUANXI* EVASION

As the Chinese are relation-orientated beings, they are naturally preoccupied with *guanxi* construction. Subsequently, the Chinese command sophisticated skills in building up connection networks. The Chinese culture has converted interpersonal relationships to an almost immaculate art. A natural question follows: How do the Chinese actually build up their personal networks?

With regard to this question, Chie Nakane (1970: 1–2), a Japanese anthropologist, has developed a useful approach by employing two contrasting criteria, i.e. "attribute" and "frame", to observe different ways of group formation. Groups, according to Nakane, may be identified by applying these two criteria: the former is based on the individual's common attributes while the latter signifies a situational position in a given frame. "Attribute" may denote, for example, being a member of a definite lineage, a clan or a social group. It may be obtained not only by birth but by achievement. "Frame" may refer to an institution and a locality, which provides a common basis to a group of individuals who are situated in it.

To demonstrate her point, Nakane describes the divergent ways of family formation in Japan and China:

The Japanese family system differs from that of the Chinese system, where family ethics are always based on relationship between particular individuals such as father and son, brothers and sisters, parent and child, husband and wife, while in Japan they are always based on the collective group, i.e. members of a household, not on the relationship between individuals.

(Nakane 1970: 1–2)

Clearly, Chinese social groups tend to be formed under the guidance of attributes, while the formation of social groups based on fixed frames is typical of Japanese social structure. Unlike the Japanese, the Chinese can have "pluralistic" identifications with other individuals or social groups based on the "attributes" they share with other individuals or social groups. In this regard, the Koreans are more similar to the Chinese. The *inhwa* (harmony) relationship binds two or more individuals, usually of unequal rank, without reference to organizational or other group memberships. There is little organizational loyalty (Alston 1989: 30).

In the attribute-guided group formation, the more "attributes" an individual has, the more *mianzi* he enjoys and the more *guanxi* (connection network) he is capable of constructing. Consequently, he will be in a more favorable position to get ahead in a competitive world. *Guanxi* network construction involves a kind of social maneuvering through which an individual builds up his own connection network. The shared attributes can be compared to a base of individual *guanxi*. In Chinese society, the often-used shared attributes for constructing networks are kinship, locality, co-worker, classmate, and teacher–student. These shared attributes are quite resilient and flexible; they can be easily contracted and expanded according to need. Locality, for instance, can imply a natural village, a county, a city, a province, a regional grouping of provinces, or even the country. There are all kinds of Chinese organizations established based on locality, such as Shandung Tongxianghui (Shandung Association of Fellow People). The concept of co-worker can be expanded to include all the people in the same profession. These attributes are used to make friendly contacts.

Since the self is located in the center of voluntarily constructed relations and takes initiative, Chinese *guanxi* construction can be characterized as an ego-centered social engineering of connection network building. With continued modernization, the second category of relationships is becoming more and more important, and the role of the self increases correspondingly. Nevertheless, while one's *guanxi* or connection network is built on the base of attributes shared by individuals, these attributes are not the only preconditions. If individual A wants to establish *guanxi* with individual B but has no opportunity to interact with B, B is a stranger to A whether B has common attributes with A or not. Under this circumstance, an intermediary has to be involved as a linking point in *guanxi* construction. Through the intermediary, individual A is able to overcome the barrier of being a stranger and associate with individual B on relational terms.

Owing to the importance of *guanxi*, it is generally assumed that the Chinese would be keen on expanding *guanxiwang* as much as possible, especially when the informal *guanxi* structure can compensate for the inefficient official system. Nevertheless, within the same Chinese socio-cultural system, socio-cultural mechanisms for *guanxi* construction exist side by side with those restricting the role of *guanxi* in order to reserve space for autonomy in rational social and economic action. There is a constant pressure to limit the role of *guanxi* at both bureaucratic and individual levels. This second aspect has not been well studied.

For bureaucracy, *guanxi* hampers the implementation of institutional rules based on instrumental rationality, leading to low efficiency and greater confusion. For individuals, *guanxi* not only brings convenience but also obligations. In short, the more benefits one gets from one's *guanxiwang*, the more obligations one incurs in one's *renqingwang*. This contradictory phenomenon leads to the ambivalent attitudes of the Chinese toward *guanxi* construction: on the one hand, a Chinese tries his best to build and enjoy his connection network; on the other, he may be reluctant to build some *guanxi* or try to evade attempts that others have made to build up *guanxi* with him. To develop *guanxi* with others is a kind of social investment and incurs responsibility and obligation. Once an individual places himself in a *guanxiwang*, either built by himself or by others, he is locked into a complicated interdependent relationship with others in which he is socially obliged to respond to any request for help from others, thereby losing autonomy and freedom. Naturally, the Chinese as often as not consciously try to avoid relating themselves too intimately with certain others in order to avoid dependence.

Therefore, in Chinese societies throughout history, there are plenty of socio-cultural mechanisms to limit the role of *guanxi*. In feudal China, for example, there was a system that strictly prohibited the assignment of officials to their native place. The logic behind this system was that an official in his native place could be compromised by his obligation to his *renqingwang* as a *guanxiwang*, whether he wanted it or not, already existed there for him. Chinese folk wisdom also advises that one should not allow oneself to be a debtor in social exchanges (or owe *renqing*) if one wants to preserve some space of autonomy in action.

In fact, a sophisticated "compartmentalization" strategy has long been developed in Chinese societies to separate the functionally specific economic exchanges from the functionally diffused social exchanges (Hwang 1987). In the Chinese business world, for example, one can often hear the saying that "*guanxi gui guanxi; shengyi gui shengyi*," which means that when good friends are engaged in business dealings they should follow the principle of separating business from their friendship in order to keep their friendship. To dispose of his property, such as a car, a Chinese may announce up front that he will not sell it to friends in order to prevent either the damage of the deal or his friendship.

Such a compartmentalization strategy not only covers ordinary friends but may even be applicable to the relationship among the most intimate members of a lineage, i.e. parents and children, brothers and sisters. As one popular expression goes, "Among good brothers, accounts should be kept clear-cut." According to the rationale of this expression, the functionally specific economic rationality should have precedence over the functionally diffuse principles in the brother–brother relationship, one of the five cardinal relations in the Confucian system. The logic underlying this expression is not to harm one of the five cardinal relations, but is, rather, used to prevent this cardinal relationship from being harmed by potential conflicts arising from possible obscure economic exchanges.

Fei Xiao-tong's description of market town behavior very vividly illustrates the "compartmentalization" strategy. In his study of rural China (Fei 1985), he notices that neighbors in the same village would often walk miles to the town market center to have their transactions done there rather than conduct transactions at their front doors. By doing that they could reduce the impact of the functionally diffuse social exchanges dictated by neighbor relationships and follow the rationality of the functionally specific economic exchanges dictated by the market principle. It was in that environment that they were able to do business with each other as "strangers." To set accounts straight is a kind of exchange accepted as legitimate and fair between strangers, in which the interference of other elements of social relations could be excluded.

Personal *guanxi* networks are also very important for the Japanese. Unlike the Chinese, the Japanese are much less dynamic in building up their own *guanxi* networks. They tend to subject their individual relationships to their relationships with their organizations, because they are basically frame-dominated as Nakane has explained. Culturally, many Japanese regard the sentiments of *guanxi* as old-fashioned and too traditional. They feel that they have or should have "outgrown" such backward ways of behaving. Compared to the Chinese, the Japanese are also much more conscious of the downside of *guanxi* networks. This is mainly because *guanxi* brings *giri/on* (duty / obligation), which "imply a more explicit sense of indebtedness and obligation than the diffusely binding Chinese concept of *guanxi*" (Pye 1992: 103).

THE INTERACTIONS BETWEEN *GUANXI* AND FACE

The relationship between *guanxi* and face is intertwined and complicated. As explained earlier, face has two dimensions, i.e. *lian* and *mianzi*. If one does not follow the rule of *guanxi*, one loses in both dimensions; if one follows the rule of *guanxi* carefully, one gains in two dimensions. In terms of establishing *guanxi*, the connection network seems to have a more direct relationship with *mianzi*. The more *mianzi* one has, the easier it will be to establish and develop one's relationship. If a Chinese is described as having no *mianzi* at all, he is virtually deprived of the right to establish and develop a connection network as others will have little interest in responding to his initiatives.

The dynamic relationship between *guanxi* and face is clearly analyzed by Huang Guo-guang (1989: 133) in his dynamic chart (see Figure 4.1). In the chart, people are divided into two groups: group one asks for help, and group two controls resources, with each having distinct psychological processes. Suppose a man named Wang from group two is asked for help, he has three relationships in mind: the impersonal relationship, a mixed relationship and an emotional relationship. For the impersonal relationship, he can easily apply rules based on fairness. In an emotional relationship, he tends to be obliged to apply the regulations based on the need of his relatives and close friends. But for the mixed relationship, he has great difficulty in deciding which are the suitable rules to be applied. If the price is smaller than the anticipated reciprocation he may be willing to help; if the price is bigger than the anticipated reciprocation he is likely to refuse to help; however, if he cannot figure out the balance of price and anticipated reciprocation he is often compelled to put off his decision.

Whatever rules Wang has applied, his decision to help or not will have direct bearing on his face. If he agrees to help, he will naturally gain face with regard to the requester. Next time, if he needs help from that person, he will be able to use his face. Should the other person not allow Wang to use his gained face, that person loses face and is morally criticized. If Wang refuses to help for some reason, he naturally loses face with regard to the requester. Next time, if he needs help from that person, he must first regain face by doing something special for that person. Therefore, when Wang makes his decision he has to consider the consequence of his decision with regard to his own face.

SUMMARY/CONCLUSION

This chapter has discussed in detail the three important Chinese social values: *guanxi*, face, and *renqing*. Though these concepts are very different from each other, they all interrelate. Among the three, *guanxi* seems to be the most important to understanding business dealings in China. In addition, there are the five basic relationships in the traditional Confucian system, and these can be broken down into voluntary and predetermined categories. As has been shown the Chinese concept of group is extremely elastic, ranging from the core family to the whole population, depending on the environment. On this basis the chapter proceeds with an analysis of *guanxi* network building and *guanxi* evasion, which seem to be contradictory phenomena. A comparison is then drawn with similar Japanese norms to bring out the cultural uniqueness of the Chinese networking system. *Guanxi* and *renqing* relationships are subsequently analyzed to explain

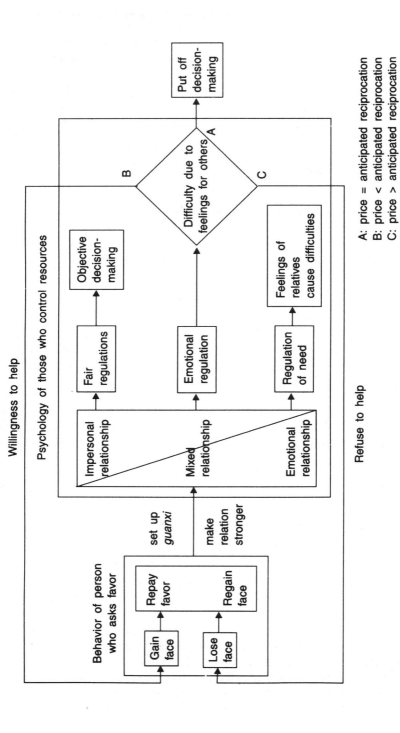

Willingness to help

Psychology of those who control resources

| Impersonal relationship | → | Fair regulations | → | Objective decision-making |

Mixed relationship | → | Emotional regulation | → |

Emotional relationship | → | Regulation of need | → | Feelings of relatives cause difficulties |

Difficulty due to feelings for others

B

A

C

Put off decision-making

Behavior of person who asks favor

set up *guanxi*

make relation stronger

| Gain face | → | Repay favor |
| Lose face | → | Regain face |

Refuse to help

A: price = anticipated reciprocation
B: price < anticipated reciprocation
C: price > anticipated reciprocation

Figure 4.1 Model on *guanxi* and face interactions
Source: Huang, 1989, p. 133.

these seemingly contradictory phenomena. In the end the dynamic interactions between *guanxi* and face are depicted to illustrate the complexity of the Chinese social process.

The Chinese, as shown, put considerable effort in *guanxi* construction and *guanxi* evasion. Obviously, *guanxi* has provided the kind of convenience and benefit that is often not available through official systems. However, the concepts of *guanxi*, face and *renqing* have long been regarded as obstructive or dysfunctional to the drive toward modernization of Chinese societies. *Guanxi* is often criticized by many Chinese, who perceive *guanxi* as much too functionally diffuse. If modernization is to prevail, *guanxi* should be done away with. Nevertheless, *guanxi* is a deep-rooted socio-cultural phenomenon, which cannot be eradicated overnight. The fact that Hong Kong, Singapore and Taiwan's modernization has not fundamentally changed the role of *guanxi* has clearly proved this point. Deng's market reform has succeeded in enriching the Chinese market, but *guanxi* has become more actively involved in social life instead of disappearing.

In sum, *guanxi* construction remains a dominant socio-cultural strategy that the Chinese consciously or unconsciously employ to maximize their social resourcefulness in everyday life. Since "attribute" rather than "frame" is the criterion of Chinese *guanxi* construction, the Chinese have developed immaculate skills in building their connection networks. In spite of various abuses, *guanxi* remains a major source of dynamics in Chinese society and provides Chinese businesses with a significant competitive edge in international competition. With the rapid economic development and modernization in various Chinese societies, *guanxi* is under increasing pressure to change and adapt. The Chinese will have to gradually combine *guanxi* with the increasing pressure of market rationality. In this respect progress is already being made. *Guanxi* will continue to play an active role in the political, economic, social and cultural life of Chinese societies. Therefore, in dealing with the Chinese, a foreign business person should acquire a basic understanding of *guanxi* dynamics, even though he/she does not necessarily have to play by Chinese rules.

QUESTIONS FOR DISCUSSION

1. What are the two dimensions of face in Chinese culture?
2. Can you define the connections and differences between *guanxi* and *renqing*?
3. In your opinion what are the voluntary constructed relationships and predetermined relationships in traditional Confucian society?
4. Can you tell the major differences between the Chinese and Japanese approaches to building connection networks?

FURTHER READING

Alston, Jon P. (1989) "Wa, Guanxi, and Inhwa: Managerial Principles in Japan, China, and Korea," *Business Horizons* (March–April): 26–31.

Barme, G. and J. Minford (1986) *Seeds of Fire: Chinese Voices of Conscience*, Hong Kong: Far Eastern Review Ltd.

Butterfield, Fox (1983) *China: Alive in Bitter Sea*, New York: Coronet Books.

Fei, Xiao-tong (1985) *Peasant China*, Hong Kong: Sanlian.

Gold, Thomas (1985) "After Comradeship: Personal Relations in China Since the Cultural Revolution," *China Quarterly* 104: 657–675.

Hofstede, Geert and Michael Harris Bond (1988) "The Confucian Connection: From Cultural Roots to Economic Growth," *Organizational Dynamics* 16(4): 5–21.

Hu, H.C. (1944) "The Chinese Concepts of Face," *American Anthropologist* 46: 45–64.

Hu, Shi (1919) *The General History of the Chinese Philosophy*, Shanghai: Commercial Press.

Huang, Guo-guang (1989) "On the Modernization of Chinese Family Business," in Jiang Yi-wei and Min Jian-shu (eds), *Ancient Management Practices*, Beijing: Economic Management Press, pp. 121–134.

Hwang, Kwang-kuo (1987) "Face and Favour: The Chinese Power Game," *American Journal of Sociology* 92(4): 944–974.

Kao, John (1993) "The World Web of Chinese Business," *Harvard Business Review* (March–April), 24–36.

King, Ambrose Y.C. (1985) "The Individual and Group in Confucianism: A Relational Perspective," in Donald J. Munro (ed.), *Individualism and Holism: Studies in Confucian and Taoist Values*, Ann Arbor: University of Michigan Press, pp. 57–72.

Liang, Su-ming (1974) *The Basics of Chinese Culture*, Hong Kong: Zhicheng Books.

Liu, Bin-yan (1983) *People or Monsters? And Other Stories and Reportage from China and Mao* (ed. by Perry Link), Bloomington, Ind.: Indiana University Press.

Montagu-Pollock, Matthew (1991) "All the Right Connections," *Asian Business* (January): 20–24.

Nakane, Chie (1970) *Japanese Society*, New York: Penguin.

Pye, Lucian (1992) *Chinese Commercial Negotiating Style*, New York: Quorum Books.

Redding, S. Gordon and Michael Ng (1982) "The Role Of 'Face' in the Organizational Perceptions of Chinese Managers," *Organizational Studies* 3(3): 201–219.

Yang, S.L. (1957) "The Concept of Pao as a Basis for Social Relations in China," in J.K. Fairbank (ed.), *Chinese Thought and Institutions*, Chicago: University of Chicago Press, pp. 291–309.

Part II
Comparative Chinese management systems

Chapter 5

The Overseas Chinese
Their origins and operational environment

INTRODUCTION

Overseas Chinese have been reputed to be astute entrepreneurs and competitive businessmen. According to a 1993 research report on the Overseas
Chinese by Ohio University, the Overseas Chinese (including those living
in Taiwan) number 55 millions and have a GDP of more than $500 billion.
Their current assets of $2 trillion surpass that of mainland China and
amount to two-thirds of Japan (*World Daily*, 19 January 1994: 4). This
chapter discusses background information concerning the Overseas
Chinese, i.e. understanding who they are and how they have developed
into their current position. Specific topics will include the origin of the
Overseas Chinese, the evolution of the environment in which they have
developed their business competitiveness, their ethnic identity and diversity, as well as the trends for change.

The term "Overseas Chinese" is ambiguous and can often be misleading.
It has been used to refer to both overseas Chinese nationals and ethnic
Chinese who are citizens of other countries. The term "Overseas Chinese"
(*huaqiao* in Chinese) also implies that these Chinese are sojourners who will
eventually "return" to China, originating from an old Chinese saying that
"fallen leaves always return to the roots." In a broad sense, the "Overseas
Chinese" are comprised of *huaqiao* (Chinese nationals who live abroad),
huaren or *huazu* (both terms mean ethnic Chinese) or *huayi* (person of
Chinese descent), and *Gangao tonbao* and *Taiwan tonbao* (compatriots in
Hong Kong, Macao and Taiwan). Overseas Chinese are found in most parts
of the world. Of the total Overseas Chinese in the world in the early 1980s,
more than 90 percent still resided in Asia. About 60 percent of the Overseas
Chinese who lived outside Asia were concentrated in the Americas (Poston
and Yu 1990: 485). This study will concentrate on the Overseas Chinese in
ASEAN nations.

THE ORIGINS OF THE OVERSEAS CHINESE

The earliest record of contact between Imperial China and Southeast Asia dates back to the third century BC (Han Dynasty). It was not until the Tang Dynasty (AD 618–907) that the Chinese began to visit the coastal regions of the South China Sea regularly. The land routes were difficult to penetrate due to rugged topography, which required that these excursions be undertaken by small groups. In comparison with the more pervasive influence of the Arabs and the Indians, the Chinese had a very limited presence in the region. For thirteen centuries from the beginning of the Tang Dynasty to the mid-Qing Dynasty, China paid little attention to the well-being of Overseas Chinese settlers. On the contrary, the Chinese rulers, given their perception of China as the center of the world and their sense of self-sufficiency, exercised varying degrees of restrictions on emigration and regarded emigrants from China as a disgrace to the nation. A sea ban was imposed at various points throughout this period of time.

In the meantime, trade was developed. Chinese businessmen traded porcelain, silk, and tea for cloves, pepper and other Southeast Asian products. But, for most of the period, the official attitude toward foreign trade was very ambiguous. While a ban on emigration was exercised by various dynasties, policies on trade were not consistent. Only occasionally did the Chinese courts make a serious effort to develop trade or establish ties with other nations via sea routes. During a brief period between 1400 and 1430, there was an extraordinary wave of maritime expeditions led by a Ming official Zheng Ho, who reached as far as the east coast of Africa. Nevertheless, this became a passing phenomenon, and China became increasingly inward-looking and virtually abandoned long-distance expeditions.

In the following centuries, succeeding Chinese governments intensified the sea ban, though it was not always successfully implemented. Those who violated the sea ban could be beheaded as traitors. According to the traditionally dominant Sino-centric view, China was supposedly the Central Kingdom. Those who sought to leave the country naturally caused national disgrace and thereby deserved severe punishment. At certain points of the Qing Dynasty, the Qing government went so far as to order that all Chinese settlers return to China within a specified time period. In 1860 the defeated Qing government was forced to grant official permission in its treaties with both Britain and France to those individuals wishing to leave China (Wu and Wu 1980: 125–127).

Therefore, in the earlier period the Overseas Chinese population in Southeast Asia was very small. It was not until the mid-18th century that the number of Chinese emigrants began to increase substantially (for historical migration patterns, see Figure 5.1). Among those were refugees escaping from various forms of turmoil and conflicts within China. They were merchants, artisans, small crop farmers and laborers (Steinberg *et al.*

1971: 216). As the colonial authorities in the region expedited the development of extractive mines and plantations, increasing numbers of Chinese were imported, kidnapped or smuggled into the region as laborers. Underground organizations were established to deal with what the Chinese called the "piggy-trade." In the late 19th century, Singapore became the major transshipment center for the redistribution of Chinese workers.

This exodus reached its climax toward the end of the 19th century with the final collapse of the Qing dynasty, which in turn brought famine and social structural disintegration. The coasts of the South China Sea attracted

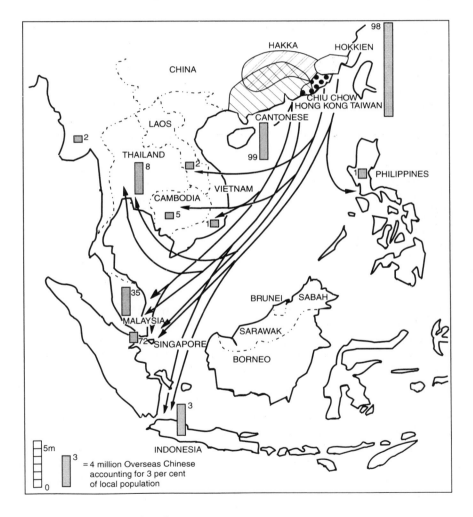

Figure 5.1 Historical migration patterns
Source: Redding, 1990, p. 22.

the most due to the fact that these regions not only needed more laborers but also had similar climate and were more easily accessible. Various Chinese communities were already established where the traditional way of life could be maintained. In the 19th century, approximately three million people left Fujian and Guangdong provinces. This was followed by another exodus in the 1930s and the 1940s, when China suffered from internal turmoil, Japanese invasion, and civil war.

Table 5.1 Major reasons for emigrating from Swatow areas, 1934

Reason given	No. of families	Percent of emigrants
Economic pressure	633	69.95
Previous connections abroad	176	19.45
Losses from natural calamities	31	3.43
Plan to expand specific enterprises	26	2.87
Bad conduct	17	1.88
Local disturbance	7	0.77
Family quarrel	7 ·	0.77
Other	8	0.88
Total	905	100.00

Source: Wu and Wu, 1980, p. 129.

Apparently, the emigrants who left China were mainly driven by the desire to earn a living and the desire to escape domestic hardship (see Table 5.1). The sense of China as the Middle Kingdom remained so deep-rooted in the minds of the Chinese people that they could hardly envision leaving their homeland without intending to return at some point. The name given to those who settled in Southeast Asia was *nanyang huaqiao*, which meant that the Chinese living in the Southern Seas were thought to be temporary sojourners. In fact, many had already sojourned for decades but still held on to their dream that they would eventually return to their motherland before their death. Though it is not the same today for most Overseas Chinese, many still feel emotionally bound to China even after centuries of family settlement elsewhere. The Overseas Chinese are a major source of tourism and investment in China, even though many of them are themselves victims or the descendants of victims of the current communist regime.

The Overseas Chinese have been remarkably successful in the economic sectors. Through years of effort, the Chinese have come to dominate retail trade and have also expanded into mining, transportation, manufacturing, plantation, and finance. Nevertheless, their experiences in Southeast Asia, especially their relationships with the colonial authorities and native Southeast Asians, have been complicated. Throughout much of China's history, the successive governments either showed little regard for the interests of the Overseas Chinese, or were hindered from truly protecting Overseas Chinese interests. This was evident in the 1603 racial massacre in the Philippines and the Red River incident of 1740 in Batavia (currently Jakarta). Some fifteen thousand Chinese lives were lost in the Philippines massacre, while more than ten thousand were lost in the Batavian skirmishes (Limlingan 1986: 26).

OPERATIONAL ENVIRONMENT OF THE OVERSEAS CHINESE

Apart from in Singapore, the Overseas Chinese are the minority ethnic group (see Table 5.2). In Indonesia, Malaysia, Thailand, and the Philippines, the extent and nature of the Overseas Chinese-dominated economy are extremely difficult to ascertain clearly; therefore, more detailed studies are necessary.

Table 5.2 Population distribution of Overseas Chinese

Country	Chinese	Percent of total population
Philippines	600,000	1.4
Indonesia	3,250,000	2.5
Thailand	3,500,000	8.5
Malaysia	3,687,000	35.5
Brunei	46,700	46.7
Singapore	1,580,000	72.0

Source: Limlingan, 1986, p. 3.

In general, the Overseas Chinese economic influence is much more powerful than what their population would seem to indicate. Due to the mixture of the Overseas Chinese economies with native economies and also to the reluctance of these governments to reveal the extent of the Overseas Chinese economic might for the sake of social stability, an absolute ethnic breakdown is difficult to acquire. The Chinese survival strategy of maintaining a low profile has made precise data all the more difficult. Since the situation varies by country, analysis is presented on a country by country basis.

Indonesia

It is the largest of the ASEAN economies and the least developed. The Indonesian economy experienced rapid growth after 1966, when the new Indonesian government led by Suharto shifted from Sukarno's inefficient planning to a market-orientated model. This provided tremendous opportunities for the ethnic Chinese to grow. By the 1980s, the Chinese share of private domestic capital was estimated to be 70–75 percent, while their business groups continued to dominate medium and large-scale corporate capital (Robinson 1986: 276). The domestic capitalistic class was predominantly Chinese. The ethnic Chinese had obviously succeeded in moving into the dominant position in the Indonesian economy. It took remarkably sophisticated political skill and business acumen for a population base of 2.5 percent to achieve ownership of 75 percent of the private domestic capital.

To understand this achievement, one has to consider a number of historical, political, and economic factors. The Dutch East India Company, which was founded in 1602, not only facilitated the import of Chinese laborers but also established a unique role for the Chinese in the economy. Acting as intermediaries between the colonial monopoly of foreign trade and the indigenous-dominated primary sectors, the Chinese began to establish wholesaling and retailing networks during this period. As a vulnerable minority, the Chinese attached great importance to an accommodation with the ruling class that put various limitations on their political powers and yet allowed them to make money in the economic sector. This was not an easy accomplishment for the Chinese because the Muslim-based successive Indonesian governments had adopted a series of discriminating governmental policies. In the Sukarno era, the Chinese suffered a major setback. To reduce the Chinese influence, Sukarno actively sought to reverse the flow of immigrants from China and force those remaining to integrate into society. In the early 1960s, more than 90,000 Chinese were repatriated to China. In the wake of a failed coup in 1965, entire communities of Chinese were expelled or murdered (Fitzgerald 1972).

The Indonesian economy has been dominated by four major groups: the state corporate sector, military-related businesses, Chinese-owned capital, and the indigenous group; among them, the state sector is the largest. As the majority of foreign and domestic investment was focused on trade and primary production, the government has, since the early 1970s, invested in heavy industry to ensure rapid industrialization. For a long time, state-owned enterprises, which were developed on the basis of the nationalized Dutch companies, contributed a larger share than the private sector to the national economy. But in reality the Chinese have heavily penetrated this sector.

The Chinese influence in the state sector can be clearly illustrated by the example of the National Logistics Board (BULOG), the institution that represents state monopolies. An important aspect of BULOG's operations has been its ability to promote or prevent private companies' access to a whole range of trade in basic commodities: import and distribution, and the manufacture and distribution of some basic foodstuffs. Under the patronage of BULOG, several private business groups have prospered. Many of those are Chinese-owned companies with long-standing connections in the Army Strategic Reserve Command. This has exemplified the so-called *cukong* system under which Chinese businessmen play the role of financiers to the military in return for political protection, licenses, and credit monopolies (Robinson 1986: 230).

In due course, this relationship won political protection for the Chinese and served to deny indigenous capitalists access to many sectors. This has allowed the Chinese to form large conglomerates clustered around military/political power centers.

From this arises an ambiguous phenomenon, in which the Chinese capitalists in Indonesia, still discriminated against by some official policies, have become close allies to the two major sources of discrimination, the government and the military. They have also forged close ties to foreign capital via joint ventures. To further insure their investment, many of them have formed business alliances with indigenous capitalists via joint ownership.

Malaysia

The Chinese in Malaysia comprise a much larger proportion of the total population but have very limited direct access to political power. This situation can be traced back to the colonial period, when the British encouraged the Chinese role of middlemen or *kapitans* in the same way that the Dutch did in Indonesia (Wu and Wu 1980: 128). The political power that the British used to hold was transferred to indigenous Malays. Consequently, the Chinese have not been interested in developing an entirely new role for themselves in the newly independent nation and have remained in their traditional economic sphere, coopting political allies where possible. Thus, the spheres of influence in Malaysia are clearly defined racially. Government is a Malay monopoly. The Chinese still control the modern economy and the Indians dominate the legal professions and unions.

The 1969 ethnic riots, in which hundreds of people were killed, to some degree reflected the inherent crisis of the ethnic division. To redress the disproportionate concentration of wealth in the hands of both ethnically Chinese Malays and foreigners, the Malaysian government enacted a New Economic Policy (NEP) in 1971 for the purpose of redistributing the wealth into the hands of the ethnic Malays (known as *bumiputras*) over an extended period. In 1971, 62 percent of the economy was controlled by foreign-based companies, a legacy of the long-term colonial rule; Malaysian nationals who were ethnically Chinese or Indian controlled the next 34 percent, while the *bumiputras* held a pitiful 4 percent. By 1990, the NEP would redistribute at least 30 percent of the domestic economic sectors to the *bumiputras*, leaving 40 percent to Chinese and Indian Malays, and 30 percent to foreigners. The NEP outlined a two-pronged strategy to achieve this objective: Poverty Eradication and Income Equalization.

The Malaysian government implemented this policy by exercising controls on business ownership, conducting government-sponsored acquisitions of foreign businesses, using business permits to manipulate ethnic participation, and imposing employment and educational quotas. These measures rapidly enhanced *bumiputra* control from 4 percent to 18 percent by 1985, while the foreign sector shrank from 62 percent to 25 percent. Interestingly enough, the Chinese/Indian sector expanded from 34 percent to 57 percent. Apparently, the designed transference of power from the original foreign sector to the *bumiputras* fell significantly short of expectations. By 1990, the *bumiputra* control was estimated at around 22 percent. This figure could have been inflated, as real control of many *bumiputra* companies was in the hands of Chinese and Indian capitalists, who hid behind a respectable *bumiputra* name on the share register and notepaper. If foreign-owned interests were taken out, the Chinese and Indian sectors together controlled 76 percent of the locally owned economy. After deducting the Indian share, Chinese nominal control of the locally owned economy could be as much as 60 percent, even without including their hidden control of *bumiputra* businesses (Redding 1990: 30–31).

The Philippines

The situation in the Philippines is similar to that in Indonesia. For many of the same reasons, the Spanish colonial authorities encouraged Chinese immigration and took advantage of their skills to benefit the export-crop economy. Since then, the Chinese have carefully extended their network into the government and military power bases. Although they represent a very small percentage of the total population, their economic power is disproportionately large. Unlike Muslim-dominated Indonesia and Malaysia, the Chinese fit better into the dominant Roman Catholic social ethos, as evidenced by the high number of Chinese–Filipino intermarriages.

Since the independence of the Philippines, successive governments have adopted a whole series of measures to prevent the Chinese from acquiring economic power or citizenship. Republic Act No. 37 in 1947, Republic Act No. 1180 in 1954, the Filipino-subsidizing project of the National Marketing Corporation in 1956, Republic Act No. 3018 in 1960, and labor regulations of 1961, were all designed to protect Filipinos from Chinese competition. Usually this was accomplished by prohibiting alien Chinese commercial activities through complicating the naturalization process for ethnic Chinese. Although this discrimination continued until the mid-1970s, the Chinese still controlled 35 percent of the local economy by the early 1980s. A study in 1982 revealed that Filipino–Chinese owned more than 33 percent of the top manufacturing firms and 43 percent of the top commercial firms (Hicks and Redding 1982: 212).

Thailand

Standing opposite Indonesia's and Malaysia's racially tinted business policies is Thailand's tolerance. For centuries, the Thais and Overseas Chinese have maintained a remarkably peaceful coexistence, with neither religion (Buddhism) nor socio-cultural norms (drinking, eating) generating friction. Certainly, there were intervals of tension. In 1942, for example, the Thai government announced that twenty-seven industries and occupations were reserved for the employment of Thai citizens only. Nevertheless, anti-Chinese policies were formerly abandoned in the late 1950s and the Chinese have since been regarded as full-fledged members of Thai society (Wu and Wu 1980: 72).

Guided by an all-inclusive Buddhist tolerance in their culture, the Thais have throughout history managed with remarkable success to restrict open discrimination against outsiders and have provided a propitious environment for assimilation. Since there is a high degree of interracial marriage and a low degree of racial separateness, it is not easy to assess how many Chinese have settled in Thailand. There remain few difficulties for the ethnic Chinese in Thailand. From the royal family to the princes, from the generals to the business tycoons, few among the elite do not possess some Chinese heritage. It is not uncommon for Thai top officials or generals to proudly acknowledge their Chinese ancestry. Many Thai Chinese have made their surnames sound "Thai."

The development policy of Thailand has also provided opportunities for the ethnic Chinese. A Sino-Thai business community has emerged as the dominant economic group, controlling a large share of virtually all major business sectors. The government policy of limiting the introduction of foreign banks and preventing those already there from building branches, for example, has enabled domestic banking to flourish, achieving a net growth of fifty times from the early 1960s to the early 1980s. Most of these local banks are owned by Sino-Thais. It is difficult to estimate the extent to which the ethnic Chinese control the Thai economy. Most estimates attribute around 90 percent of all investment in commercial and manufacturing sectors to Sino-Thai ownership. More than 50 percent of all investments in the banking and finance sectors are in the hands of the Sino-Thais (Clad 1989: 150).

Except for Singapore, most of the newly independent ASEAN countries have at various stages tried to redress Chinese dominance in their economies through heavy governmental involvement, including policies to cut off or even reverse the flow of Chinese immigrants, exclusion policies, preference policies, support policies and indigenization policies. The need for a certain degree of economic rationality has constrained the ASEAN governments from radically changing the ownership structure. This has provided the Overseas Chinese with an opportunity to tap into capitalist development in those countries and achieve dominance. By coopting various indigenous governments, the Overseas Chinese have managed to turn various governmental barriers to their advantage.

THE DIVERSITIES AND COMMONALITIES OF THE OVERSEAS CHINESE

Although the Overseas Chinese are relatively distinct from their host cultures in Indonesia, Malaysia, the Philippines and Thailand, various degrees of integration and assimilation into local societies have already taken place. Yuan-li Wu and Chun-hsi Wu's research divides the Overseas Chinese into two broad categories (see Figure 5.2). The second category consists of those born of mixed parentage, with only those whose fathers are ethnic Chinese classified as Chinese, reflecting the dominance of the male line of succession.

In reality, the Overseas Chinese are even more diverse. The Chinese in Indonesia can culturally be separated into Indonesian-speaking *perranakans* and Chinese-speaking *totoks*, with the former being the dominant group. The majority are already naturalized Indonesians; the resident aliens are comprised of PRC nationals, Taiwan nationals and those with ambiguous national status. The Chinese community in Malaysia also presents a complex picture and mainly consists of three groups. The group A Chinese identify themselves with either China or Taiwan, both politically and culturally; Group B (the majority) is interested in low-profile politics of trade and associations; Group C has cultivated some sort of Malayan loyalty. Due to the large size of the Chinese population, the majority remain culturally more Chinese than those in Indonesia, the Philippines and Thailand. The Philippines Chinese can be divided into Chinese *mestizos* and ethnic Chinese. The first group identify themselves completely with Filipinos; the second group has varying degrees of acculturation into the larger Filipino society. The Chinese in Thailand are also heterogeneous, though there is a higher degree of assimilation into the local Thai population. In Singapore, the Chinese can be broadly classified into English-educated and Chinese-educated groups, with very different values and behavioral patterns belonging to each group (Suryadinata 1985: 11–15).

The extent of acculturation depends on a number of factors: the size of the Chinese community in proportion to the non-Chinese population, the

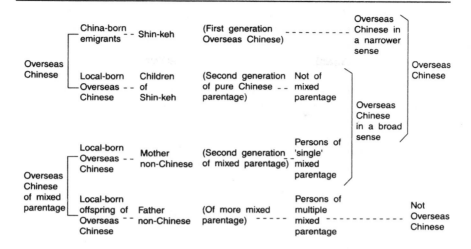

Figure 5.2 Overseas Chinese identity
Source: Wu and Wu, 1980, p. 208.

degree of religious and custom similarities between the Chinese and the indigenous population, and the willingness of the indigenous governments to integrate the ethnic Chinese. As a result of religious and cultural tolerance in Thailand, the Chinese in Thailand seem to have achieved the most rapid acculturation, with a high rate of mixed marriage. They are followed by the Chinese in the Philippines and Indonesia. The least acculturated are those in Malaysia, since the Chinese minority accounts for a substantially larger proportion of the total population. As they are the majority group in Singapore, the Chinese can hardly be expected to be acculturated into the "indigenous" minority group, but the Singapore Chinese are different from those in Taiwan, Hong Kong and Macao; many have a sense of local character, hints of Indian and Malayan influences and are more conscious of Singaporean identity.

In spite of a gradual process of assimilation and an increasingly greater mobility in the Overseas Chinese communities with many already acquiring Western education and passports, there is a strong sense of consistency and continuity among the Overseas Chinese in identifying themselves with Chinese civilization. Remarkably, this sense of "Chineseness" seems to have faded very little over time and geographic separation. This is the single most outstanding feature of the Overseas Chinese. In an attempt to define the key aspects characterizing their relationship with their environment, Redding (1990: 33–40) has identified a set of influences shared by many Overseas Chinese which have played an important role in molding much of their contemporary thinking and are indispensable fundamentals for understanding the Overseas Chinese.

First, they have lived in not-so-friendly social environments that have time and again displayed open hostilities throughout history, thereby forcing them to rely on their own resources. This environmental hostility is not only characterized by occasional eruptions of anti-Chinese violence, but more often by constant Chinese feelings of being separate from the environment and uncertain of the future. Such feelings can be derived from racial quotas for university access, cost and difficulty in acquiring citizenship, government-sponsored economic favoritism to indigenous businesses (e.g. restrictions on certain Chinese business activities, and specific restrictive rules with regard to the use of Chinese language). Mainly in response to these discriminatory measures, the Chinese have followed the principle of caution, hedging bets and avoiding publicity.

For different reasons, such separateness and long-run uncertainty even influence the predominantly Chinese societies in Hong Kong, Singapore, or Taiwan. The source of the threat for Hong Kong and Taiwan is communism and the prospect of eventually being brought back to the mother country. Their reactions are complicated and ambivalent. The common factors of separateness and uncertainty turn the environment into one very similar to those of their cousins throughout the region. Chinese families in both Hong Kong and Taiwan can hardly take the future for granted. Although Singapore is a country with a Chinese majority, it is surrounded by countries with non-Chinese majorities. The nation has always felt a sense of threat and isolation.

Second, the Chinese feelings of being separate from their environment and uncertainty about their future have given rise to a heightened sense of cooperativeness within the Overseas Chinese world. The traditional network systems, which are constructed on the basis of special personal relationships, can facilitate their cooperation. Ironically, the sense of cooperativeness is usually much lower in a predominantly Chinese society such as Hong Kong or Taiwan because fierce competition among various family businesses and their networks overshadow the mood of cooperativeness. To illustrate the lack of cooperativeness among the Chinese, a famous Chinese scholar Lin Yu-tang compared the Japanese to a piece of granite and the Chinese to a tray of loose sand. Each grain represents a separate Chinese family, while the Japanese society is not so divisive. But when the Overseas Chinese become the minority in the major ASEAN countries they are compelled to turn their competitiveness toward non-Chinese majorities, who have been identified as a major threat to Chinese survival. Their tendency to weave networks helps consolidate their cooperativeness; these networks bind not only blood-related relationships but also people from the same regions in China.

Third, the first two factors have served to strengthen the natural tendency of the Overseas Chinese to identify with Chinese civilization, especially when it is set against very different cultural traditions in Southeast Asia. The sense of Chineseness has become a powerful unifying force. Except for Thailand, which has maintained its independence throughout history and has a strong Buddhist-based cultural identity, the other ASEAN countries have suffered from the damaging impact of colonialism on the development of their native national cultures. With a deep-rooted pride in their own unified form of civilization, the Overseas Chinese tend to hold on to their own culture and take an often condescending attitude toward the diversified indigenous cultures in Southeast Asia. Many Overseas Chinese believe their strength lies in the legacy of their sophisticated cultural tradition.

Finally, the initial hardship of migrating has cultivated values for economic survival, such as pragmatism, a work ethic, and thriftiness that also correspond to traditional Chinese values. Since the majority of Chinese immigrants left the country for similar reasons, i.e. to escape turmoil and poverty, three sets of values became dominant in their struggle for survival. To begin with, the Confucian value of family was greatly strengthened as the immigrant family became the central scene of life for its members, providing a safe haven and welfare. Next, the survival of individuals and their families entailed hard work, which also embodied individual members' obligations to their families. Those who were considered lazy and selfish or made little contribution were regarded as social outcasts, thus being slighted and isolated by their families. Last but not least, the prospects of long-term insecurity promoted the value of chasing and accumulating material wealth and money.

SUMMARY/CONCLUSION

This chapter has reviewed the origins of the Overseas Chinese and found that most of them came to Southeast Asia not as traders but as laborers who were either attracted by the opportunities or were refugees of political and economic disasters in China during the mid-19th century to the early 20th century. The discussion subsequently led to an analysis of the overall operational environment of the Overseas Chinese businesses in Southeast Asia with the focus on Indonesia, Malaysia, the Philippines, and Thailand. In the end the diversity and commonalities of these Chinese were identified and analyzed.

Generally speaking, the social environment of the Overseas Chinese has not been favorable. In spite of their early start during the colonial period as the intermediaries between colonial authorities and the indigenous people, they have become major targets of rising nationalism throughout the region. In addition to being victims of sporadic racial rioting, the Chinese have endured a whole range of discriminating policies carried out at different stages by governments of independent Southeast Asian nations. With a few exceptions, their integration and assimilation have been slow, with many Chinese societies still remaining quite aloof from society as a whole. But through hard work, effective organization and dexterous co-option of the indigenous governments, they have excelled in business competition and consolidated their positions in the region. The Overseas Chinese success in the economic area in Southeast Asia has been phenomenal. With a mere 6 percent of the region's 460 million people, they dominate virtually every national economy. In all of the ASEAN countries the Overseas Chinese have generated powerful businesses and financial interests. Most of these people are either immigrants or descendants of immigrants who escaped the insecurity and poverty in China during the hundred years from the mid-19th century to the mid-20th century.

QUESTIONS FOR DISCUSSION

1 What was "piggy-trade" in the last century in Southeast Asia?
2 What is the implication of the term *nanyang huaqiao*?
3 How do you assess the overall operational environment of the Chinese in Southeast Asia?
4 What are the key commonalities of the Overseas Chinese?
5 In your opinion what factors have been the major influences on the acculturation process of the Overseas Chinese?

FURTHER READING

Clad, James (1989) *Behind the Myth: Business, Money and Power in Southeast Asia*, London: Hyman.

Fitzgerald, Stephen (1972) *China and the Overseas Chinese: A Study of Peking's Changing Policy 1949–1970*, Cambridge: Cambridge University Press.

Hicks, George C. and S.G. Redding (1982) "Culture and Corporate Performance in the Philippines: the Chinese Puzzle," in R.M. Bautista and E.M. Pernia (eds), *Essays in Development Economics in Honour of Harry T. Oshima*, Manila: Philippines Institute for Developmental Studies, pp. 199–215.

Jesudason, James V. (1989) *The Origin of Modern Capitalism in Eastern Asia*, Hong Kong: Hong Kong University Press.

Lim, Linda Y. and L.A. Peter Gosling (eds) (1983) *The Chinese in Southeast Asia* (Vols 1 and 2), Singapore: Maruzen Asia.

Limlingan, Victor Simpao (1986) *The Overseas Chinese in ASEAN: Business Strategies and Management Practices*, Manila: Vita Development Corp.

Pan, Lynn (1990) *Sons of the Yellow Emperor: The Story of the Overseas Chinese*, London: Secker & Warburg.

Poston, Dudley L., Jr. and Mei-Yu Yu (1990) "The Distribution of the Overseas Chinese in the Contemporary World," *International Migration Review* 26 (3) (Fall): 480–509.

Redding, S. Gordon (1990) *The Spirit of Chinese Capitalism*, New York: Walter de Gruyter.

Robinson, Richard (1986) *Indonesia: the Rise of Capitalism*, Sydney: Allen & Unwin.

Steinberg, David J. *et al.* (eds) (1971) *In Search of Southeast Asia: A Modern History*, New York: Praeger Publishers.

Suryadinata, Leo (1985) *China and the ASEAN States: The Ethnic Chinese Dimension*, Singapore: Singapore University Press.

—— (ed.) (1989) *The Ethnic Chinese in the ASEAN States: Bibliographical Essays*, Singapore: Institute of Southeast Asian Studies.

Wang, Gungwu (1991) *China and the Chinese Overseas*, Singapore: Times Academic Press.

Wu, Yuan-li and Chun-hsi Wu (1980) *Economic Development in Southeast Asia: The Chinese Dimension*, Stanford, Calif.: Hoover Institution Press.

Yoshihara, Kunio (1988) *The Rise of Ersatz Capitalism in Southeast Asia*, New York: Oxford University Press.

Chapter 6

The Chinese family business
Organizational challenges and competitive edge

INTRODUCTION

The Chinese family business (CFB) has become the dominant form of Overseas Chinese business organization and one of the major forms of Asian business. The CFB has two dimensions: one refers to the core family business, which includes only family members and is normally very small. This is the purest form of family business. The other refers to a sort of clan business, which hires nonfamily members. The core family still controls the ownership while the owner and key family members hold the most important positions of management. As these companies continue to grow, they are confronted with the challenge of either modernizing the management system with the help of professional managers or holding on to the traditional mode of management. The transition will have a tremendous impact on the direction of the CFB itself.

The dominant managerial ideology of the CFB can be summarized by the word "patrimonialism," which covers a wide range of themes such as paternalism, hierarchy, mutual obligation, responsibility, familialism, personalism, and connections (Redding 1990: 155). Several interrelated influences are derived from these themes: the notion that power and authority are closely connected to ownership; autocratic leadership, which is sometimes coated with benevolence; and a personalistic style of management. These three influences have led to a number of organizational features, such as the importance of ownership, small structural size, informal and simple structure, factionalism, etc.

There are basically two schools of thought on the study of the CFB. One school, as reflected in Professor Huang Guo-guang's writing (1989: 121–134), emphasizes the negative influence of the Chinese business culture on the development of the CFB. In this view, the CFB should radically introduce advanced Western management technique while minimizing the interference of traditional Chinese culture. The other school, typified by the research of Professor S. Gordon Redding (1990), tends to emphasize the positive role that the Chinese business culture plays in shaping the competitive edge of the CFB. In the opinion of this school, the CFB should not lose its cultural uniqueness in the process of modernization. While these two schools do not differ in their description of the organizational and managerial features of the CFB, they do have fairly different approaches toward the impact of Chinese business culture on the development of the CFB.

This chapter is intended to present a balanced view on the strengths and weaknesses of the CFB in terms of its organizational structure and management process. Both the positive and negative influences of Chinese business culture will be examined in proper proportion. In the end, there will be a discussion on an ideal modernization process for the CFB, which will combine some Western management techniques with positive elements of the Chinese business culture.

ORGANIZATIONAL STRUCTURE

The distribution of power and authority provides an institutional framework for an organization's internal culture and behavior. There are a number of dimensions for organizational structuring, such as centralization, specialization, standardization, formalization and configuration. Among them, specialization, standardization and formalization seem to be closely related because they all represent the degree to which a company is organized. These three dimensions are concerned about designing and elaborating organizational structures and their activities. In contrast to these, there is the practice of telling people what to implement. If a boss wants to retain absolute authority in everything, he is not interested in delegating power and does not need elaborate structures. High centralization results in a low structure, whereas delegation requires structure.

Ownership

According to Confucian ethics, "family" is the most fundamental revenue and expenditure unit, within which every member contributes his or her income to the common family fund while each one has a right to obtain a portion of it, with the rest belonging to the family as a whole. The interests of the family take precedence over those of the society and of other society members. The family is an elastic concept, which can be expanded or contracted according to need. Five subgroups can be identified within the family business; and these are the core family members, close relatives, long-term employees (honorary family members), distant relatives, and non-related employees, with core members clearly in the dominant position.

Under the influence of this concept, the business owner tends to regard the business as the private property of the core family, and thereby is reluctant to share the ownership with others. As long as the business itself can provide capital or borrow capital from friendly sources, the business owner will be unwilling to share proprietorial rights with others – even friends. Some large Chinese corporations, though technically public, are still heavily influenced and controlled by the family because of this view.

Consequently, the top management positions in the family business are filled by key family members. The chief financial officer is typically either the boss himself or a key member of the family, often the son or wife. Secondary key management positions are often reserved for close relatives and those who have worked for the family for an extended period and are qualified as quasi-family members. Family ownership also means that the bulk of the contributions made by nonfamily members will be passed on to the family purse, thus undercutting the link between individual effort and reward.

Size

The majority of the CFBs remain small, despite rapid economic development in the non-communist Chinese societies where the CFBs typically thrive. In fact, the size of the CFBs in Hong Kong has decreased. In 1951, 79 percent of all manufacturing enterprises in Hong Kong employed fewer than 50 people. This percentage had grown to 88 percent by 1971 and to 92 percent by 1981. In the same period, the proportion of the workforce in the small-business sector had expanded from 26 percent to 41 percent. In contrast, medium-sized companies hiring 50 to 500 employees had declined in number from 19 percent to 8 percent of the total, and the proportion of the workforce employed in this sector had dropped from 47 percent to 43 percent. In 1981, companies with more than 500 people only took 0.4 percent of the total and employed 16 percent of the workforce (Redding and Wong 1990: 275).

According to a 1981 statistic on Taiwan's manufacturing industries, there was a total of 280 state-owned enterprises, which hired 347,818 employees, averaging 1,242 employees per enterprise. On the other hand, 98 percent of the enterprises on the island were privately owned enterprises that numbered 513,133 and each employed fewer than 50 employees. On average, each privately owned enterprise hired about eight employees. Businessmen in Taiwan joke that if one "throws a rock out of a top floor window of a Taipei skyscraper, the odds are good that the rock will hit a president of a Taiwan company" (Huang 1989: 127). The reason for the plentitude of small CFBs is the great diversity of interest among the populace. One cultural explanation is the "*laoban* syndrome" (the desire to become a boss) in the Chinese business world. A popular expression clearly reflects this mentality: "Better to become the head of a chicken than the tail of an ox." As will be shown later, the ownership and organizational structure of the Chinese family business have also made it difficult to grow.

Structure

The CFBs are not only small but also simple in structure. Most of them can only concentrate on either production, sales or service. Even in the larger businesses, very few develop large functional departments. The overwhelming majority of the CFBs do not have ancillary departments for R&D, labor relations, public relations, or market research. All employees are expected to be involved in the main products or the services of the company, which directly create profits.

Moreover, as most CFBs do not have a complete set of rules and systems, various functions within the CFBs are not clearly defined and roles of various posts are not clearly assigned. The level of specialization is very low, with fewer job specifications and more people dealing in a range of activities across a number of fields. With less standardization, there are fewer routine work procedures. Employees can be assigned to various jobs at the whim of business owners.

The organizational structure is not only simple but also very informal. The rules of an organization have the function of restricting the abuse of power. Without such rules, a business owner tends to wield all the power in his own hands and makes his decisions in order to prevent transgressions from his managers. When the organization grows to the extent that he can no longer handle all the decisions, he will appoint family members or relatives to the most important posts within the business. Thus, the CFB becomes a social organization orientated toward connections: a Chinese businessman manages as an owner, while his family members fill the senior ranks and the middle-ranks are occupied by those having close long-term ties with the family. Those who do not have close ties will have to work at the lowest level.

Due to the lack of formal structure and rules, personal relationships and feelings about other people are likely to take precedence over more objectively defined concerns such as organizational efficiency. As a result, the CFB becomes an organization where who one knows tends to be more important than what one knows. One consequence is the suppression of professionals. Setting up a personnel department, or hiring a financial analyst, is tantamount to inviting challenge to managerial authority. Expert power threatens the power of patronage and personal relationships. This may also explain the reluctance to build up the staff.

The lack of formal structure and rules also allows the CFB to be a breeding ground for cliques, which form on a number of levels stemming from regional affiliations, clannish relationships, and even job similarities. These cliques substitute the function of a formal structure and tend to place their own interests above those of their organization. When the contest between cliques evolves into a major dissension, the cooperative framework on which day-to-day operations depend can be severely damaged.

MANAGEMENT PROCESS

Management processes embrace such activities as leadership, decision-making, and the communication methods through which organization goals are achieved. The way by which the process is implemented is influenced by the interaction between the structural characteristics of the organization and the individuals.

Leadership and decision-making

The leadership style is authoritarian and can be best described by the word "didactic" (Silin 1976: 63). In order to maintain his power, the boss controls information and transmits it piecemeal to subordinates so that they become dependent and unable to outperform him. The amount of information given to a specific subordinate depends on the degree of trust that the leader has for that individual. With the control of information, the subordinates frequently have to ask the leader for instructions.

The boss's concern with the retention of power is also reflected in the careful maintenance of a large power distance. He should not be openly challenged by his subordinates. In the Chinese family business system, subordinates are supposed to think what the boss is thinking and tailor their ideas accordingly. Dissenting opinions and proposals should be conveyed to the boss through private and personal channels, with a duly respectful tone. Given this style of leadership, it can be expected that the boss can take for granted his frequent interference and unaccounted-for changes of direction.

Since a business owner regards his business as the private property of the family, the goal-setting is often treated as an affair internal to the family. The financial situation of the CFB is often regarded as a family secret and many important decisions are made after discussion within the family. Those who are not a part of the family often have the obligation of implementing the directives, without sharing in the decision-making process.

The decision is usually made by the boss himself and the process is very simple, with the boss making most of his decisions based largely on intuition and/or experience. Given his monopoly over the information of the business, he is probably in the best position to make all the important decisions. As most of the bosses of the CFBs have started from scratch, and have taken care of every aspect of the business, they have accumulated precious experiences and are capable of powerful intuitions. The family ownership and simple structure discussed earlier make this an acceptable practice. This type of decision-making process is also justified by the need of the CFB to seize each opportunity immediately.

Management control

Management control involves the processes of translating organizational goals into action codes, monitoring the results across a whole range of activities, comparing results against projected goals, and adopting a measure to overcome deviations from the plan. In Western organizations it is thought to be a rational and open process.

Due to the lack of structure and rules, the authority and responsibility of each position in the CFB are not clearly defined. Therefore, it is difficult for managers at different levels to make objective assessments of employee performance. Consequently, the top management in the CFB often pays special attention to the degree of "manager loyalty." For those highly loyal to top management and capable of special skills integral to the business, the boss will give substantial personal rewards in the form of year-end bonuses and/or a "little red bag" (the bag containing money). For those deemed "less loyal," and less competent, any reward is also correspondingly lower. For those having no special relations or special skills that the business depends on, the boss will typically employ them with lower wages and will not even give them "face" by refraining from public humiliation.

Given the family ownership, the corporate and personal goals of key executives from the family are identical, thus providing for strong motivations to achieve organizational goals. Nevertheless, this culture also fosters a tendency for top managers to hold control over decisions relating to bonuses, pay increases, employee discipline, or even the social behavior of employees. In other words, while the operating responsibility may be delegated to lower-level managers, effective control over employees is retained at the top of the organization. As a result, mid- and lower-level managers are frequently bypassed and employees are obliged to side with the boss who controls the paychecks, even when he may be wrong. This tends to suffocate the creativity and talents of mid- or lower-level managers who are not closely associated with the family. The result is that professionals are tempted to leave as often as they are actually squeezed out (Deyo 1983: 215–217).

Two implications for organizational behavior can be identified from this (Redding and Wong 1990: 285–286). First, many Western managerial techniques in the area of human resources management may be very difficult to transfer to the context of the Chinese family business. A suitable example is related to the principle of management by objectives (MBO), which relies on notions of individual competitiveness, self-actualization, personal achievement, accountability, and open confrontation. All of these notions clash with the prevalent perceptions and feelings about relationships in a

Chinese organization. Chinese management control is tantamount to the subtle art of weaving and balancing obligation networks. Individually measured performance is hardly a major concern in assessment unless it takes place in mechanical production systems and in the control of component-type operations.

Second, the lack of a nonobjective assessment mechanism enhances the role of personalism. To reduce unpredictability, employees tend to spend a great deal of time developing their connections in the organization. Subsequently, informal sub-organizations become very important. Various factions tend to rival each other within the larger organization. One measure of management control tends to involve a number of employees forcing management to take into consideration the implications of a specific control measure over employees. The apparent harmony conceals perennial internal dissension within the organization.

The management of external relations

The influence of personal relationships also extends to the management of external business relations. These small companies are linked together in networks, like a spider's web. It is not organized in a formal way, nor is there any formal contract. All business contacts are virtually based on personal relationships, whether they are with relatives or friends. It is established and consolidated on the value of *xinyong*, which refers not only to "credit," in the sense of services and goods offered against the promise of future repayment, but also to the "credit rating" of the person who applies for credit (Barton 1983: 50).

If personal relationships provide business, *xinyong* allows them to keep that business connection or expand those business ties. Business connection networks make up for the limited resources of a small family business. Once again, there is very little need of institutional support for that connection network. This type of business relationship is often informal, with many agreements being achieved orally. Flexibility is the key to managing such a connection network. In this way, a small family business is able to respond to shifts in international trade and investments with great efficiency. The CFB can handle almost any business by joining forces with its business connections.

Subcontracting relationships, for example, are often managed in a less formal way than might be the case in other cultures. According to Redding (1990: 149–153), 31 percent of the subcontracting firms in Hong Kong are in that position because of "personal ties" with the firms they supply. In 34 percent of the cases, only a verbal contract existed. In 53 percent of the cases, price was determined through discourse between the parties concerned rather than as a result of unilateral decision. Most of the orders required delivery within one month, indicating the need of a swift market response in operation. In spite of the fact that 71 percent of the responding subcontractors noticed an inherent instability and irregularity in subcontracting, 81 percent claimed to be satisfied with the formula.

INHERENT WEAKNESSES AND COMPARATIVE STRENGTHS

The above discussions of the organizational structure and management process of the CFB have shown that the Overseas Chinese seem to be doing many things contrary to mainstream management in the West. Matthew Montagu-Pollock (1991: 20–21) has listed a number of contrasts in Western theory (w) versus Eastern theory (e): larger firms are competitive because they can profit from economies of scale (w); companies perform the best when they stay small (e); management development is the key to raising company effectiveness (w); the business tycoons leading Asia's revival have no regular management training (e); the CEO should delegate management authority to his subordinates and employees (w); it is dangerous to delegate (e); a new leadership is needed every few years to revitalize the company (w); stability and consistency are important (e), etc.

For many in the West, the management style of the CFBs represents a worst nightmare scenario. There is a great deal of truth to such a conclusion. Among the prominent features of the CFB's organizational structure and management processes is the inability to separate power away from ownership, its small size, its simple and informal structure, a didactic leadership style, and personalistic management control. These features can have a number of harmful impacts on the organization and its management.

First of all, the trust and loyalty that the CFB seeks to build is difficult to accomplish. Except for a few family members and those very close to the owner, members of Chinese businesses usually lack the consciousness of identifying with the business itself. Nonfamily members and ordinary employees often feel as if they are outsiders, and thus have a low degree of loyalty and a low level of responsibility. Even those holding high positions in the CFB feel more loyal to the specific superior in the business rather than to the business itself. This is reflected in the relatively high transfer rate among the CFBs. In Taiwan, the transfer rates in small and mid-sized companies reach as high as 50 percent each year (Hall and Xu 1991: 573).

Second, the leadership style tends to repress professional talents. The narrowly defined family, which emphasizes bloodlines (Hsu 1985: 35), tends to exclude professional talents from the inner circles of company management that have access to key company information and company ownership. Those with professional talent can change their position in one of the following ways: (1) they marry themselves into the family pedigree, thus gaining quick promotions; (2) they control the kind of skills that the CFB depends on to an extent that the owner must cultivate a special relationship with them and promote them to key positions after being convinced of company loyalty; (3) they endure long-term repression of their talents and eventually win the status of honorary family member and thereby obtain a promotion; (4) they pack up and leave in a short period.

Third, the lack of an institutionalized succession mechanism often undermines the longevity of the CFB. As a popular Chinese saying goes, "no family can stay rich for more than three generations." The inheritance in the CFB tends to be equally divided among all sons, and daughters are now also included in some CFBs. As companies are passed from one generation to another, a typical pattern can be identified. As the owner passes away, the second generation succeeds and begins a cycle of fragmentation. In the event that they cannot break up the company, they often are involved in endless power struggles and clique strife. The emergence of the third generation further fragments the CFB. Thus, it is not surprising that a CFB rarely survives for more than 100 years (Wong 1985).

Finally, all these negative impacts have worked to restrict the growth of the CFB either in terms of size or diversification. The use of centralization rather than the use of structuring as a means of exercising management control naturally hampers the growth process. The larger the company grows, the higher the pressure on top management to delegate: it either has to delegate or face the consequence of overburdening at the top. Chinese-style centralized management can function in large companies only on the condition that the company sticks to one business – such as retailing, shipping, property, or banking, where decision-making can be more centralized. When complicated decision-making is involved, this centralization will make the CFB very inefficient. Therefore, many CFBs either choose to remain small in order to survive or choose to grow to become extinct.

Consequently, the vast majority of Chinese family businesses are either small or specialized in one field of expertise. Large Chinese family businesses are still very rare, but the ones that do exist concentrate on specific businesses and are still run as if they were small. Therefore, the characteristics of their management style do not differ from those of the small CFBs. A "typical" larger Chinese-owned company will have people ranging from fifty to a few hundred performing a specialized activity such as toy manufacturing or subcontracting. The owner, who most likely is also the CEO, would be the majority shareholder.

In spite of these problems, one should not ignore the competitive edge of the CFB. As noted earlier, the CFBs have contributed to some of the most impressive national growth records ever achieved. If their business is generally successful, it is not unreasonable to suppose that the internal efficiency of the CFB is higher than may have been recognized. In order to achieve this efficiency, the CFB tends to follow fairly consistent forms of management and organizing, which have been discussed earlier in this chapter: these include family domination, paternalistic leadership style, centralized decision-making, small size, personalism, and loose structure.

As a result, the balancing of forces is a delicate process that leads to high levels of vertical and horizontal cooperation while allowing productive drive to set personal and organizational goals in equal manner. If the CFB grows too large, it goes beyond the reach of the personal relationships which bind people tightly together. Too much delegation may risk abuse by managers, while too little will strain top leadership. Too much nepotism may undermine organizational effectiveness, while too little may foment distrust. In the subtle balance of the CFB organization, the central point is that being small is beautiful (Redding and Wong 1990: 293–294). Ironically, this is a lesson being relearned by many Western companies, which are downsizing, getting meaner, leaner, and fitter.

In addition to their advantage of networking, the CFBs have been and will continue to be successful in two regards (Montagu-Pollock 1991: 23). The first is the situation where flexibility is necessary. The CFBs have been very good at reducing costs due to their small size and concentration on labor-intensive industries, as well as their ability to maintain flexibility in order to seize business opportunities. As many Chinese businesses upgrade their technology they will gradually lose their reputation as cheap producers, but their flexibility will continue to be their competitive edge. The size, the leadership style and family support will help maintain this flexibility. In the manufacture and design of machinery and parts, Chinese organizations will continue to be competitive because of their superior flexibility. The second is the situation where deal-making skills are crucial. The management structure and style of the CFB, though authoritarian, is well suited for speedy decision-making. The Chinese business owners' abilities to excel in deal-making will continue to allow them to maintain their competitive edge in retail finance, hotels, shipping, and other areas where decision-making can still be centralized with efficiency.

SUMMARY/CONCLUSION

This chapter has analyzed the organizational structure and management process of Chinese family businesses. The organizational structure of a CFB can be typified by closed family ownership and small size with a simple and informal structure. In terms of management practice, CFBs have a distinctive authoritarian leadership style that is didactic in nature; the decision-making process being intuitive and swift. Management control is characterized by emphasis on loyalty and a subjective assessment mechanism. Owing to high dynamism in developing connections at work, Chinese companies manage external relationships very well. In the end the comparative strengths and weaknesses are identified. Among the major problems are high turnover rates of employees, suppression of professional talents, and lack of an institutionalized succession mechanism. The comparative advantage of CFBs lies in their small size, flexibility, connection network, and deal-making skills.

The Chinese family business is the product of Chinese culture and tradition. Many features of the CFBs' organization and management must be understood in the cultural and traditional context, without which wrong conclusions will be reached. Like business organizations in other cultures, the CFBs have been under constant pressure to change and modernize. The new generations of Chinese managers, who have been trained in the West, have also been pushing for the kind of change that is aimed at closing the gap between the West and the Chinese organizations. With the upgrading of their technological levels, many CFBs will have to readjust their traditional distrust of professional employees and allow them to display their creativity.

Nevertheless, all these changes do not mean that the CFBs are becoming a passing phenomenon, nor are they losing their uniquely competitive features, as evidenced by the slow pace of Westernization in the Overseas Chinese companies. Even among the pioneers of modernization – large Chinese corporations – the trend toward Westernization is surprisingly slow. Out of the 100 largest Taiwanese companies, for example, all but two are owned either by a family, a single owner, or by very close partners (Montagu-Pollock 1991: 23). The Western-trained MBA graduates have often found that they need to reconcile their Western training with the Chinese environment, as complete application tends to backfire.

What the CFB really needs to do is to expand the cohesiveness within the core family members to include all employees by institutionalizing the organization and the management style. With clear-cut organizational structures and rules, professionals and ordinary employees will be able to identify themselves with the CFB. In a sense, this is to apply the concept of family to all employees so that they feel emotionally attached to the company. The role of personalism in management should be restricted so that everyone will have real incentives to work hard for the company. Only in an institutionalized organization will such Confucian ethics as loyalty (group identification), diligence (work initiatives), sincerity (open atmosphere) and harmony (good interpersonal relationships), be given full display.

QUESTIONS FOR DISCUSSION

1 Can you describe the key organizational features of a typical CFB?
2 Why do you think factionalism is an inherent problem in CFBs?

3 What does it mean when the leadership style of a CFB is described as didactic?
4 What options do you have to consolidate your position as a professional in a CFB?
5 In what areas do you think CFBs need to modernize the most?

FURTHER READING

Barton, Clifton A. (1983) "Trust and Credit: Some Observations Regarding Business Strategies of Overseas Chinese Traders in South Vietnam," in L.A. Peter Gosling and Linda Y.C. Lim (eds), *The Chinese in Southeast Asia* (Vol. 2), Singapore: Maruzen Asia, pp. 46–64.
Deyo, Frederic C. (1983) "Chinese Management Practices and Work Commitment in Comparative Perspective," in L.A. Peter Gosling and Linda Y.C. Lim (eds), *The Chinese in Southeast Asia* (Vol. 2), Singapore: Maruzen Asia, pp. 215–229.
Hall, Richard H. and Xu Weiman (1991) "Run Silent, Run Deep – Cultural Influences on Organizations in the Far East," *Organization Studies* 11 (4): 569–576.
Hsu, Francis L.K. (1985) "The Self in Cross-cultural Perspective," in George DeVos, Anthony J. Marsella, and Francis L.K. Hsu (eds), *Culture and Self*, London: Tavistock, pp. 31– 45.
Huang, Guo-guang (1989) "On the Modernization of Chinese Family Business," in Jiang Yi-wei and Min Jian-shu (eds), *Ancient Management Thinking and Chinese-Style Management*, Beijing: Economic Management Press, pp. 121–134.
Limlingan, Victor Simpaol (1986) *The Overseas Chinese in ASEAN: Business Strategies and Management Practices*, Manila: Vita Development Corp.
Montagu-Pollock, Matthew (1991) "All the Right Connections," *Asian Business* (January): 20–24.
Oh, Tai K. (1991) "Understanding Managerial Values and Behavior Among the Gang of Four: Korea, Taiwan, Singapore and Hong Kong," *Journal of Management Development* 10(20): 46–56.
Redding, S. Gordon (1990) *The Spirit of Chinese Capitalism*, New York: Walter de Gruyter.
—— and Gilbert Y.Y. Wong (1990) "The Psychology of Chinese Organizational Behavior," in Michael Harris Bond (ed.), *The Psychology of the Chinese People*, New York: Oxford University Press, pp. 267–295.
Silin, R. (1976) *Leadership and Values*, Cambridge, Mass.: Harvard University Press.
Wong, S.L. (1985) "The Chinese Family Firm: A Model," *British Journal of Sociology* 36(1): 58–71.

Chapter 7

Competitive Chinese business strategies in ASEAN

INTRODUCTION

As mentioned in previous chapters, Overseas Chinese in ASEAN states number roughly 6 percent of the total regional population and yet despite this dominate the national economies of all six member countries. In addition to their traditionally-controlled commercial sector, the Overseas Chinese have successfully expanded into the industrial sector. Throughout the region, millions of small and mid-sized Chinese family businesses and some very large multinational Overseas Chinese groups have developed. The Overseas Chinese clearly possess a competitive edge, which stems not only from the close ties they have developed with the indigenous governments and shared management organizations and styles but also from their shared competitive business strategies and techniques.

The Overseas Chinese excel in expanding their market share by implementing a high inventory turnover and realizing rapid returns on investment. Their exquisite deal-making techniques allow them to seize multitudes of business opportunities and thereby dominate the commercial sector. They have also successfully initiated development and industrialization programs in an effort to expand into new industries. In addition to collaborating with indigenous governments, they have succeeded in overcoming various governmental policy prejudices in industry and commerce through organizing counter-strategies and relying on their own resources.

THE CHINESE COMPETITIVE STRATEGIES IN THE MARKETPLACE

In his seminal book on Overseas Chinese business management, Limlingan (1986: 68–69) describes the dilemma confronting most of the Overseas Chinese businesses during the colonial period: while the Chinese were among the earliest to start in business, a Chinese businessman in any of the ASEAN countries (with the exception of Singapore) faced a bleak reality;

he not only belonged to an unpopular minority group but also had to look for business opportunities outside that group. Moreover, the indigenous majority controlled the government market – state purchasing and state-owned enterprises – which accounted for as much as 30 percent of the economic sector. Consequently, the Chinese businessman entered the marketplace with considerable disadvantages: i.e. he had to develop his market outside his own Chinese community against great odds, since both the majority of his potential clients and the official policies favored his indigenous business competitors.

At the same time, the Chinese businessman had a distinct business advantage *vis-à-vis* his indigenous competitors. The Chinese business community or network constituted an exclusive and useful resource base for reliable business information, easily accessible capital, credential checks on other Chinese businessmen, and resolving disputes through arbitration. The Chinese business community or network was a kind of a social organization designed to promote and facilitate business activities. The most important group to a Chinese businessman was probably the local Chinese Chamber of Commerce, which functioned as a mini-government for the Chinese community. A Chinese Chamber of Commerce typically handled not only business-related issues but also represented the interests of the Chinese community as a whole. Some even provided such social services as matchmaking and mediating in family disputes. Although the organizational basis of the Chinese business community or network may vary in different places and may have changed over time, the Chinese business network has always existed. Indigenous businessmen often have no way of proving themselves to the Chinese and thus are commonly excluded from these networks. As a consequence, they cannot compete with Chinese businessmen on an equal basis (Yoshihara 1988: 54; Williams 1976: 171).

Chinese businessmen successfully penetrated the indigenous marketplace as middlemen due to the fact that there was a great demand for people who could perform as intermediaries in ASEAN countries (Limlingan 1986: 70). In a developing environment there is often imperfect market information and a poor transportation system that cause many business opportunities to arise. As a result, prices of products and commodities vary among local communities. The Chinese businessman, therefore, was needed to link consumers and suppliers, separately located, via the Chinese business community.

Take importing and distributing foreign goods as an example. The foreign supplier usually required cash payment and only the consumer was expected to pay cash. Since transferring these products from the foreign supplier to the consumer required a great deal of time and distance, well-versed intermediaries were indispensable. In comparison with indigenous groups, the Chinese businessmen were at a clear advantage because of the resourceful Chinese business communities. In a Chinese business network, foreign products were imported with cash and then transferred on credit through Chinese wholesalers to the retailers, who then collected the cash. This form of networking was an institutional alternative to contract law. It could also contribute to high levels of business efficiency by the reduction of costs or enhancement of organizational flexibility and strategic adaptiveness (Redding 1991: 146).

To make this network an efficient operation, one needs mutual trust. For example, once a verbal agreement is reached it is expected to be kept. If a Chinese businessman promises to sell certain goods at a specified price he must sell the goods at the agreed-upon price. If he breaks his promise he will lose trust and will be required to deal on a cash basis. For Chinese businesses that have limited capital, such a virtual exclusion from the network can be disastrous. The mutual trust established among Chinese traders ties them closely together. In her studies of the ethnic Hokkien Chinese middleman group in the rubber business in Singapore and Malaysia, Landa (1983) interviewed a number of Chinese businessmen, who almost universally pointed out the importance of trust. Once a verbal agreement is made, it is expected to be kept, as their business is based on "100 percent" mutual trust.

> Because of the risk involved in advancing money without security, based purely on trust, we tend to trade with those whom we trust; they are often kinsmen, friends, people from the same place in China and those who speak the same dialect . . . we find it easier to give credit to a fellow Hokkien, because there are ways of finding out the creditworthiness of that person – about his background, his associates, his ethical code, and so on.
>
> (Landa 1983: 90–91)

Indigenous businessmen and government corporations have also tried to duplicate this process, but because of their less efficient network and inadequate market entry strategies they have not seen the same level of success. As an outsider to this Chinese network, an indigenous business-man would find it much harder to get credit from the Chinese.

There are two different market entry strategies: one is to retain the bulk of surplus, and the other is to transfer the bulk of surplus to the consumer. The Chinese entry strategy was based on transferring most of the surplus to the consumer, which was advantageous for the Overseas Chinese in two respects. First, lower prices could often soften the negative connotation most indigenous patrons place on non-indigenous firms. On the other hand, lower pricing might help to squeeze out the less competitive in-digenous businesses which adopted the first strategy, thereby allowing Chinese businessmen to dominate the marketplace (Limlingan 1986: 73–74).

In fact, this second entry strategy of low-margin/high-turnover concealed the huge profits that were possible under this strategy. The lower gross margins on sales were often offset by a greater turnover of assets. The turnover may have contributed as much to the return on equity as the gross margin on sales (see Figure 7.1).

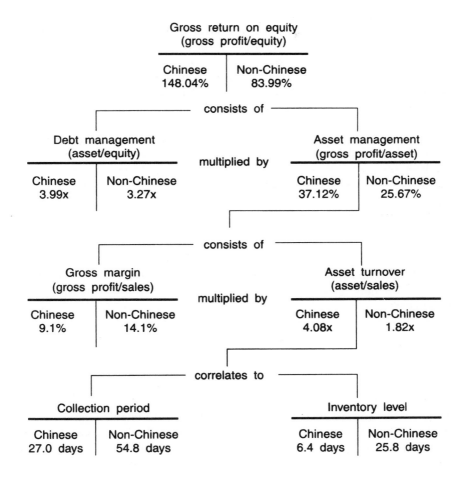

Figure 7.1 Comparative financial performance
Source: Limlingan, 1986, p. 75.

After a Chinese businessman has broken into the indigenous market through application of the aforementioned strategy, he could prepare for further business expansion. On the basis of enlarging his market share, the Chinese businessman could choose to upgrade his operations or branch into other businesses. According to Limlingan (1986: 82–86), he has five options: (1) integrating forward into the distribution system; (2) integrating backward into the distribution system; (3) integrating backward into production; (4) branching into other product lines; and (5) diversifying into other businesses.

Integrating forward into the distribution system, i.e. moving from dealership to mass merchandising, was an option open basically to Chinese businessmen running their operations in the major urban centers. For those who succeeded in integrating forward, the increased volume of their business transactions enabled them to take advantage of economies of scale, such as in-house transportation, warehousing, etc. Integrating backward into the distribution system was an option that only a few firms could take advantage of; those who attempted to integrate backward into the distribution system would have to survive fierce competition from the few existing large and powerful Chinese trading firms. Integrating backward into production was an option in which a Chinese trader lost some of his comparative advantage in trading and had to develop skills in organizing production. But, as will be shown in the next section, more and more Chinese followed this course.

The fourth option of branching into other products was utilized by many Chinese businessmen. They simply functioned as intermediaries between the cities and the countryside. Many of them expanded from simply purchasing commodities for export into trading in products from the cities, acting as dealers for urban and foreign producers. Several advantages to this option could easily be identified to explain its popularity. To begin with, Chinese businessmen were able to expand their business activities by distributing products from the cities to the countryside, where the need existed. This enabled them to consolidate their trading positions. Next, their existing access to the market could significantly reduce their marketing costs. Credit risks could be minimized while transportation costs could be sharply reduced, as trucks were used in both directions. Finally, and most importantly, adding another line of business would enable Chinese businessmen to access an additional source of credit, thereby expanding the base of financial resources. The cash that was advanced by second-level dealers to pay for purchases from the countryside could be used for other businesses if they chose to pay the farmers in products rather than in cash. The last option of diversifying into other businesses concentrated in a few areas, such as transportation and financing.

RIDING THE WAVE OF DEVELOPMENT AND INDUSTRIALIZATION

The emergence of a large number of Chinese industrialists in ASEAN has been viewed with dismay by many who believed that the Chinese had absolutely no incentive to expand into industrial areas for a number of reasons (Limlingan 1986: 97). To begin with, the Chinese were reluctant to make long-term investment due to the unfavorable political environment in these countries. Except in Singapore and Thailand, the Overseas Chinese had experienced various degrees of discrimination. Second, the small and simple business structures utilized by the Chinese were more suitable to trading than to manufacturing because the family-style management complicated growth. Third, as successful traders, they would not seem to have incentives to move into a relatively unfamiliar area. Finally, even if they wanted to, they did not have the pool of capital to move into industrial sectors.

Nevertheless, the industrial policies of some ASEAN countries have virtually catapulted Chinese businessmen into making this strategic expansion (Yoshihara 1988: 46–52). As the post-Second World War period witnessed the decline for Western capital, Chinese capital experienced rapid expansion. As an element of domestic capital, it benefitted from the nationalization of Western capital, restrictions on the entry and operation of foreign capital, and promotion and protection of domestic capital. After independence, all the Southeast Asian governments made policies to put their economies on a new path. Although the Chinese businesses suffered from various discriminations, they were situated in a much better position than their Western competitors.

In Indonesia, for example, the government forced the Chinese to move by declaring in 1955 that the ownership of rice mills was limited to indigenous Indonesians. The Chinese were required to transfer ownership to indigenous citizens within a two-year period. In 1957, fifteen industries were designated for Indonesian citizens only, and the Chinese had to transfer their ownership to Indonesian citizens. In 1960, the Chinese, together with other aliens, were prohibited from retailing in the rural areas below the agency level. The divested money of the Chinese became an important source of capital. At the same time, the Indonesian government implemented an economic development plan that focused on achieving industrialization via import-substitution. The government plan allowed it to intervene in the country's development by raising tariff rates on foreign products and lowering tax rates for domestic firms, as well as offering domestic firms government credit, protection from expropriation, exemption from some government regulations, and regulation of the market. This plan provided tremendous incentive for the Chinese to make the strategic shift into industrial areas.

The economic plan opened new opportunities for the Chinese to invest in priority industries with their divested capital. Governmental policies, such as tariff barriers for foreign products and low interest rates for governmental borrowing and market monopolies, virtually guaranteed the profitability of these investments. As a result, not only could the Chinese be privy to cheap capital and monopoly rights through coopting government officials, they could also enjoy some institutional guarantees for the success of their businesses.

Since the government virtually provided assurance against expropriation for investment in priority industries, Chinese businessmen had an incentive to make long-term commitments. Moreover, government policies on allowing foreign investors to enter into joint ventures with Indonesian businesses further secured the Chinese position and enabled them to acquire technical and managerial expertise. In addition, many foreign investors desired to form partnerships with the Chinese.

The growth of the Salim Group perhaps provides the best example (Schwarz 1991: 46–53). Born in Fujian, China, in 1916, Liem Sioe Liong began his business career in a town in Central Java at the age of twenty. After a ten-year apprenticeship in his uncle's peanut-trading business, Liem started his own business by buying the kretek cloves from farmers and then selling the product to clove cigarette producers. During the Indonesian struggle for independence against the Dutch (1945–1949), Liem actively supported the Diponegoro division of the Indonesian army in Central Java with food, clothing, medicine, and military supplies. Through this arrangement, Liem got to know the officers quite well, one of them being the young Suharto. It was the very nature of the Indonesian army that gave Liem his opportunity. Since the early 1950s, the Indonesian army had been deeply involved in the business life of the country.

During Sukarno's reign in the 1950s, Liem moved into the manufacturing industries of textiles, bicycle parts and small hardware while the nationalistic Sukarno government began to restrict Chinese traders in the local areas. With the collapse of the Sukarno government and the rise to power of Suharto in 1966, Liem's traditional ties to the new president paid off. When the new government decided to restrict the import of cloves to only two companies, Liem and Suharto's brother were chosen. Although Indonesia was a major producer of cloves, huge domestic consumption required large imports. In addition, he made a substantial amount of money in the export of rubber and coffee. He developed such an intertwined relationship with the Suharto family that Suharto's son, daughter, and his stepbrother all became big shareholders of some of Liem's businesses.

The import and export licenses themselves, though very profitable as business deals, could not bring about institutionalized and long-term businesses. Thanks to governmental loans and contracts, the Salim Group refined their manufacturing activities by the late 1960s and early 1970s. Liem expanded his textile manufacturing, and then pursued flour-milling, where he achieved a monopoly through government licensing. Meanwhile, he branched into the cement industry, which thrived on large public-works spending. He also expanded into the steel industry, which was completely under government monopoly. Liem's endeavor to institutionalize his

business deals is vividly illustrated in the Krakatau Steel–Cold Rolling Mill
Indonesia Utama deal.

Krakatau Steel was a state-owned Indonesian enterprise that possessed
the country's only integrated steel complex in Cilegon, West Java. The steel
complex was comprised of a direct reduction plant with a total capacity of
two million tons, a slab mill with a capacity of one million tons a year, a
billet plant with a capacity of 500,000 tons a year, a sections mill, a bar mill,
and a wire-rod mill. Nevertheless, due to poor management, Krakatau had
been run at a loss. To turn Krakatau around, the Indonesian government
asked Liem for assistance. This agreement with the government enabled
the Salim Group to sell Krakatau Steel's production at full capacity, whereas
only 50 percent of the steel had been disposed of earlier. The major components of the deal included the establishment of a cold rolling mill (Cold
Rolling Mills Indonesia Utama), the imposition of tariffs, and the monopoly
of importation and exportation rights.

By the mid-1980s, the Salim Group already accounted for about 5 percent
of Indonesian GDP and had become truly multinational. Presently the
largest private corporation in Indonesia (see Table 7.1), the Salim Group
consists of about 75 companies in 24 countries with a turnover of more than
$1 billion per year, and an estimated employed workforce of 25,000. The
group not only covers the traditional business of trade and distribution but

Table 7.1 Salim Group's Indonesian companies

Company	Description
Bogasri Flour Mills & Berdikari Sari Utama	Controls 100% of flour milling
Bank Central Asia (Rps 7.5 trillion assets)	Indonesia's largest private bank
Indocement	Accounts for 44% of the country's cement capacity and owns the world's third-largest cement complex
Indomobil	The sole agency in Indonesia for Mazda, Nissan, Suzuku, Hino, and Volvo cars and trucks
Indomilk	Control 35% of Indonesia's condensed and pasteurized milk market
Sarimie Asli	Controls 80% of the domestic noodle market
Bimoll	Commands more than half the bottled cooking-oil market
Cold Rolling Mill Indonesia	The country's only producer of cold-rolled steel plates and sheets

Source: Schwarz 1991, p. 48.

also handles manufacturing, construction, financial services, and properties. There remains hardly any area of Indonesian economic life that is not represented by some presence of the Salim Group. Liem is also quite ubiquitous in the international arena where he has been building up an offshore empire in the industries of trade and finance through his acquisitions of American and European companies. His corporate empire spread from Hong Kong to the Netherlands, from the west coast of Africa to North and Central America. While Liem Sioe Liong has been one of the most successful Overseas Chinese industrialists in the country, he is by no means alone in his success.

EXPANDING AGAINST UNFAVORABLE POLITICAL ENVIRONMENTS

In Malaysia, the economic and racial rivalry made the situation more complicated for the ethnic Chinese. The racial riots in 1969 amplified the message to the Malaysian government that unless something was done to redress the economic balance between the rich minorities (primarily Chinese) and the poor majorities (*bumiputras*, "the sons of the soil" referring to the Malays), the racial disparity would worsen and cause more trouble in the future. In 1971, the Government of Malaysia launched the New Economic Policy (NEP) to raise the Malay's share in the country's economy from around 4 percent to 30 percent by 1990. In order to accomplish this goal, the NEP offered preferential treatment to the majority – *bumiputras* – which left the minorities at a disadvantage.

In an attempt to boost the development of *bumiputra* businesses, the Malaysian government carried out a radical strategy of taking the leap to managerial capitalism without having to go through entrepreneurial capitalism. To expedite this process, the Malaysian government actively sought to transfer professionally managed British companies' expertise, such as the Guthrie Corporation, to the hands of Malay businessmen. The Permodalan Nasional Berhad (PNB, or National Equity Corporation) was established to facilitate just such a transfer (Limlingan 1986: 108–109). The strategy that PNB adopted to achieve this objective consisted of several phases.

PNB received interest-free loans from the Bumiputra Investment Foundation, which was funded by the Malaysian government. With this money, PNB sought to buy shares in the corporate sector chiefly from two major sources. The first was the shares in private companies owned by government institutions such as Perbandanan Nasional (PERNAS, or National Corporation of Malaysia). PNB was able to acquire a large amount of these institutions' investment portfolios at preferred pricing. The second was the publicly listed shares of foreign companies operating in Malaysia. Several top foreign companies, such as Sime Darby, the Guthrie Corporation, and Harrison and Crosfields, were purchased by PNB. Then, PNB arranged the transfer of its acquired shares in the corporate sector to individual *bumiputras* at very good installment terms via Sekim Amanah Saham Nasional (SASN), a mutual fund established and managed by PNB. The *bumiputra* investor only needed to invest 10 percent of the price of the mutual fund shares in return for the PNB's guarantee that the dividends from the mutual fund would be sufficient to pay off the 90 percent balance within nine years.

Many small and medium-sized Chinese businesses were badly hit by the partiality of the Malaysian government. Larger Chinese firms were also under increasing pressure. In order to protect their interests in the Malaysian economy, the Malaysian Chinese were compelled to develop a counter-strategy to make use of their own resources. In comparison with Indonesia, the Chinese in Malaysia occupy a much larger percentage of the total population and are better organized.

Unlike the Chinese in Indonesia, the Malaysian Chinese have been actively involved in politics. The most important Chinese political organization is the Malaysian Chinese Association (MCA). Since its founding in 1963, Malaysia has been governed by a coalition called the Barisan Nasional (National Front), which consists of three major political parties representing the three races – the United Malays' National Organization (UMNO), the Malaysian Chinese Association (MCA), and the Malaysian Indian Congress (MIC). Therefore, the Malaysian Chinese had more access to political power than the Indonesian Chinese (Milne and Mauzy 1986: 43–46).

The Malaysian Chinese also had a diversified pool of capital and were much less dependent on the Malaysian government. First, the pool of capital among the Malaysian Chinese was much larger because of the large number of Chinese in the populace. Second, Singapore and Malaysia had well-developed stock exchanges in which Malaysian and Singaporean company shares were openly traded. Many Malaysian Chinese businessmen could easily acquire capital in these exchanges through new stock offerings. Third, the large Singapore banks, such as the Overseas Chinese Banking Corporation (OCBC) and the United Overseas Bank (UOB), had retained their Malaysian branches, which were founded when the two countries still belonged to British Malaya (Limlingan 1986: 110). Naturally, they would prefer to deal with the Malaysian Chinese.

The goal of the Malaysian Chinese was not only to maintain their existing percent share of the corporate sector but also to expand their share in the post-independence Malaysian economy. This meant that not only would the *bumiputras* have to increase their share at the expense of foreigners rather than the Chinese but also that the Chinese, as Malaysian citizens, should be allowed to take over some foreign companies. The strategy adopted by the Malaysian Chinese was to create a parallel business organization – Multi-Purpose Holdings (MPH) – which served to help Malaysian Chinese establish themselves as industrialists.

From its inception, MPH has maintained close ties with MCA (Yoshihara

1988: 239–240). The company was established in 1975 as part of the Chinese reaction to the controversial Industrial Coordination Act (ICA), which required those Chinese businesses employing twenty-five or more people and having a capital of M$100,000 to comply with the terms of *bumiputra* participation. Politically, MCA responded by proposing amendments in Parliament to soften the impact of the Act. The economic response was the incorporation of MPH. MCA urged its members to subscribe to the initial capital of MPH. The first public issue of about 30 million shares (of M$1 each) had produced an enthusiastic response by the Chinese community, which had been worried about the growing share of *bumiputra* businesses in Malaysia. The first institutional investor in MPH was Koperasi Sebaguna Malaysia (KSM or Multi-Purpose Cooperative Society of Malaysia). Formed nine years earlier by MCA, KSM organized the Multi-Purpose Investment Fund to facilitate the transfer of MPH ownership to its members.

Unlike its counterpart PNB, MPH had a much more diversified financial source. In addition to the Malaysian Chinese contribution, MPH actively sought international sources, including listing its shares in the Singapore Stock Exchange, placing some of its London shares for sale, and getting loans from international banks such as Chase Manhattan, Chartered Bank, and the Overseas Chinese Banking Corporation. Shareholders once numbered around 40,000, but KSM held over 50 percent of the total equity.

With these diverse sources, MPH became a super-organization representing the interests of the Malaysian Chinese without causing much outcry from the Malays. On the surface, it had a semblance of international ownership and the financial backing of multinational banks. In essence, it was closely associated with MCA. The example of MPH was followed by the state organizations of the Malaysian Chinese Association. Various Chinese regional and professional groups also established their own versions of MPH.

In the first few years of its founding, MPH acquired controlling interests in Malaysian Plantations, Bandar Raya Developments (a property developer), and Magnum Corp., whose main source of profits was a license to operate a lottery. In the early 1980s, MPH intensified its acquisition activities. It took over Dunlop Estates Bhd and Promptship Holdings, which had a fleet of more than 30 vessels. MPH also acquired a 40 percent interest in United Malayan Banking Corp. (UMBC). By acquiring the Singapore-based British trading company, MPH attempted to build a Japanese-style trading house, renaming it the Multi-Purpose International Trading Corporation (MITC).

Rapid expansion came to a sudden stop in 1985, when MPH lost about M$190 million, the bulk of which came from shipping and trading operations. This fiasco was followed by the arrest of the founder of MPH, Tan Koon Swan, in Singapore, on charges of criminal breach of trust in connection with the bankruptcy of Pan Electric Industries in 1985. A Harvard Business School graduate, Tan once promised to revolutionize the way the Chinese did business in Malaysia. Then, later in the year, Bank Negara Malaysia suspended the operation of MPH's controlling shareholder, KSM, on charges of corrupt management. To overcome the deteriorating situation, the board of directors reorganized in 1987, with the former MCA-related directors being replaced by non-politicians in an effort to make it a more business-orientated organization.

DEAL-MAKING SKILLS: A CHINESE COMPETITIVE ADVANTAGE

The combination of governments' nationalistic development policies and Chinese business acumen has enabled Chinese businessmen to become the dominant force of business throughout ASEAN. Yoshihara has compared the relative positions of foreign, Chinese and private indigenous capital in Table 7.2.

One key to understanding Chinese success lies in the fabulous Chinese deal-making skills (Engardio 1991: 60–62). Deals refer to business activities practiced to correct sudden and unexpected deviations in the marketplace, such as abrupt changes in governmental trade and industrial policies.

Table 7.2 Relative position of Chinese capital

Industry	Foreign capital	Chinese capital	Private indigenous capital
Banking	moderate	substantial/ dominant	moderate/ substantial
Property development		substantial	substantial
Construction	moderate	moderate	moderate
Mining	moderate	moderate/ substantial	moderate
Oil exploration	dominant		
Plantation agriculture	minor	substantial	moderate/ substantial
Export/import trade	substantial	substantial	minor
Manufacturing	substantial	substantial	minor
Light industries	minor	dominant	minor
Machinery	substantial	substantial	minor
Metals & petrochemicals	dominant	minor	

Source: Yoshihara 1988, p. 51.

Therefore, deals can hardly be prearranged and prepared. Owing to the high rate of change in the marketplace, a good deal requires an immediate and effective business response. On the other hand, bad decisions can result in heavy losses. The high pressure of closing a deal may restrict one's ability to differentiate a good deal from a bad one or weaken one's ability to bargain for good terms on a deal. Thus, there is a high degree of speculation involved in deal-making.

The rapid business expansion of the Thai agribusiness conglomerate Charoen Pokphand (CP Group) provides an illuminating example (Goldstein 1993: 66–70). The CP Group started business in China immediately after Chinese leader Deng Xiao-ping launched the open door and reform policies in 1979. At the time most Western companies balked at the political and economic uncertainty of China, which had just come out of the Cultural Revolution. In 1981, Dhanin Chearavanont, the owner of the Group signed the group's first joint venture, which was the first foreign investment in the newly established special economic zone. One of the comparative advantages of the Overseas Chinese companies in China is their ability to operate in its underdeveloped legal environment. The Overseas Chinese excel in risk-taking.

The Chinese business framework of the cash-generation cycle provides a competitive advantage in deal-making. Since deals cannot be programmed in advance, the Chinese businessman must keep some cash on hand or be capable of raising cash on short notice so as to seize a fleeting business opportunity. For a Chinese businessman involved in a business deal, cash metaphorically falls asleep until it is awakened into cash again. This is the so-called cash generation cycle (See Figure 7.2). In order to get quick cash, a good Chinese businessman focuses on accelerating the cash generation cycle.

Accelerating the cash generation cycle is conducive to a fast turnover. Due to political uncertainties in these countries, the sleeping period is the most dangerous, as cash may never awake from its deep slumber. The Chinese tendency to trade a smaller margin for a shorter sleeping period leads to a fast turnover orientation. The Chinese businessman recognizes that by being satisfied with a lower price and a smaller margin he can sell much faster, thus reducing the slumber period. For these reasons, he would rather get a margin of 10 percent than a margin of 20 percent. If the business deal requires a long slumber period, the Chinese businessman would demand much higher rates of return to justify his risk. The mentality of "fast-in and fast-out" is prevalent among Chinese businessmen throughout the ASEAN region.

The Chinese businessman does not follow the Western management practice of separating marketing from financing (Limlingan 1986: 88–89). When a Chinese trader, for example, offers a cash advance to a coffee grower, he is not interested in separating the income from financing the

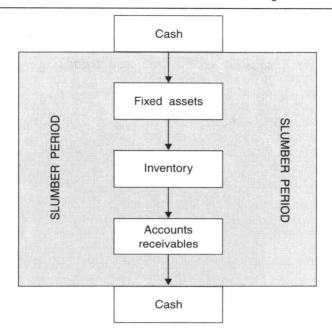

Figure 7.2 Cash generation cycle
Source: Limlingan, 1986, p. 87.

farmer, the income from transporting the coffee, the income from extending receivable financing to the coffee manufacturing, and the income from the sale of the coffee – and has great difficulty in doing so. His sole concern is to generate an amount of cash at the end of the cycle large enough to compensate for the sleeping period of his money.

A good Chinese businessman is capable of simultaneously conducting several deals at different stages of completion. Treating them as sub-deals of his larger deal, he manipulates them to enhance his benefits. He may sell some goods at a loss in order to generate badly needed cash in another sub-deal, thus considering voluntary losses as financing costs. Those who are not familiar with these tactics may easily sustain losses. Many Chinese businessmen took advantage of the liberal credit terms of Western multi-national corporations by "dumping" their products in the market for cash.

Sometimes, concern over "sleeping" cash can reach absurdity. Chinese businessmen may borrow from a non-Chinese bank only to put the cash right back in again on deposit with the same bank. They are willing to absorb the cost of the interest differential if such a practice assures them of instant access to ready cash. Multi-layered interest rate policies of the

ASEAN governments can significantly reduce the cost of this insurance policy. They can also reinforce this practice by getting a better credit-line through their connection network.

Within the framework of the cash generation cycle, according to Limlingan (1986: 90), a Chinese businessman can easily identify the two most attractive deals. The first is a deal which, after the process is begun and the invested cash has already been recovered, continues to bring cash inflows. Such a deal becomes a self-generating cash-cow that no longer needs any further paid-in investment. In business jargon, it is a deal that can yield "gravy profits." The second is a deal that is self-financing, thus requiring no cash investment. It is vividly described in business jargon as "frying in its own fat" or "cooking in its own juices."

The deal-making skills are also reflected in the formation of alliances. Over the years, a good Chinese businessman would know that a government policy favoring indigenous businessmen need not always be an obstacle to his own business activities. He can form a business alliance with the favored indigenous businessman. This is the so-called Ali–Baba relationship, in which Ali the Indonesian or Malay becomes the "sleeping" or "blind" partner of a business but gives it a "native" front, while Baba the Chinese businessman runs the actual business, enjoying Ali's protection. Since Ali obtains financial benefits from the deal, the alliance can be very solid (Clad 1989: 52–53). This strategy is used elsewhere, not only in Southeast Asia; Chinese companies adopt this approach when they invest in countries where the overall political environment is not transparent and stable. For example, the CP Group's investment strategy in China is based on joint ventures with mainland partners. In most cases they formed partnerships with provincial authorities and city government officials. The partner of its Shanghai Motorcycle Venture is the China North Industry Group (Norinco), which is the country's biggest defense conglomerate (Goldstein 1993: 67).

Having said all this, one should not forget another important advantage of the Overseas Chinese, i.e. a culture that encourages hard work and high savings. In the course of developing their businesses, many Overseas Chinese tycoons worked long hours and lived very moderate lives. The strong desire to succeed and the uncertainty of the environment has driven them to pursue their goals ruthlessly. For years, many of them have had very few vacations and have worked consistently long hours. Even after their businesses succeeded, many still kept their modest lifestyles and maintained the same work pace. The strong Chinese entrepreneurship constituted one of the most important bases for their success (Jing 1992: 3–16).

SUMMARY/CONCLUSION

This chapter has reviewed the Chinese competitive strategies in the Southeast Asian market. In the emerging economies of ASEAN, the Overseas Chinese have developed a successful series of business strategies, which are first of all based on a low-margin/high-volume strategy aimed at capturing market share. On the basis of a substantial market share, the Overseas Chinese have sustained their competitive advantage by pursuing economies of scope rather than economies of scale. Next, the process of the Chinese traders being transformed into industrialists was analyzed. As shown earlier, they have benefitted from governmental development policies by cultivating good relations with the government, skilled political bargaining, and sophisticated use of their comparative strengths. Finally, the deal-making skill of the Chinese was analyzed, with discussions on cash generation processes, the quick-in quick-out strategy, and the Ali–Baba relationship. By applying these strategies the Chinese have been extremely successful in market competition.

This is not to say that all Chinese businesses outperform indigenous businesses. Besides numerous failures of small and mid-sized Chinese businesses, larger Chinese businesses have also met with disaster. One major cause is the speculative nature of many Chinese businesses, which are driven by a sense of insecurity as they hold out hoping to earn fast money. The application of the traditional small family management style to large modern businesses constitutes another major reason for the failures. The above-mentioned MPH was a classical case in point. The widely cherished Ali–Baba relationship can also become a liability as disputes between the two sides can place the Chinese businessman at the mercy of his indigenous benefactor. The story of the Malaysian Chinese business tycoon Khoo Teck Puat is just one example (Clad 1989: 158–160); his business empire ran into serious trouble after he developed conflicts with the Sultan of Brunei. As a result the Sultan jailed his son, who at the time was chairman of the National Bank of Brunei, which was then dominated by the Khoo family. Such cases of failures are not uncommon in the Chinese business community in Southeast Asia, and challenge the widely held view that Overseas Chinese businesses are invulnerable.

QUESTIONS FOR DISCUSSION

1   According to Limlingan what were the major comparative advantages and disadvantages for a Chinese businessman in entering the Southeast Asian market?
2   What are the chief advantages of using a low-profit-margin /high-turnover strategy?

3 What insights do you get on Overseas Chinese business advantages from the rise of the Salim Group?
4 How do you assess the role of Multi-Purpose Holdings in the
development of Chinese businesses in Malaysia?
5 How do you evaluate the Chinese deal-making skills? Are they
uniquely Chinese or can they be transplanted to other business
groups?

FURTHER READING

Clad, James (1989) *Behind the Myth: Business Money and Power in Southeast
Asia*, London: Unwin.
Cushman, Jennifer and Wang Gungwu (eds) (1989) *Changing Identities of the
Southeast Asian Chinese Since World War II*, Hong Kong: University of
Hong Kong Press.
Engardio, Pete (1991) "The Chinese Dealmakers of Southeast Asia," *Busi-
ness Week* (11 November): 60–62.
Goldstein, Carl (1993) "Full Speed Ahead," *Far Eastern Economic Review* (21
October): 46–70.
Jing, Sheng *et al.* (1992) *The Success Secrets of the Overseas Chinese Businessmen*,
Shenyang: Liaoning People's Press.
Landa, Janet T. (1983) "The Political Economy of the Ethnicity and Entre-
preneurship in a Plural Society," in Linda Y.C. Lim and L.A. Peter
Gosling (eds), *The Chinese in Southeast Asia* (Vol. 1), Singapore: Maruzen
Asia, pp. 86–116.
Limlingan, Victor Simpao (1986) *The Overseas Chinese in ASEAN: Business
Strategies and Management Practices*, Manila: Vita Development Corp.
Milne, R.S. and Diane K. Mauzy (1986) *Malaysia; Tradition, Modernity and
Islam*, Boulder, Colo.: Westview.
Pan, Lynn (1990) *Sons of the Yellow Emperor*, London: Secker & Warburg.
Redding, S. Gordon (1991) "Culture and Entrepreneurial Behavior Among
the Overseas Chinese," in Brigitte Berger (ed.), *The Culture of Entrepre-
neurship*, San Francisco: Institute of Contemporary Studies, pp. 137–227.
Schwarz, Adam (1991) "Empire of the Son," *Far Eastern Economic Review* (14
March): 46–53.
Sender, Henny (1991) "Inside the Overseas Chinese Network," *Institutional
Investor* (September): 37–42.
Williams, Lea E. (1976) *Southeast Asia: A History*, New York: Oxford Univer-
sity Press.
Yoshihara, Kunio (1988) *The Rise of Ersatz Capitalism in Southeast Asia*,
Singapore: Oxford University Press.

Chapter 8

The evolving environment of the Chinese State Enterprises

INTRODUCTION

The firms designated as being Chinese State Enterprises (CSEs) include those whose properties are owned by the state. According to current policies, the State Council can exercise its right of property ownership over these state enterprises at any time. Since the inception of the People's Republic of China (PRC), the CSEs, especially large and medium-sized CSEs, have been at the center of China's economic development. As of 1992, China had 11,000 large and medium-sized state enterprises which occupied 2.9 percent of all industrial enterprises in the country. Together, they made up nearly 50 percent of China's total industrial value and 67 percent of the nation's tax revenue (Wu 1992: 17). Since 1979, it has been the effort to improve the performance of state-owned enterprises that prompted the reform of China's socialist economic system into a market system. Without market reform it would not have been possible to reform the CSEs. The development of the CSE itself has been subject to the heavy influence of its operational environment. This chapter concentrates on an analysis of the operational environment affecting the CSE's development.

PRE-1979 OPERATIONAL ENVIRONMENT OF THE CSEs

There are a number of key environmental factors influencing the development of the CSEs, including the nature of the economic system, the role of the market, and various state policies. Since the founding of the PRC, the CSEs have had more than 40 years of operating experience. During this period, the CSEs' operational environment has undergone continual changes. Generally speaking, this period can be divided into two parts, with 1979 as the demarcation line. Although the pre-1979 period can be divided into several minor parts, the major points which follow can be applied throughout the period.

Before its defeat in 1949, the nationalist government took under its control much of the heavy industry, including all the Japanese and German enterprises after the end of the Second World War. By 1946, state and foreign capital dominated the industrial sectors of China. By the time of the communist takeover, the bureaucratic capitalists controlled major banks, the heavy industry, all railroads, highways and airlines, several large trading companies, nearly 50 percent of shipping tonnage, the largest industrial enterprises and the bulk of light industry. After the communists took power, they quickly confiscated all enterprises belonging to the bureaucratic capitalists and foreign interests and converted them into state enterprises. During the following years of socialist transformation, national capitalist industrial enterprises were transferred from private hands into state property (Xue 1981).

The socialist economic system of China had tremendous influence on the development of these CSEs. Owing to various historical and political reasons, the People's Republic began to follow the Soviet way of industrialization in 1953 by introducing its Five-Year Plan. It adopted a highly centralized product economy model and negated the necessity of commodity production and the existence of a market. The State Council of the central government commanded the decision-making and control power of the whole national economy and managed through its imperative plans. These plans were forcibly implemented and included almost every aspect of the economy. By 1957, the Central Planning Commission planned for 60 percent of the gross value of industrial output and the central government controlled 75 percent of the country's financial resources (Xu *et al.* 1982).

The relationship between the government and enterprises under this system was a kind of administrative relationship in which the government controlled the operation of enterprises through directives and/or imperative plans. The state was the owner, operator, and employer, and therefore the state planned, directed, and funded all its enterprises. Under the system of unified control over income and expenditure (*tongshou tongzhi*), the state provided land, plant, equipment, basic materials, working capital, managers, and everything else used in production. It also set the prices of the finished goods regardless of their cost and quality. The state enterprises were required to remit all profits and depreciation funds to the central government. In addition the state covered all the losses.

China adopted the Soviet centralized system of macro-management organized around a network of several branches of industry. Each industrial branch was managed by a hierarchy of authorities, starting from the central governmental ministries, to provincial bureaus, to city governments' sections and finally, down to the enterprises (see Figure 8.1). The deficiency of the centralized management system has been obvious since the 1950s. Several reforms were implemented before 1979, but they did not radically change the structure of state planning. Generally speaking, reforms alternated between centralization (*tiao tiao*) and decentralization (*kuai kuai*). During the Great Leap Forward of 1958, decision-makers at the local level were granted greater independence in the realm of production. Provinces were allowed to plan industrial development on a territorial basis. More than 80 percent of state enterprises were transferred from the jurisdiction of the central ministries to the lower levels, and the central control of financial resources was cut down to 20 percent. In 1961, the decision-making balance was shifted back to the central government. But during the Cultural Revolution, decentralization became popular again, and the central government's power to plan was seriously weakened by the nationwide chaos. During that time even some of the largest enterprises, such as the Anshan Iron and Steel Complex, were turned over to provincial governments.

Consequently, large and medium-sized CSEs were often subject to two systems of leadership: the line (an industrial ministry of the central government) and the block (local governmental institutions), which were difficult to coordinate with each other. The CSE, therefore, had a problem with too many "mothers-in-law" (Pan 1988: 52). Such administrative ambiguities demoralized enterprise management for they caused uncertainty over who was responsible for enterprise goals. This situation also led to the development of a large bureaucracy in both the CSEs and the government, with corresponding low levels of efficiency and a lack of accountability. In addition, management became extremely risk averse, and their decision-making virtually became administrative reactions to instructions from the government institutions.

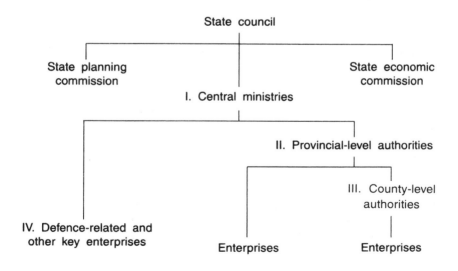

Figure 8.1 Industrial management and planning hierarchy in China
Source: Jackson, 1992, p. 17.

Under such an economic system, there was no recognition of the "law of value" or the principle of supply and demand. Various measures were taken to de-marketize or restrict the development of the market. Apart from some markets for consumer products, all the markets of production materials, capital, labor, technology and information ceased to exist. The result was gross misallocation of resources, leading to stockpiling of unneeded goods in certain areas or to chronic shortages in certain other areas. One notorious example was the story of the 34.5 million tons of steel produced in 1979, 20 million tons of which were wasted in warehouses as unmarketable either because they were the wrong assortment or were of poor quality. From the 1960s to 1970s, 81 huge industrial complexes failed, with 40 being poorly located, 27 never operating at full capacity, and the rest unfinished (Prybyla 1982: 3–24).

Even the market for consumer products was fragmented and limited in coordinating power. The prevailing situation under this arrangement was a shortage of supply. Thus, the state had to adopt measures to restrict consumption and impose a rationing system. Rationed products included cotton cloth, food grain, vegetable oil, sugar, meat, soap, and a few other products that were considered to be basic essentials. Every month each person received a fixed number of ration coupons for these goods. Table 8.1 gives the supply of rationed goods from 1957 to 1960. Some years during the 1960s and 1970s proved to be even worse.

There was a whole series of state policies corresponding to the model of the product economy. In terms of financial and taxation policies, the state had responsibility for all costs incurred by the CSEs while also collecting

Table 8.1 Supply of rationed goods from 1957–1960 (in units of 10,000)

	Region							
	Beijing				Shanghai			
	Ration supplies				Ration supplies			
Year	Total retail sales	Type of product	Total sum in RMB*	Percent in retail sales	Total retail sales	Type of product	Total sum in RMB*	Percent in retail sales
1957	138,047	6	33,923	24.6	255,537	7	75,590	29.6
1958	178,100	6	47,738	26.8	269,995	9	84,047	31.1
1959	214,700	12	57,118	26.6	297,987	15	97,531	32.7
1960	248,235	50	101,239	40.8	321,417	25	125,398	39.0

Source: CERI, 1984, p. 164.
* = Renminbi, or Chinese Yuan

all profits, though they were nominally independent accounting units. The CSEs had neither independent economic interests nor responsibilities. The state was the only investor. During this period of time, banks were only an extension of the state. The state either allocated funds directly or offered "gratuitous" credits through banks at very low interest rates. The CSEs did not have to worry about the source of financing or the efficiency of investment. The financial and taxation policies provided for minimal economic leverage.

In regard to pricing policies, there was only one form of price, i.e. the state-set price, except for those agricultural products sold in the free markets in some years during the period. Most of the prices neither reflected the costs of production nor the supply/demand of the market, and they remained unchanged for decades. Since demand was greater than supply, the government imposed strict control over the distribution of products. Most products were bought and sold by the state. The most typical selling process went as follows: the state set specific factory output quotas and bought the output at state-set prices. The first-level state-owned wholesalers distributed the collected products to the second-level state-owned wholesalers according to plan, which in turn supplied to the third-level wholesalers within their region. The third-level wholesalers finally transferred these goods to their subordinate retailers. The end result would be either a stockpiling of unneeded goods or chronic shortage (CERI 1984).

Four administrative bodies responsible for the general distribution of goods were:

1 The Ministry of Commerce, which included the bureaus of commerce in various levels of government as well as numerous state-owned businesses. Its basic responsibility was the distribution of manufactured consumer products, mainly in urban areas.
2 The National Federation of Supply and Marketing, which included supply and marketing cooperatives at different levels of government as well as a considerable number of supply and marketing cooperatives throughout the countryside. Its main responsibility was the distribution of agricultural and agricultural sideline products (except for grain and edible oil) to the whole country and the distribution of the means of agricultural production and manufactured daily necessities to rural areas.
3 The Ministry of Food, which included offices related to grain production at the various levels of government and numerous grain stores. The main function of this system was the distribution of grain and edible oil.
4 The Ministry of Materials, which included bureaus at various levels of government as well as associated state-owned companies.

The system was responsible for the distribution of machines and materials used in the production process and divided into three categories: Category

One comprised widely used key materials that were distributed by the State Planning Commission (*tongguan*). Category Two comprised specialized key materials that were distributed by central ministries (*buguan*), and Category Three were materials under local distribution (*diguan*) (Koziara and Yan 1983).

Under state-set pricing, the relationship between production costs and product prices was greatly distorted. Processing industries benefitted considerably from higher prices. The relative profitability of industries was more related to the arbitrary price of their inputs and outputs than related to their production efficiency (Riskin 1987: 168). For example, the prices of China's cigarettes and wine were usually significantly higher than cost, which enabled manufacturers to register huge profits. On the other hand, the prices for various raw materials and public services were set so low that the enterprises involved in these areas could not stay in business without the support of the state.

As mentioned earlier, the CSEs were subordinate organs of governmental institutions. Managers naturally became government officials since they were governmental appointees. All the managers, technicians and workers were allocated by the state according to state plans. The CSEs had no power to allocate income on the basis of performance or job quality. The state set general wage standards according to region and profession. Wage standards were set artificially low and remained unchanged for a long period of time. Although China had practiced a complex system of wage ranking sales since the 1950s, the differences between the wages of top administrative and technical personnel and ordinary employees were small. Even before the puritanical Cultural Revolution, the ratio between the highest and the lowest in an industrial enterprise was only 3 to 1 (Richman 1969: 799). Egalitarianism was the norm while there was no leverage of wages and bonuses.

Under such a system the CSEs had neither independent management power nor managerial responsibility. There were no distinctions made between good and bad performances. The CSEs had neither internal vitality nor operational pressures, and they lacked the ability for self-development. By resorting to administrative ordinance and imperative plans, the government directly controlled the CSE operation. Thus, these enterprises became mere subsidiaries of government institutions without any autonomy in management. The productive activities of the CSEs, ranging from the acquisition of the factors of production to business operations, were all controlled by the imperative plan and administrative ordinance. The operational environment of the CSEs restricted the development of the CSEs and in return led to the slow development of the national economy. This was the main reason for the introduction of the 1979 reform. (For a summary of this section see Figure 8.2.)

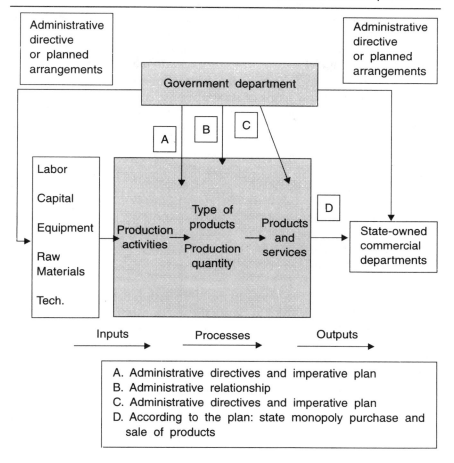

Figure 8.2 Pre-reform CSE operational model

POST-1979 CHANGING OPERATIONAL ENVIRONMENT

Since 1979, an ambitious reform program has been instituted in China, first in the countryside and then in the cities. The reform has greatly changed the operational environment of the CSEs, providing unprecedented opportunities for their development but also presenting some serious challenges. In order to follow the line of analysis, one should understand the key aspects of the CSEs' operational environment on the basis of the three major factors used earlier.

First, most of the Chinese have agreed that the old highly centralized model was obsolete because it prevented the promotion of productivity.

Since 1979, the government no longer relies on administrative directives and imperative plans in employing economic and legal means, policy guidance, or market mechanisms in the coordination of the national economy.

In terms of a planned system, the general trend has been a gradual reduction of content and scope of state planning control. By 1984, only 30 to 40 percent of industrial production could be attributed to central planning. According to the authorities concerned, the imperative output quota that originated in the State Planning Commission had been reduced from 120 to 60 by September 1991. Throughout the national economy, the industrial sector controlled by state planning has significantly declined, with those still controlled by imperative plans occupying a small proportion of around 20 percent. This means that the CSEs have obtained more decision-making and control power and also that the role of the market has greatly increased. The CSEs now need to get more material from the market in order to sell more products. By 1991, the national goods and materials system obtained 72 percent of its sources from the market, and many cities 50–60 percent (Cao 1991: 4).

Some progress has been made in the relationship between the government and enterprises. In order to clarify the relationship of the state as CSE owner, the state has gradually separated ownership from the power of management in many CSEs. The state enjoys ownership, while the CSEs have the right to manage. More concretely, the state has implemented a contractual responsibility system through leasing or responsibility contracts that spell out the sharing of interests, responsibilities and powers between the state and the CSEs. In addition, some cities introduced bankruptcy laws, and in August 1986 the city of Shenyang announced China's first case of bankruptcy since 1949 (*People's Daily*, 9 August 1986). Thus, many CSEs have begun to experience relative autonomy.

Second, the traditional prejudice against the role of the market has gradually changed, and the market system has experienced great development. Since 1979, not only has the consumer market been expanded significantly but other types of markets have also achieved various levels of development. The market for production materials already parallels the consumer market while the service tertiary industries are expanding rapidly. Similarly, China is quickly developing its financial markets as well as markets for technology, labor, and real estate. Thus, a relatively complete market system has taken shape.

The system of supply and demand has also improved greatly. Since 1979, greater varieties and quantities of goods have been supplied to the market. Before 1989, however, the general demand always surpassed supply due to inflation of investment, consumption habits, and oversupply of money. The austerity program combined with rapid augmentation to productivity has changed this situation. In a market investigation in 1991, for example, the Ministry of Commerce found only six kinds of goods were in slightly short supply among 700 consumer goods (Cao 1991: 4). Many goods that were previously rationed are now readily available. Nevertheless, this has also created competitive pressures. Before 1989 it was basically a seller's market, but after 1989 it has turned into a buyer's market. The competition is becoming increasingly heated.

Third, the state has readjusted and promulgated a series of policies since 1979. First was the change in financial and taxation policies by which the CSEs began to enjoy the status of an independent accounting unit. On 1 June 1983, the government replaced profit remission with an income tax: large and medium-sized state enterprises were required to pay 55 percent of their profits as tax, and small enterprises paid on the basis of an eight-grade progressive tax schedule, thereby severing their direct relationship with government institutions (Jackson 1992: 102–107); any after-tax profits were then retained by the companies. Therefore, there is an incentive to better manage the enterprise, since profits can now be retained by the firm. Furthermore, the state is no longer the only investor. The CSE can raise funds through a variety of channels, with one of the most used being bank credit. The state has also begun to emphasize the importance of leverage financing. Policies of priority credit and discount credit are granted to certain better-managed CSEs, or to CSEs in key developmental areas. The CSEs, however, still have much higher income tax rates than other types of enterprises, whose taxes are exacted at the rate of 33 percent.

The number of goods with prices controlled by the state has been diminishing. Not only are more of the prices for consumer products freely set, but more and more prices for production materials are being regulated by the market. According to statistics of the State Pricing Administration, 97 percent of all retail goods were traded at prices set by the government in 1978. For agricultural and sideline products purchased by the state, 92.6 percent were sold at fixed prices. By the end of 1991 the proportion of the state-set prices for the purchase of agricultural products occupied 22.2 percent, with 20.9 percent for retail prices of general consumer goods and 36 percent for the selling prices of production materials. In 1992, China opened the prices for 593 materials for production and for communication/transportation services. By 1992, only 89 production materials, seven agricultural products (such as cotton, grain and tobacco), and 30 light-industrial consumer products were still subject to state price control (Ling 1992: 23–25). Thus, enterprises have basically obtained control of the right to set prices. In addition, except for the few products still under the imperative plans, most goods can be freely purchased and sold in the market since the original state-controlled wholesale channels no longer exist. Also, market and commodity exchange centers have emerged to ease transactions.

There have also been fundamental changes in personnel and labor policies. Contract systems have been instituted for both cadres and workers, and the traditional lifelong employment system has been significantly weakened. The CSEs have increasingly begun to enjoy the right to hire managers, employ workers, and decide on the establishment of institutions as well as the scope of the organization. The state only controls, to some extent, the total sum of wages and the general level of wages. If the CSEs are well managed, the total sum of wages can be augmented so that the welfare and wage allocation can be increased. As for how wages are to be allocated within enterprises and in what form, the enterprises themselves have substantial power to decide. (For details, see Chapter 9.)

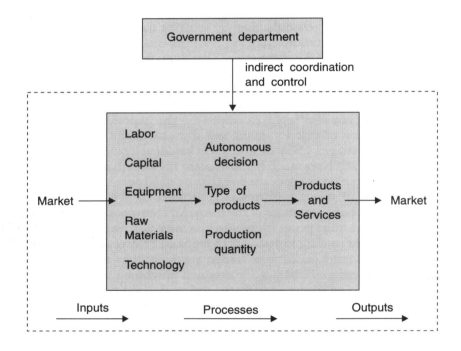

Figure 8.3 Post-reform CSE operational model

In sum, the general operational environment of the CSEs has been shifting from the product economy model to the market economy model. The state has begun to reduce substantially its role in the economy, which has facilitated the transformation of the CSEs. The significance of the change lies in the fact that the CSEs have begun the process of changing into independent entities operating freely within the market. Apart from the few key state enterprises that remain under governmental control because of their strategic importance to the national economy of China, most of the CSEs have already changed into the model shown in Figure 8.3.

THE FUTURE TRENDS OF THE CSEs' OPERATIONAL ENVIRONMENT

In spite of significant improvements in the development of the CSEs over the past decade, many serious problems still stand in the way. While market pressure has become more intense, many CSEs have been unable to adapt to the heated competitive environment. A large number of these CSEs have been sustaining losses. The state subsidies paid to cover their losses grew by 34 percent in 1989 compared with 1988 (Jackson 1992: 111). In comparison to joint ventures, private enterprises, and township enterprises, the majority of the CSEs have lagged behind in development. There are a number of reasons, both operational and internal, but only the operational obstacles will be analyzed here.

First, in order to become a really independent manufacturer of commercial goods, a CSE must be completely separated from the government. Right now, the state has adopted the method of separating ownership and management rights through the implementation of the contract responsibility system among the majority of the CSEs. Although such a contract system has vitalized many CSEs, it cannot solve the fundamental problems in the relationship between the state and the CSEs. This has led to a proliferation of short-term endeavors on the part of the CSEs and constant bargaining between them and the state. Many believe that the only way out is through the introduction of stock ownership. Since the definition of ownership is not clarified, the government still retains much of the power for macro-management (Gao 1992: 23). Many ministries of the government still interfere in the economic activities of the CSEs. Therefore, the government must streamline its administrative structure through the conversion of its functions and loosening of control.

Second, in order for the CSEs to become independent competitors in the market, the state must further cultivate and develop the market system. Right now, a market system is taking shape, but its development has been uneven. Transfers among the financial, technological, labor, information, and real estate markets, as well as the property rights market, are still relatively immature. There are still regional and departmental divisions and blockades and the market is beset with confusion and lack of order. The 1991 riot in Shenzhen's Stock Market, where large fluctuations in prices are still quite common, is a case in point.

Finally, a series of state policies need to be further readjusted. The reform of finance and taxation should serve to establish more firmly independent accounting for the CSEs. Many enterprises are responsible for gains only and not for losses. The gaps in the burden of taxation between the CSEs and others should be closed. Financial reform should further vitalize financial markets, making transparent the central bank's role of coordination and promoting the vitality of specialized banks. Price reform should be aimed at further relaxation of prices and to quick-fix the "dual" price system. Reform of the personnel and labor system should focus not only on the smashing of the "three irons" system, i.e. the "iron chair," the "iron rice bowl," and the "iron wage," but also on the establishment of a national social welfare system, without which it would be impossible to lay off unnecessary workers (Gao 1992: 22–23).

The operational environment of the CSEs is still undergoing rapid changes, as China's economic reform continues to develop with full force. It was significant that the Chinese communists were committed to market-ization of the Chinese socialist economy by writing the principle of market socialism into its Constitution in the 14th National Congress of the Chinese Communist Party in 1992. Undoubtedly, the general trend of reform will have tremendous influence on the operational environment. To predict the CSEs' operational environmental trend for the 1990s, several key factors influencing this operational environment need to be analyzed.

The first is the political and ideological trend, which has exerted consid-erable influence on the operational environment of the CSEs throughout the history of the PRC. This was obvious in the anti-rightist campaign of the 1950s and the Cultural Revolution of the 1960s and 1970s. In the course of the reform, this has had significant influence on the debate of the relationship between the plan and the market, and the issue of "capitalism" versus "socialism." While economic reform has proceeded rapidly, China's political reform has lagged far behind.

The second is social endurability, or how much a society can bear within a short period of time. Social endurability has two layers of meaning, i.e. psychological endurability and material endurability. The Chinese eco-nomic reform has covered every stratum of society and influenced the interests of everyone. There is a process by which people accept change. Reform will not come without certain costs. Resolution of the "three irons" issue, for example, can hardly be conducted without a complete social security system.

The third factor is the development of the economy. If the current dynamics of rapid economic development can be maintained without causing a major imbalance, structural reform will have a more propitious environment in which there will be greater social endurability. Otherwise, high inflation, major economic imbalance, and social disorder will hamper the process of reform.

Based on the dynamics of the reform in the past decade, there would seem to be three possible scenarios. The first is accelerated marketization whereby the Chinese government would expedite its reform, streamline its administrative structure, reduce the role of planning to a minimum, and give more autonomy to local governments. Except for a few key CSEs in the national economy, the state would turn most of its enterprises into stock companies. For some of them, the state would maintain dominant share-holdings; for others, the state would hold a substantial portion of stock. The CSEs would become really independent competitors, having no adminis-trative relationship with the state. Macromanagement would be characterized by a small role for government and a big role for society. All the markets would experience rapid development. Legal and financial leverage would be the main recourse for government coordination of the economy.

The second scenario would be a slow but stable evolution. In macro-management, the central government would maintain a substantial amount of control for an extended period, while giving local governments and enterprises more autonomy and further clarifying the division of labor among the three. While gradually diminishing the role of imperative and indicative planning, the state would gradually increase the market's role. The CSEs would continuously improve their responsibility system, and a small number of the CSEs would be turned into stock companies. Markets would also continue to develop and expand. The government would thereby emphasize the employment of combined administrative, eco-nomic, and legal means to coordinate economic operations and gradually rationalize the economy.

The third possibility is a scenario involving limited retraction of current policies. While the state would continue its reform, it could rescind some of the present policies to a certain extent, thereby reemphasizing the com-bination of a planned commodity economy and market coordination. The state would continue to exercise planned control over major industries, enterprises and products while allowing market coordination for other sectors. The central government would continue to strengthen its macro-management by resorting to administrative, economic, and legal means aimed at clarifying the relationships between central and local govern-ments. The CSEs would continue their responsibility system and, while paying attention to the development of the market system, the state would emphasize the management of markets. While actively developing com-modity, service, and information markets, the state would exercise strict control over security, real estate, and labor markets.

SUMMARY/CONCLUSION

The chapter has traced the evolution of the operational environment of Chinese State Enterprises. The central line of the evolution has been de-veloped around the centralization and decentralization in the relationship between the state and the CSEs. Nevertheless, before 1979, this centraliza-tion and decentralization was merely shifted between the central and local governments. After 1979, the Chinese government began to consider the decentralization of decision-making and management from the governmental institutions to enterprises, so that they become full-fledged participants of market competition. As mentioned earlier in this chapter, the government has adopted a number of measures to change the operational environment of the CSEs, including the development of a market system in China, and the separation of ownership and management in the CSEs. In spite of improvements in many CSEs, there still exist tremendous problems. By the end of the 1980s there were many CSEs operating in the red. Their problems are partly attributed to the operational environment of the CSEs, such as continued governmental control, an underdeveloped market system as well as the lack of necessary social structures such as a social welfare system, etc. In the end, three scenarios of development are compared and analyzed: accelerated marketization, stable evolution, and the limited retraction of current policies.

Based on the current dynamics of Chinese reform, the first scenario holds the highest probability, and the third is the least likely. China's reform has developed to such a stage that the relationship between the government and the CSEs must be radically reformed. Without these changes, the CSEs will not only remain a burden to the government but also will become the single most important obstacles to reforms. Therefore, it is generally agreed that the government should conduct further reform on the operational environment of the CSEs. The continually changing operational environment has provided the CSEs with good opportunities to reform their managerial mechanisms, yet it also presents tremendous challenges to their survival. Although the CSEs' development has been hindered by state control in the past few decades, they have also been protected by the state from market competition. When the state began to remove these controls, the CSEs started to feel the pressure of competition. Therefore, the reform of the managerial mechanisms of the CSEs has become critically important. Without such reform, the changing operational environment will simply spell the end of many CSEs in the years to come.

QUESTIONS FOR DISCUSSION

1   How important are large and medium-sized state enterprises to the Chinese economy?
2   What are the key characteristics of the Soviet centralized system of macromanagement as reflected in China?
3   What are the four administrative bodies responsible for the distribution of goods in China before the reform?
4   How do you assess the progress of China's marketization?
5   Do you think the Chinese government will eventually have to give up ownership in order to revitalize state enterprises?

FURTHER READING

Cao, Zhi-hu (1991) "Establishing and Perfecting A New-Type Socialist Economic Operational System," *Liberation Daily* (4 September).

Chossudovsky, Michael (1986) *Toward Capitalist Restoration? Chinese Socialism After Mao*, New York: St Martin's Press.

Commercial and Economic Research Institute of the Chinese Commerce Ministry (CERI) (1984) *The History of New China's Commerce*, Beijing: Finance and Economics Publishing House.

Feuchtwang, S., A. Hussain and T. Pairault (eds) (1988) *Transforming China's Economy in the Eighties. Vol. 2: Management, Industry and the Urban Economy*, Boulder, Colo.: Westview Press.

Gao, Shangquan (1992) "New Operating Mechanism," *Beijing Review* (15–21 June): 18–24.

Henley, John S. and Mee-Kau Nyaw (1986) "Reforming Chinese Industrial Management," *Euro-Asia Business Review* 5(3) (July): 10–15.

Jackson, Sukhan (1992) *Chinese Enterprise Management*, New York: Walter de Gruyter.

Koziara, E.C. and Chiou-shuang Yan (1983) "The Distribution System for Producer's Goods in China," *The China Quarterly* 96: 689–702.

Laaksonen, Oiva (1988) *Management in China During and After Mao*, New York: Walter de Gruyter.

Ling, Bin (1992) "Market Plays Dominant Role," *Beijing Review* (23–29 November): 23–25.

Lippit, V.D. (1987) *The Economic Development of China*, Armonk, N.Y.: M.E. Sharpe, Inc.

Noland, Peter and Furen Dong (eds) (1990) *The Chinese Economy and Its Future*, London: Polity.

Pan, L. (1988) *The New Chinese Revolution*, Chicago: Contemporary Books.

Prybyla, Jan (1982) "Where is China's Economy Heading? A Systems Analysis," *Journal of Northeast Asian Studies* 1(4) (December): 3–24.

Richman, Barry M. (1969) *Industrial Society in Communist China*, New York: Random House.

Riskin, Carl (1987) *China's Political Economy: The Quest for Development Since 1949*, London: Oxford University Press.

Solinger, Dorothy J. (1984) *Chinese Business Under Socialism: The Politics of Domestic Commerce, 1949–1980*, Berkeley: University of California Press.

Xu, Disin, *et al.* (eds) (1982) *The Chinese Economy Since 1949*, Beijing: New World Press.

Xue, Muqiao (1981) *China's Socialist Economy*, Beijing Foreign Languages Press.

Wu, Naitao (1992) "State-Owned Enterprises: No Longer State Run," *Beijing Review* (16–22 November): 17–21.

Chapter 9

Reforming managerial mechanisms of Chinese State Enterprises

INTRODUCTION

Owing to the restrictions of their overall operational environment, the CSEs were born with some major structural and managerial problems. After more than 30 years' practice, these problems had become so obstinate that mild reform measures could not remove them. Since 1984, the Chinese government has focused its attention on reforming and revitalizing the state-owned industrial sector, which accounted for more than 70 percent of the total national industrial output at the time. Two responsibility systems have since been introduced. The first was the "enterprise responsibility system" which was intended to decentralize responsibility for the operation and performance of the CSEs down from higher administrative ministries and bureaus to the enterprises themselves. The second was the "director responsibility system" which was intended to concentrate internal executive authority into the hands of the enterprise director, supervised by the Party committee and workers' congress. The goal of these two responsibility systems was to transform the CSEs from being merely factories taking administrative orders from the state into competitive business units which could carry out market transactions based on their own strategic judgements. This chapter will examine major structural and managerial problems of the CSEs, analyze the key features of the ongoing reform and their implications for the CSEs, and discuss options for the CSEs in their attempt to break away from inveterate inertia.

STRUCTURAL AND MANAGERIAL PROBLEMS OF THE CSEs

The development of the Chinese management system has gone through four major stages since the beginning of the People's Republic in 1949. After the transformation to state ownership, a Soviet model of management was introduced. In large and medium-sized state enterprises, executive authority was concentrated in the hands of directors – the so-called "one director management system" (Laaksonen 1988: 197–199). This management system laid a foundation for current management practices and made considerable contribution to the heavy industrial development in China in the 1950s. Nevertheless, this imported bureaucratic top-down management did not fit very well with the Chinese communist aspirations of greater roles for Party officials and the workers' congress (which were the legacies of revolutionary mobilization), as it relied heavily on technically trained managers that China had very few of at the time. This system was weakened by reforms in 1956 and 1961, which strengthened the role of factory party committees and workers' participation. Factory directors were placed under the leadership of Party committees and became responsible for implementing decisions made by those committees. This system was disrupted again by the model of the Cultural Revolution, in which managers were discredited while the representatives of revolutionary workers were given power to control, subject to the guidance of ideologically loyal Party committees. The current reform was based on the second model.

Whatever models were adopted, the CSEs were more or less organized along the line-function system of management (see Figure 9.1). Under this system, people in functional departments acted in their professional capacity of providing guidance and advice both to their superiors and subordinates, but had no authority to give directions and commands. This group of people included technicians, accountants, engineers, etc. who normally had professional training. Factory directors, managers, workshop heads and production team leaders had the authority to direct and command their subordinates within their divisions. They were supposed to be both red (ideologically loyal to the Party) and specialist (in managing their own fields), though being red was more important. Moreover, the CSEs, whether large or small, were designed to be operationally complete. Each factory had an independent system that included nearly all functions. Their levels of specialization and socialization were very low. Such a structure made it difficult for many CSEs to reach the expected economic scale.

In addition to this inefficient structure, the responsibilities of enterprise leaders were not clearly defined. The most prominent problem was the existence of the Party structure in each enterprise, which operated parallel to the administrative structure. The Party branch served as an ideological control over what happened within the enterprise, ensuring that enterprise activities conform to general Party policies. It also acted as a protecting mechanism for the interests of the workers, allowing them to complain against management. There were no clearly defined patterns of power distribution between managers and Party officials, which really depended on the connections and styles of individual managers and Party officials. However, the Party secretary has always been a powerful "watch dog" and had significant decision-making power (Andors 1977: 60–61). In the course of management reform, the factory directors who wanted to get back some of their own management powers would try to wear two hats in the

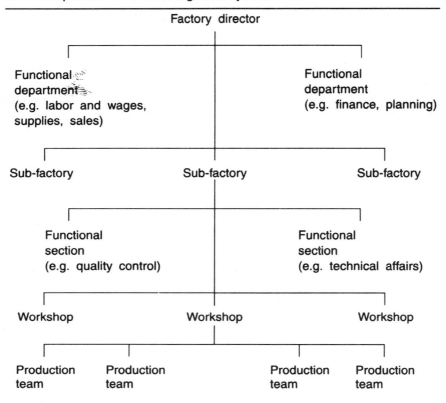

Figure 9.1 The line-function system of management
Source: Jackson, 1992, p. 214.

enterprise, i.e. to be both director of the enterprise and the secretary of the Party committee. This ambiguity was further complicated by the fact that organizational structures and their respective responsibiiities as well were often decided by higher-level governmental institutions and not based on the need for production activities (*Shang-xia-dui-kou*). The CSEs were also expected to mirror their divisions to those of their respective government authority.

Besides supporting a Party system, a CSE also had to support activities of two additional systems that were not linked to core business activities. These systems put an extra drain on the enterprise, without bringing visible benefits to the enterprise. John R. Schermerhorn Jr. and Mee-Kau Nyaw (1991: 11) give a good description of these two systems. The first was called a life-support system, which was designed to provide workers and their families with a whole set of facilities supporting their off-work activities, such as housing, nursery schools (or elementary and high schools for larger enterprises), entertainment centers (or cinemas and theaters for larger enterprises), a transportation system for commuting and recreational trips, and clinics (or hospitals for larger enterprises). To deal with the extent of this life-support system, a fairly large bureaucracy was established.

The second system Schermerhorn and Nyaw call a sociopolitical support system, which was to assist the Party in cultivating a loyal workforce and exercising control. It included a workers' union, which belonged to the All-China Federation of Trade Unions (ACFTU) and was designed to advance workers' welfare; the women's federation, which was related to the All-China Women's Federation (ACWF) and was organized to safe- guard women's rights and take care of such daily problems as patching up family quarrels and providing advice on maternity and child care; the Communist Youth League, which was a branch of the national organization and subject to Party leadership; and, finally, a militia, which was a para- military self-defense organization with multiple functions.

In terms of personnel management, enterprise leaders and other cadres were governmental officials appointed by higher-level government institu- tions. These cadres could not be fired or demoted and, in effect, enjoyed "iron ruling chairs." Enterprise workers were also deployed by various governmental labor departments according to state plan. A CSE did not have the right to hire its own managers and workers. Furthermore, once these people entered a CSE they would enjoy lifelong employment and an "iron rice bowl." The CSEs could not lay off their workers, and workers could not choose their own jobs. As for promotion and wage levels, a CSE had to unconditionally implement various relevant state rules. In addition, due to the loose management system and fragmented rules within the CSEs, managers often resorted to political indoctrination rather than to economic or legal incentives for promotion of efficiency. Under these arrangements there was little incentive for workers to perform. Thus, they tended to eat out of the "iron rice bowl of the enterprise."

In financial management, a CSE was directly subject to state financial control. Thus, a CSE belonged to the unified balance of the state, and had only a nominally independent system of accounting. Funds needed for operations were allocated by the CSE's higher-level government institution according to imperative plans. These funds were restricted and could be used by the CSE only under the guidance of certain governmental rules. The CSE was also obligated to deliver to the state all income it generated. The state appraised enterprises mainly in terms of whether they had fulfilled or overfulfilled state plans. The standard of the appraisal focused on product quantity and value. It did not really matter whether a CSE was efficient or profitable. Since a CSE was responsible only for meeting pro- duction quotas it became dependent upon "the iron rice bowl of the state" to meet its financing requirements. Consequently, the CSEs generally did not pay attention to the use of funds, business accounting practices, or economic benefits.

MAJOR REFORM MEASURES AND EXISTING PROBLEMS OF THE CSEs

In 1979, when China began its reform program, there was a consensus among the Chinese leadership that the management system should be reformed, but they could not agree on suitable models to be used for reform. Therefore, they adopted an experimental approach. By mid-1979, over one hundred provincial-level state enterprises in Sichuan province began to experiment with some management powers over production and the marketing of products. By 1980, such pilot experiments were spread to include a total of some 6,600 state enterprises in the province. In October 1984, based on the results of these experiments, the Party Central Committee passed a major policy document on "China's Economic Structure Reform," which provided a comprehensive guideline for Chinese economic reform, with a focus on enterprise management reform (*China Daily*, 23 October 1984).

The focus of the reform beginning in 1984 was an industrial responsibility system, whereby a CSE signed a "profit and loss contract" (*yinkuibaogan*) with its supervisory governmental institution. After paying a quota of profit to the state, the CSE could retain a share of basic profits above the quota. Starting in 1985, all state industrial enterprises were required to implement a "responsibility" system under the leadership of the enterprise director, which replaced the director (or manager) responsibility system under the leadership of the Party committee. Thus, the director (or manager) was located at the apex of the enterprise and represented the highest decision-maker fully responsible for management activities. Party committees, under the new system, mainly played a supervisory role, even though the opinion of the Party secretary could not be brushed aside lightly (Henley and Nyaw 1986: 268).

The CSEs had the right to form their own internal sub-organizations in accordance with the needs of production activities, particularly for the purpose of augmenting and strengthening market sales, and information (Child 1987: 27–30). The CSEs began to enjoy partial rights in personnel management and employment, such as an appointment system for managers, a contract system for workers, and reassignment of surplus laborers. The old "iron ruling chairs" and "iron rice bowls" began to be reformed. Employees, for their part, began to have freedom in choosing their own professions and jobs. The CSEs also started to institute independent accounting practices and retained the income remaining after the payment of taxes and fulfillment of contracted responsibilities. Investment funds were no longer solely provided by the state but were also generated by the CSEs themselves. The CSEs began to pay attention to the rational use of funds, management of costs, and the increase in interest rates. The CSEs also obtained substantial freedom in bonus and wage setting, and in distinguishing between good and bad work.

As a result of rapidly rising interest among the CSE managers in Western management techniques, management concepts (such as PERT, network analysis, critical path analysis, value analysis, TQC, system analysis, and MBO) had become increasingly familiar to many of those managers. During the 1980s, a number of foreign management programs were set up in China, including the Canada/China Enterprise Management Training Center (Chengdu), the China Europe Management Institute (Beijing), the Sino-American National Center for Industrial Science and Technology Management Development (Dalian), the Sino-German Shanghai Industrial Management Training Center, the Sino-Dutch Management Training Center (Changsha), and the Sino-Japanese Enterprise Center (Tianjin). Strong management skills began to be seen as a ticket to a promising career (Borgonjon and Vanhonacker 1992: 14). State enterprises have been experimenting with many Western management techniques, though the results have been mixed.

On 13 April 1988, the Seventh National Congress of the People passed a series of laws on state enterprises. The law stipulated that "enterprises are socialist commodity production and accounting units which operate independently, assume sole responsibilities for gains and losses, and conduct independent accounting"; that the "property of state enterprises is owned by the people, and the state grants enterprises their management power in accordance with the principle of separating ownership from management"; and that "the legitimate rights and interests of enterprises are protected by the law and should not be violated" (Wu 1992: 17).

According to an investigation in 1989, more than 60 percent of production in the majority of the CSEs was already made in accordance with their own plans; more than 70 percent of the used raw materials were purchased from the market; and approximately 80 percent of their products were sold by CSEs themselves. The CSEs had obtained substantial autonomy in investment decisions, product pricing and wage setting. In 1989, their autonomous rights in these three areas reached 58 percent, 74 percent and 78 percent respectively (*World Daily*, 16 December 1992: 9). Into the 1990s, more policies have been issued to revitalize large and medium-sized state enterprises, including the 11 measures issued in May 1991 and 20 policies issued in September 1991 which have given more power to the managers of CSEs.

With these measures, many large and medium-sized state enterprises have been revitalized by reforms. Among them are the Shoudu (Capital) Iron and Steel Corp. (SISC), the Shanghai No. 2 Textile Machinery Plant and the Yanshan Petrol-Chemical Company. The SISC, for example, became one of the first experimental enterprises to be reformed in 1979 and adopted a contract system in which it increased its tax contribution by 7.2 percent a year while the rest of its income was used for production funds, welfare, and wages and bonuses using a proportion of 6:2:2. The company now has a payroll of nearly 200,000 employees, more than 100 plants, over 60 joint ventures, and six overseas companies and offices. The contract will last from 1981 to 1995. The raising of wages is related to the profits at the ratio of 0.8:1. The SISC has the right to sell 15 percent of its planned iron and steel products. The contract system is applied to all the people working in the company, who are fully responsible for their performances. The director is the real leader while the Party committee only exercises political guidance. A greater role is given to the workers' congress in management and for strategic decisions workers will be consulted. In 1990 and 1991, the SISC ranked first in profit-making and tax turnover among the large and medium-sized state enterprises. In 1991, its profit amounted to 2.36 billion RMB, an 11 percent increase compared to 1990; the company also made foreign exchange income of US$210 million in the same year (Wu 1992: 20–21).

In spite of substantial advances, major problems still remain. Many CSEs have not been able to adapt to the changes and demands of the market and are inferior competitors as a result. The state has essentially pushed the CSEs into the market to purchase their own production inputs and to develop their own products. Since the latter half of 1989, the supply and demand balance has shifted to bigger supply, leading to heated market competition. Many CSEs cannot compete effectively due to their low-quality, dated stocks, and backward sales methods, often resulting in large inventories and inefficient work. The incentives of managers and workers in many CSEs remain low. Many CSEs still lack the desire to maximize profits and expand production. Low levels of efficiency and economic benefits are plaguing many CSEs, with many directors and managers failing to handle their everyday tasks and managerial duties efficiently. Thus, many CSEs still operate at a loss and depend upon state subsidies.

In fact, a crisis in CSE management took place in 1990, when more than 30 percent of them were reported to be operating at a loss. In 1990, profit and taxes collected from all state enterprises dropped by 18.5 percent compared with the previous year, while their total loss nearly doubled (*China Daily*, 13 April 1991: 4). A large number of state enterprises became interlocked into a chain of debt default payment, called the "triangular debt" cycle, in which producer enterprises were in debt to the enterprises supplying raw materials, but they themselves were owed money from their clients. The manufacturing enterprises were among the worst hit. In spite of the state injection of temporary loans to keep funds circulating for production purposes, the debt problem remained serious among many CSEs in the following two years.

These problems have stemmed from a number of factors, including both overall environmental factors as well as problems associated with the internal enterprise managerial mechanisms. First, the CSEs have not really become independent units of production because they have not yet obtained true autonomy. Although greater surplus production means higher retained earnings for the enterprise, various higher-level institutions still manage to obtain a portion of generated profits. In addition, officials of these higher-level institutions tend to increase the base figures of the responsibility contract, and this increases the burden placed on the enterprise. In China this is called the "whip hitting the fast-running cow" phenomenon, meaning that companies are punished for increasing their productivity; the government sets higher production quotas as companies become more efficient, thereby negating any benefits from the rise in output. Such government interference is common in CSE operations. According to a 1991 survey, more than 90 percent of self-management power was poorly implemented in a majority of the CSEs (Wu 1992: 18–19).

Second, while the overall planning system has been reformed, many related policies in finance, pricing and taxation lag behind. The CSEs may have more autonomous rights than before, but they are still restricted by these various policies, some of which are discriminatory. Large and medium-sized state enterprises, for example, were until recently required to pay a fixed 55 percent tax, while township enterprises paid much lower progressive tax rates. Also, large and medium-sized enterprises were allowed depreciation rates of just 5.3 percent of manufacturing cost.

Third, many CSEs have not established good sales mechanisms (see Figure 9.1). Until 1989, the state controlled a substantial portion of the market and the CSEs focused their efforts solely on production and paid little attention to sales. The marketing and sales departments in the CSEs remain ineffective. One stumbling block is their traditional penchant for selling whatever is produced rather than basing production on market need. Therefore, the CSEs have neither devoted enough attention to market research and forecasts, nor have they aggressively pursued technological advancements and new product developments. They continue to manufacture many unsalable and unwelcome products lacking in quality, variety, color, model, packaging, and trademark. In contrast, township enterprises and joint ventures have adopted much more aggressive strategies.

The competition between Shanghai Soda Water Factory and the Sino-American joint venture Shenmei Drink and Food Ltd. during 1990–1991 is a case in point. Shanghai Soda Water Factory, an aged state-owned enterprise, dominated the market in Shanghai with its product Zhengguanghe. But, the much smaller and newer Shenmei introduced two brands "Xuebi" and "Fangda" which rapidly absorbed Zhengguanghe's Shanghai share, eventually squeezing it out of Shanghai's central commercial district. One major contributing factor was Shenmei's adoption of a Coca-Cola-type sales mechanism that is characterized by a large sales department, free delivery of goods, high-quality service, powerful advertisement, and public relations (*Liberation Daily* from July to September 1991).

Fourth, most of the CSEs still hold on to the old straight-line functional model, in which departments and management levels are often laid out irrationally with many redundancies. There is a symbiosis of overstaffed organizations on the one hand (such as the life-support and sociopolitical support systems discussed on p. 131) and an absence of some necessary departments on the other (such as R&D, information services, and consulting departments). For example, the staffs dealing with general affairs, personnel, Party affairs, secretarial work, etc. occupy close to 30 percent of the total employees in the CSEs compared to only 11 percent in Sino-foreign joint ventures (*World Daily*, 16 December 1992: 9). The ability of directors to integrate and reconstitute the typically large number of functional and staff departments also remains low. Divisions of labor and responsibility between different departments and among different managerial levels are ambiguous. Consequently, there is considerable organizational duplication and serious trouble in interdepartmental cooperation.

Fifth, the CSEs still have to carry heavy social burdens by maintaining their life-support systems. In addition to maintaining a large staff to deal with various non-production activities, they have to support a relatively large number of retired workers. The bulk of extra benefits resulting from the rise in productivity has to be used to resettle redundant workers and staff. Until very recently, they have also had to pay a fixed tax rate of 55 percent while other types of enterprises paid much less.

Sixth, although traditional political education and administrative control have gradually been replaced by various new methods designed to boost work incentives, too much emphasis has been put on material incentives at the expense of sociological, psychological, as well as scientific managerial methodologies (such as quality control, systematic engineering, etc.) There is a general lack of a modern managerial control mechanism. Product quality, for example, has been a serious problem among many CSEs. For most of the CSEs, good managers are in severe shortage. There are many factors conducive to this shortage: management schools have only been a recent phenomenon; since China has developed by leaps and bounds, many managers have been unable to follow the dynamics of development; and the rigidity of the personnel system precludes many talents from being promoted. Furthermore, professional training has not received necessary attention.

Lastly, the "three irons" problems are still very serious. Although some measures such as the implementation of appointment systems for managers have been taken, obstacles to full implementation still remain. The governmental inclination to restrict tightly the laying-off of permanent workers remains strong due to China's lack of a social security system and the government's real concern about possible social instability. Therefore, most of the CSEs have not been able to lay off permanent workers but only those newly hired contract workers. On the whole, however, contract workers are less of a problem compared to those hired on a permanent basis who tend to resist radical reform of the personnel system. Abrogating the "three irons" would influence the interests of everyone hired under the old system, meaning that everybody has to work harder and compete more, thus increasing the risks and pressure placed upon them. Traditionally formed habits are still deeply rooted. The CSEs on the whole do not have the full right to promote general wage scales and the state tends to be very conservative when approving wage motions. In sharp contrast, township enterprises and joint ventures do not suffer from the consequences of the "three irons."

NEW GOVERNMENTAL MEASURES OF REFORMING THE CSEs AND THEIR LIKELY IMPACTS

By the early 1990s, the revitalization of the CSEs, especially of large and medium-sized state enterprises, had become a top priority for the Chinese leadership. A working session of the State Council in October 1991 determined that the State System Reform Committee, led by Vice-Premier Zhu Rong-ji and assisted by the Office of Economy and Trade of the State Council, and the Legal Bureau of the State Council, would study and draft the necessary documents. After a study of more than half a year, in July 1992 certain managerial reforms were formally promulgated under the name of "the Regulations for Transforming Managerial Mechanisms of the State Owned Enterprises" (*Liberation Daily*, 27 July 1992). The regulations stipulate 14 kinds of power to ensure self-management. Some of them serve to clarify ambiguities in the existing laws and rules, but the majority are new rules aimed at transforming management mechanisms and governmental functions.

Included in the 14 kinds of managerial power are production management power, power to price service and products, power to sell their products, import and export power, power to make investment decisions and use their own funds, power to dispose of their properties, power to merge and make alliances, power to determine workforce, personnel management power, power to set up various sub-organizations, power of wage and bonus distribution and power to refuse governmental apportionment. Detailed rules are created to protect each of these powers from interference or infringement by government institutions. Among these managerial powers, the following are deemed to be the most significant: to manage production; to make investment decisions; to price products and services; to import and export; and to manage human resources.

Power to manage production: one regulation stipulates that "enterprises may decide to adjust the scope of their production and business in and outside their trade." This serves to guarantee state enterprises the right to move away from government dependence and become largely independent businesses. According to the regulations, enterprises, when asked to meet mandatory production plans, have the power to demand contracts with their clients signed under the auspices of the government department concerned. Without such contracts they have the right not to make any commitment to production. Also for the mandatory production plans, the CSEs have the right to demand a readjustment if the state cannot fully guarantee the normal supply of energy, key materials and transportation. Previously, only the state could exercise such controls, but now the CSEs may also place restraints on the state.

Power to make investment decisions: the new regulations allow the CSEs to use reserve capital to undertake productive projects in various regions under the guidance of state industrial policy and industrial and regional development plans. Subject to governmental approval, they can also freely make international investments and set up enterprises overseas. Most of the CSEs were handicapped by the subordinate relationships between central and local governments and could not previously keep up with investment changes and lost many good opportunities.

Power to price products and services: in spite of reforms in pricing, the state still maintained control of the prices of many products. Most of the prices controlled by the state affected the products of the CSEs. There existed virtually two price systems: one was free while the other remained subject to the control of the state. Obviously, those subject to more control suffered more. This system resulted in some well-managed companies losing money, while some poorly managed ones made profits due to pricing. Under the new regulations, except in very special circumstances, the CSEs can freely set prices for their products for daily use and means of production, as well as for their technical services.

Power to import and export: for a long time, the CSEs were only able to import and export goods via state-designated foreign trade institutions. The new regulations stipulate that "enterprises may choose any foreign trade institution in China to import and export for them and have the power to participate in negotiations with foreign businesses." Moreover, "enterprises may determine their own foreign currency reserve expenditures and transactions within guidelines set by relevant state regulations on foreign currency control. No department or unit can demand use of foreign currency reserves of enterprises."

Power to manage human resources: this is aimed at smashing the "iron rice bowl" in human resources management. Under the new regulations, the CSEs are allowed to "decide the time, conditions, methods and numbers when hiring new employees." The contract system of hiring people can be applied to those who previously enjoyed the lifelong employment legacies of the Maoist period. More significantly, the CSEs have also obtained the power to hire managerial and technical staff from abroad, subject to approval from relevant departments. The power to allocate wages and bonuses has also been expanded. The total wages of the individual CSEs can be decided on the basis of combining the state-stipulated total wages with economic efficiency. The CSEs have the power to freely allocate wages and bonuses within the scope of the total wages assigned by the state. They can freely determine the scales of wages and bonuses according to each employee's work skill, work intensity, work responsibility, working conditions, and actual contribution.

Besides ensuring the managerial power of the CSEs, the state also tries to intensify their responsibilities in the new regulations, i.e. with all their newly acquired power, directors of the CSEs have direct management responsibility for any gains and losses while workers have corresponding indirect responsibilities. In order to establish self-controlling mechanisms in the CSEs, the government has decided to enforce the following managerial components: (1) the link between total income of employees and economic benefits; (2) the responsibility of the directors for gains and losses; (3) the responsibility of the CSEs to function as a profitable entity and, if unprofitable they must cover their losses or file bankruptcy.

Even more significantly, the role of the government is clearly redefined. The government is mainly responsible for creating conditions and providing services assisting the transformation of the management mechanisms of the CSEs in four areas: (1) it should establish a macro-control management system to facilitate economic operation; (2) it should continue to promote the role of the market system; (3) it should set up a comprehensive social security system; (4) it should take more responsibilities for developing public facilities and welfare institutions to reduce the burden on the CSEs. To curb administrative intervention, the new regulations also stipulate that governmental institutions will have to bear legal consequences for trespassing on enterprise autonomy.

In addition to the 14 kinds of power, the state has also taken measures to improve the situation of the CSEs. Notably, one of them is the most recent attempt to unify the tax rate, which will bring the tax rate of the CSEs down to the level of township and private enterprises. These changes may give those already well-reformed and competitive CSEs a strong boost if they are enforced. But they may exert more pressure on those already suffering from the unfavorable impact of market competition, resulting in either their eventual collapse or absorption by other enterprises. Therefore, the performance of the CSEs will be mixed, contributing to a polarizing tendency, with the gaps between well-managed and poorly managed companies continually growing. There will likely be constant reorganization of various state enterprises either among them or within each one of them. For the next few years, the development of many CSEs may be characterized with upheaval and uncertainty. In order to survive, the CSEs must quickly modernize their own management and become competitive in the market.

One major problem with these new regulations lies in the fact that the ownership issue is still not fundamentally solved. Until the solution of this problem, the separation between the government and the CSEs will continue to be subject to various limitations. One option that has proved to be effective at solving the problem is the adoption of a shareholding system. Some of the CSEs, like the Shanghai No. 2 Textile Machinery Co. Ltd., have made substantial progress (Dai 1992: 25–31). Converted into a joint-stock business in 1991, the company now has a registered capital stock of 178.99 million RMB and a total of some 17.9 million shares. In addition, 14.08 million shares, or about 78 percent of the total, are held by the state (mainly in the form of factory buildings, machinery and equipment), 800,000 shares, or close to 5 percent of the total, are held by other enterprises, and three million shares, or around 17 percent of the total, are held by individuals. Beginning in 1992, the company formally issued A-stocks (for Chinese purchasers in Chinese RMB) in China and B-stocks (for foreign purchasers in foreign hard currencies). However, not all the companies can successfully adopt this approach.

Besides turning the CSEs into stock companies, in the author's view the CSEs should also be encouraged to form joint ventures or cooperations with foreign companies. There are many advantages to forming joint ventures. For example, once the CSEs become joint ventures, their relationships with the government are clarified with regard to problems of autonomy and associated responsibilities for gains and losses. Furthermore, since the Chinese government pays special attention to protecting foreign companies' interests for the sake of maintaining a good reputation, it tends to refrain from directly interfering in the management of joint ventures. The "three irons" problem can also be easily overcome, as most of the workers are already aware of the "strictness" of management in joint ventures and are willing to work harder for more benefits. More important, by forming joint ventures, the CSEs can absorb foreign technologies and apply advanced management, thereby adapting themselves to the demands of a market economy in an international market. Foreign partners will find it to their benefit that the CSEs are better candidates than other companies in China. This is especially true in terms of historical records, facilities and equipment, the quality of employees, supply and demand channels, social relations, reputation and risks.

There are also some other major problems not well addressed by the new regulations. They mainly lie in the managerial mechanisms: the problem of enterprise leadership or the selection and cultivation of managers, for example, need to be quickly solved. Whether an enterprise can perform well depends largely on the leadership. Although the aforementioned Chinese "Enterprise Laws" emphasize a system of director (CEO) responsibility, in practice there are many ambiguities to be clarified, such as the relationship between the director (CEO) and the Party committee, the appointment and removal of the director (CEO), and the responsibility, power and interests of the director (CEO). Furthermore, China lacks professional managers while many CSEs do not have good in-house training programs. If this shortage is not quickly addressed, the CSEs will be further inhibited from taking advantage of their newly acquired autonomous powers.

Last but not least is the need to restructure organizations. The CSEs should not only streamline their organizations by reducing, if not entirely deleting, life support and sociopolitical support systems, but also reduce operational functions by focusing only on their comparative advantages and forming strategic alliances with other enterprises. In fact, since the mid-1980s, many state enterprise groups have already been formed to transform loosely connected management of production and marketing into an integrated management, thereby enhancing the optimum use of production factors and rationalization of the CSEs' organizational structure. In the Chinese auto industry, for example, there were about 757 automobile factories, most of which had only an average annual output of 4,000, with some having output as low as 100 cars per year. Cars were assembled through a handicraft type of production line. The Hubei No. 2 Automobile Plant, one of the largest in China, took the lead in forming the Dongfeng Automobile Group, which now includes 300 enterprises of different scale. This auto industrial group has established a specialized and socialized mass production system (Yao 1992: 18–23). While such reorganization can help alleviate the management problems of many CSEs, they should not be encouraged to develop into monopolies.

CONCLUSION

This chapter has reviewed the structural problems of the CSE prior to the 1979 reform and discussed the reform of the CSE since 1979. It is far more complicated than many Chinese would have expected in the early 1980s. In a sense, the reform of the CSE has spurred on the reforms of China's economic system and of the government's role, the development of the market system, as well as reforms in investment, finance, taxation, price, circulation, labor and personnel, etc. It has also called for the necessity of creating a social security system. Therefore, the success of the reform of CSEs is critically important to the success of the Chinese economic reform. The Chinese government has adopted a whole series of measures in an attempt to separate ownership from management, while instituting a contractual responsibility system and giving more power to enterprise directors. Nevertheless, the experience of reforming the CSEs in the past decade has shown that it is not an easy process. When the problems are very serious, mild measures will not achieve the hoped for results. The crisis of the CSEs in the early 1990s is a case in point. Many thorny problems, such as the ownership of the CSEs, the role of the Party in the enterprises and the structural deficiency of the CSEs, have yet to be solved. The polarizing trend of the development of the CSEs will further strengthen some strong state enterprises and gradually eliminate the weak ones.

On the whole, the role of the CSEs in China's economy will diminish. Statistics show that the industrial output value of state enterprises decreased from 78 percent in 1981 to 55 percent in 1991; and in the same period that of collectively owned enterprises rose from 21 percent to 35 percent, and private and foreign-funded enterprises increased from 0.7 percent to 10 percent (*Beijing Review*, 24–30 August 1992: 10). This trend will certainly continue, as it is widely believed that the state will eventually give up its ownership to most of the state enterprises, keeping only a few strategically important large enterprises. If so, many of the existing CSEs will no longer be categorized as CSEs and the reform process will be completed.

FURTHER READING

QUESTIONS FOR DISCUSSION

1   Why do many directors in the CSEs want to wear two "hats"?
2   Can you briefly describe the line-function system of management in a pre-reform CSE?
3   Comment on the "life-support system" and the "sociopolitical support system" in a CSE.
4   What are the major problems still besetting the CSEs since the introduction of a series of industrial reforms in the 1980s?
5   What do you think is a feasible way to get the CSEs out of their current troubles?

Andors, S. (1977) *China's Industrial Revolution*, New York: Random House.
Borgonjon, Jan and Wilfried R. Vanhonacker (1992) "Modernizing China's Managers," *The China Business Review* (September-October): 12–18.
Byrd, William (ed.) (1992) *Chinese Industrial Firms Under Reform*, New York: Oxford University Press.
Child, John (1987) "Enterprise Reform in China," in Malcolm Warner (ed.), *Management Reform in China*, London: Frances Pinter, pp. 24–52.
Dai, Gang (1992) "A Multi-Economic Sector Enterprise," *Beijing Review* (September–October): 25–31.
Fukuda, John (1989) "China's Management: Tradition and Reform," *Management Decision* 27(3): 45–49.

Granick, David (1990) *Chinese State Enterprises: A Regional Property Rights Analysis*, Chicago: University of Chicago Press.

Henley, John S. and Mee-Kau Nyaw (1986) "Development in Managerial Decision Making in Chinese Industrial Enterprises", in Stewart R. Clegg, C. Dunphy, and S. Gordon Redding (eds), *The Enterprise and Management in East Asia*, Hong Kong: Center of Asian Studies, University of Hong Kong, pp. 267–299.

Jackson, Sukhan (1992) *Chinese Enterprise Management*, New York: Walter de Gruyter.

Laaksonen, Oiva (1988) *Management in China During and After Mao in Enterprises, Government and Party*, New York: Walter de Gruyter.

Schermerhorn Jr., John R. and Mee-Kau Nyaw (1991) "Managerial Leadership in Chinese Industrial Enterprises," in Oded Shenkar (ed.), *Organization and Management in China (1979–1990)*, Armonk, N.Y.: M.E. Sharpe, Inc., pp. 9–21.

Tidrick, Gene and Chen Jiyuan (eds) (1987) *China's Industrial Reform*, New York: Oxford University Press.

Tung, Rosalie L. (ed.) (1982) "Chinese Economic and Management Systems Reform," *International Studies of Management and Organization* 22(2) (Summer).

Wu, Naitao (1992) "State-Owned Enterprises: No Longer State Run," *Beijing Review* (November): 17–21.

Yao, Jianguo (1992) "Experimenting With Enterprise Groups," *Beijing Review* (May): 18–23.

Chapter 10

Comparative Chinese managerial systems

GENERAL

The Chinese residing in mainland China, Taiwan, Hong Kong and ASEAN share a common cultural and religious tradition – Confucianism – which instills the belief of hierarchy and order in society as well as harmonious interpersonal relationships. A Chinese should first and foremost know his place in society and how to interact with others in a proper manner. *Guanxi*, face and *renqing* are important components in regulating interpersonal relationships.

Nevertheless, they do have some outstanding differences as a result of living in different countries or entities and under different social systems. Among their major differences is the fact that the Overseas Chinese constitute the minority in Southeast Asia while Chinese living in mainland China, Taiwan, and Hong Kong are the majority. Therefore, the Overseas Chinese in Southeast Asia have had to cope with a social environment in which the indigenous majority have not always been friendly. There is a greater uncertainty and insecurity among those Chinese.

Another major difference lies in social systems. The Chinese residing in mainland China have been living under a socialist system, with communist domination and a command economic system. However, the Chinese living in Taiwan, Hong Kong, and Southeast Asia have enjoyed various versions of free market and capitalist economic systems. Major differences in social systems have inevitably left imprints on the management systems of the Chinese living in different areas.

Two major forms of Chinese companies have been identified: the Chinese family business (CFB) and the Chinese State Enterprise (CSE). The two are now compared under the headings which follow.

ORGANIZATIONAL STRUCTURE

The CFBs are very much different from the CSEs in their organizational structures, though there are some outstanding similarities. Many of these differences are determined by the differences in social systems.

First, the CFBs are owned by families and are regarded as private family properties. Even though some CFBs have grown into multinational corporations, the ownerships are still under tight control of core family members. In addition, top management mainly consists of family members.

In contrast, the CSEs were established and owned by the state. Top management does not lay claim to ownership of the businesses. For a long period, CEOs of the CSEs were assigned by the state and were themselves government officials. The economic reform in mainland China has made major changes in the appointment systems of CEOs, but has not changed the ownership into that of family. The direction of change would most likely be to a stock company.

Second, the overwhelming majority of the CFBs are small companies, with an average number of employees under 50, while a large number of the CSEs are large or mid-sized enterprises. While a growing number of the CFBs are expanding in size, the majority remain small. Owing to structural features and management style, many CFBs ostensibly do have difficulty in growing very large. Many of those that have grown to substantial size are experiencing difficulty in management control and are under the pressure of downsizing or have split into several smaller companies.

The economic reform in mainland China has allowed millions of small family businesses to spring up, but at the same time there is a trend toward forming large enterprise groups. Size is often cited as an important advantage in terms of access to raw materials and market share, as well as the right to conduct export and import business. Many of them have been trying to follow the example of *keiretsu* and *chaebol*. The trend has also been strongly encouraged by the Chinese government.

Third, the CFBs are also noted for their simple structure, with very few ancillary departments that are not directly related to profit-making, such as R&D. Neither structure nor rules are clearly defined. The level of standardization is also very low. In contrast, the CSEs have been overburdened with large bureaucracies. In addition to complicated and rigid organizational structures, the CSEs have had to support a Party system. At the same time, many important ancillary departments have been absent, such as the marketing and/or R&D departments. The structures and rules were also not clearly defined. The Chinese economic reform has been aiming at reducing the presence of the Party system and unnecessary bureaucracies, while at the same time adding the necessary ones. An increasingly vigorous responsibility system is being instituted in the CSEs to streamline management.

In terms of structure, they do share an important similarity, i.e. informalism. The important posts in the CFBs are either controlled by the core family members, dominated by the owners themselves, or given to close relatives or long-time associates. Those enjoying good *guanxi* in the CFBs may have larger powers than their posts justify. In the CSEs, informalism has also been prevalent. *Guanxi* has been playing an important role in the appointment and the sharing of power, with small cliques still rampant in both the CFBs and CSEs.

MANAGEMENT PROCESS

The management processes in CFBs and CSEs are strikingly similar. This phenomenon has mainly resulted from a commonly shared cultural tradition.

First, the CFB owners tend to adopt a didactic style of leadership. In order to maintain their authoritative position they generally keep tight control of information, especially financial information. The subordinates are dependent upon the owners for information. The owners also tend to suppress talents. There is a large "power distance" between the owners and the subordinates. Major decisions are almost all made by the owners themselves. Finally, those managers who are not among the core members of the family do not have access to the key decision-making processes.

Similar dilemmas are found in the CSEs, where the CEOs tend to be authoritative. The delegation of power is very limited, with most of the decision-making power concentrated in the hands of the CEOs or in small groups of top managers and party officials. Traditionally, party secretaries have held the dominant power. This situation has been changing; more and more directors having taken over power formerly held by party secretaries, but the "power distance" still remains very high.

Second, the control process in the CFBs is characterized by the lack of clear criteria on employee performance. The owners tend to attach great importance to the "degree of loyalty" of their subordinates rather than to their actual performance. They give special rewards and develop special ties with those who have loyally implemented their directives. These rewards are normally conducted in a concealed way. For those who do not enjoy special relationships with the owners, or those who do not have the kind of skills that the owners are dependent upon, the owners try to keep wage levels as low as possible and openly criticize such employees in public. Therefore, there is greater turnover among these people in the CFBs.

The control process in the CSEs has also been very similar. The loyalty of managers to the Party in general and to the top executives in particular has been the most important factor for their promotion and well-being. There has also been a notable lack of clearly defined criteria on employee performance. One of the focuses of the Chinese economic reform has been trying to overcome these problems by setting up more concrete criteria, but this has not proved to be an easy process.

Third, both the CFBs and CSEs are highly dependent on *guanxi* to develop their external relationships. Many CFBs are virtually dependent on *guanxi* for survival. They form all kinds of connection networks to acquire business opportunities. *Xinyong* has played an important role in maintaining these kinds of business ties. This is also true for many CSEs, but to a lesser extent. *Guanxihu* can help the CSEs get what they cannot get through regular channels. The economic reform in mainland China has so far encouraged this tendency rather than eradicated it.

COMPETITIVE STRATEGIES AND TACTICS

The competitive strategies of the Overseas Chinese in Southeast Asia have been known as low margin/high turnover to get market share, and economy of scope rather than economy of scale in order to seize business opportunities. The Chinese business community serves as an important basis for successfully carrying these competitive business strategies.

To secure their competitive positions as a minority, they have developed political sensitivity and a high degree of sophistication in forming alliances of convenience with officials in indigenous governments or with indigenous businesses. They have been remarkably successful in coopting various indigenous governments and taking advantage of economic development strategies of those governments to develop their businesses.

Many Chinese living outside China have been very good in managing money and making deals. Good deals need quick decisions, immediate action and ready cash. For them, the most important principle in managing money is to shorten its slumber period. Investment should also be made in deals that can either generate "gravy" profits or be self-financing (frying in its own fat). Flexibility is the key for the Overseas Chinese companies to seize business opportunities and to make profitable business deals, though the short-term and speculative behavior of many Overseas Chinese businesses also lead to business disasters.

In contrast, the CSEs in mainland China have not been able to develop competitive business strategies until only recently. Under the rigid economic system, the CSEs were dominated and overprotected by the state in terms of industrial material input, market share, and financial support. They were also dependent on the state in almost every aspect of the production process. With the support of the state, they became monopolies in their respective fields, yet they were not good at seizing business opportunities or in coping with changes in the market.

Their sense of security has gradually been shattered by the economic reform in mainland China. The CSEs had to study basic principles of market operation from input of industrial materials to marketing their products. This has proved to be a difficult process. They are under growing competitive pressure from the newly emerging and often small township, private and joint venture enterprises. Although they do enjoy the advantage of size, pool of talents, possession of good technology and solid financial base, they still have to develop their competitive strategies to be able to expand or even maintain their traditional market shares.

SUMMARY

There is a growing pressure to modernize both the CFBs and CSEs. For the CFBs, modernization may help them cope with the challenges of the high-technology era, when professional people are playing an increasingly important role in management. The modernization may also help promote size and longevity of the CFBs, but for many it would seem unlikely that this will happen in the near future. Their small size has also been cited as the very source of their success and competitive edge. Many CFBs have fared and continue to fare very well. Therefore, for a relatively long period small CFBs will remain the dominant actors in the Overseas Chinese economies.

The modernization of the CSEs has been commonly viewed as the only way out for them, as many of the CSEs are either profitless or operating at a loss. Large enterprises clearly need delegation of power and structural standardization and rules. The bureaucracy should be downsized while the management should be streamlined. Therefore, there is a greater urgency among the CSEs to modernize their organization and management. The result will very likely be the relatively rapid modernization of the CSEs in organization and management compared to the CFBs. As discussed earlier, there is a tendency to form large groups of state enterprises in the course of the reform. Furthermore, the government currently does not have laws to curb this trend as anti-trust laws do in the United States. Therefore, large groups of CSEs will likely emerge within the next decade to play a dominant role in the Chinese economy.

For a relatively long period, some aspects of the management process will continue to be heavily influenced by Chinese cultural tradition. The didactic style of leadership, for example, will remain the dominant mode of leadership in Chinese businesses for both mainland Chinese and Overseas Chinese. Large power distance will also remain an outstanding feature of Chinese management. *Guanxi* will continue to play an important role both within Chinese organizations and between them. Any successful modernization will be a compromised or mixed form of traditional Chinese management and modern or Western management techniques.

Part III

Comparative Japanese and Korean management systems

Chapter 11

Government–business relations in Japan and Korea

INTRODUCTION

The rapid industrialization process in Japan and Korea was not only spectacular but also unprecedented in modern history. The active role that the Japanese and Korean governments played in bringing about such dynamic economic growth has often been cited as one of their major sources of strength. Both governments were involved in the process by developing industrial policies and fostering close relationships with priority industries and related big businesses. Their interventions were justified on the grounds that they wanted to catch up with advanced industrialized nations within the shortest possible time.

However, the existence of intimate government–industry relations in Japan and Korea does not testify to a "Japan Inc." or "Korea Inc." conspiracy. Japanese and Korean businessmen are not motivated much differently from their Western counterparts, despite their differing interests. Their willingness to collaborate with government is not because they are exceptionally patriotic, or culturally devoted. Rather, it is because they have known through their experience that such collaboration can bring material benefit. It is also true that industrial policy is not unique to these two countries. Close governmental relationships with priority industries and related big businesses are also quite commonly seen elsewhere in the world. For many developing countries, these phenomena are more sources of trouble than of strength. This is because they contribute to widespread favoritism, corruption, and the suffocation of competition. Nevertheless, in Japan and Korea the result seems to have been quite remarkable and the channel seems to have been fairly effective.

By the late 1980s, pressure to change these government–business relationships had developed. More criticisms were heard about the defects of heavy governmental involvement in industries and there was a growing voice among the industries to restrict governmental roles. This chapter will focus on the study of governmental relations with business in both Japan and Korea. It will include discussions of their historical legacies, the outstanding features of such relationships, and an analysis of their strengths and weaknesses, as well as their trends of development.

HISTORICAL PERSPECTIVE OF GOVERNMENT–BUSINESS RELATIONS

Japan

The Meiji Restoration in 1868 marked a turning point in Japanese history, when the new government took upon itself the responsibility to industrialize the nation within the shortest possible time. The situation was critical: after the arrival of the American fleet in 1853, Japan's doors were forced open and the threat that she would become another colony of the West was very real. The imposition of unequal commercial treaties in 1858 and 1866 stripped Japan of tariff protection and introduced a flood of imports that amounted to 71 percent of Japan's foreign trade by 1871.

The only viable option open to the Japanese government seemed to be a rapid political and economic transformation so that Japan could match Western development and thereby deal with the West on equal terms. This option was reflected in the popular slogan of *"fukoku kyohei"* (rich country – strong amy). The lack of private capital, modern commercial skills and techniques, a modern economic infrastructure, as well as a modern liberal merchant class meant that if Japan was to catch up with the West progress would have to be initiated by the government or not at all.

The existing channels of economic control, which were established from the Tokugawa period (1603–1868), facilitated governmental involvement in transforming the Japanese economy (Lockwood 1955). The reform measure in the Meiji period further strengthened the role of the government by allowing the state to borrow private capital and invest it in the development of strategic industries such as mining, shipbuilding, communications, armaments and textiles. When these enterprises became mature, the state transferred them at extremely low prices to selected private hands. The large-scale transfer of major state-owned enterprises in 1880, the first attempt to privatize, paved the way for the formation of the large industrial and financial combines called *zaibatsu*.

The government intervention in business had not only benefitted emerging modern industrial firms, especially *zaibatsus*, but also brought the active support of big business to the government. Time and again, *zaibatsus* loyally supported many important international and domestic policies of the successive governments. The armed revolt at Satsuma in 1877, for example, was suppressed by government troops paid by Mitsui Bank and transported by Mitsubishi's ships. The government's expansionist policies during the First and Second World Wars received vigorous support from *zaibatsus*, which in return benefitted from the government's war efforts (Morikawa 1992).

The defeat of the Japanese Empire at the end of the Second World War, and the ensuing democratic reform instituted by General Douglas MacArthur, did not fundamentally change the relationship between the government and big business. Although the family-dominated and vertically-linked *zaibatsus* were dismantled under the charge of war crimes, they were quickly replaced by large horizontally-linked *keiretsus*. These new groups were not strict monopolies because they competed against each other, but they together formed an oligopoly. Some used the old *zaibatsu* names, such as Mitsubishi, Mitsui and Sumitomo (Yanaga 1968: 30–62). While the militarists were tried and disgraced, the old theme of catching up with the West was further reinforced. It was generally agreed that Japan's defeat resulted from its backward economy and technology. The focus shifted from military expansion to economic revival.

Big business was once again endowed with the historical mission of reconstructing the war-shattered Japanese economy (Johnson 1982: 308). A strong link between the government and big business was reestablished in Japan. The government bureaucracy, the ruling political party (LDP), and the private sector combined to form a powerful intertwined triangle in which the government implemented a system of "administrative guidance." Key governmental departments, such as the Ministry of International Trade and Industry (MITI) and the Ministry of Finance (MOF), have been actively involved in business by giving favors to and subsidizing those businesses whose activities conformed to national priority. On the other hand, big business has exerted tremendous influence on the political process through informal communication links with the LDP leadership. Money has been channeled from big business to those political candidates who strongly support the interests of big business.

Korea

Korea's industrialization took place at a much later time. More than one-half of the industrial base that was left behind by Japanese colonial rule in 1945 was destroyed during the Korean War, which lasted from 1950 to 1953. In the 1950s the Korean economy lived on American military and economic aid. While some import substitution projects, such as sugar refining and textiles, were introduced during the 1950s, the US-educated President Syngman Rhee was more interested in introducing free market principles than in heavy governmental intervention.

The few earliest *chaebols*, such as Sambo, Samsung, Kaepoong, Lucky (later Lucky-Goldstar), Taehan, and Tongyang, experienced relatively rapid development in the 1950s. As Rhee's government dispensed with favorable concessions in the form of import licenses, foreign exchanges at favorable rates and governmental properties expropriated from the Japanese, these early starters became a ready target of the civil revolution in 1960 that led to the collapse of Rhee's government. In August 1960, twenty-four companies were required to pay a total fine of $65 million for tax evasion and unfair profiteering. The military government of Park Chung Hee, which replaced the civilian government in a coup in 1961, continued the campaign against the corrupt *chaebol* owners (Park 1982).

These events had a number of effects on the developments that followed later. First, the Korean government established its superior position *vis-à-vis* big business. This later allowed the government a relatively free hand to push big business into the priority industries. The Korean counterpart of Japan's MITI is the Ministry of Trade and Industry (MTI), which helped the government to create and implement its industrial policies. Second, the government took over some commercial banks previously dominated by private businessmen. This laid the foundation for the governmental control of bank credit. Third, the badly tarnished *chaebols* learned the importance of developing good relations with the government and also established their own organization, the Federation of Korean Industries.

In the 1960s and 1970s, Korea experienced an unprecedented economic boom, in which the government and business firms formed a team. The government made five-year economic plans and set economic targets. Business firms that had developed a close relationship with the government received strong support in developing their businesses according to the government plans. As a former general trained in Japan, President Park was impressed with the Japanese governmental involvement in business. With the support of the government, large *chaebols* had achieved rapid development and were able to survive on their own by the mid-1970s.

The dramatic ascendence of *chaebols* did cause concern for the government. Beginning from 1974, President Park adopted a series of measures to limit the excessive growth of *chaebols*. Some private firms were pushed to list their stocks on the open capital market. The tax payments and bank credits to big businesses were closely monitored. These were followed by compulsory sales of real estate not used for business purposes, forced divestment of many subsidiaries of the top twenty business groups, and the revocation of some large trade associations. Ultimately, however, these measures were not strongly enforced and the share of the ten largest *chaebols* in the manufacturing sector consequently grew from 21.8 percent in 1975 to 24.2 percent in 1982 (Song 1990: 115).

By the early 1980s the Korean economy became so heavily dependent on *chaebols* that it was almost impossible to curtail their activities without hurting the growth of the economy. The decade of 1975–1985 witnessed a new trend in which *chaebols* intensified competition between each other and began to focus their attention on advancing their specific skills by investing in technology, marketing, and managerial know-how. Meanwhile, the *chaebols'* social status had also been remarkably improved. In the economic downturn of the late 1970s and the early 1980s, the government was forced to openly acknowledge that its interventionist attitude could be very harmful to economic development, and began to allow the private sector to take more initiatives. The *chaebols* had also come to realize that in spite of major advantages there could be some undesirable and severe consequences. For instance, ICC-Kykje, then Korea's seventh largest, was severely punished by the government and lost its credit line almost overnight for not paying the donations expected by two quasi-governmental organizations that had ties with the then President Chun Doo-Huan (Kearney 1991: 41–42).

In short, Japan and Korea shared a similar historical legacy of heavy governmental involvement in business which was justified on the ground that, in order to catch up with the advanced nations, the government should assume the responsibility for defining industrial policies and for using whatever means were available to achieve identified goals. Although the Korean government was heavily influenced by the Japanese government's relationship with its industry, the government–business relationship was developed much later than in Japan and in a much more volatile way, with one major difference being that the partnership between the government and business in Japan had been institutionalized ever since the Meiji Restoration.

GOVERNMENT–BUSINESS RELATIONS IN JAPAN

The major players

The three major players in Japan – bureaucracy, business, and the LDP – have developed extensive channels of communication in their triangular relationship.

Bureaucracy

The Ministry of International Trade and Industry (MITI), formed in 1949, is the most important institution in Japan's industrial policy-making process. The Ministry is responsible for: (1) constructing the structure of industry and adjusting dislocations; (2) guiding the development of industries and their distribution activities; (3) coordinating Japan's foreign trade and commercial ties; (4) managing specific areas such as raw material and energy to supply industries, small businesses, etc. The Ministry of Finance (MOF), a major rival of MITI, controls important tools to implement industrial policies, ranging from the budgetary process and cheap government loans to selective tax measures (Magaziner and Hout 1980: 40–43).

Business

Zaikai, which translates as "business world," represents the peak associations of big business, including the Federation of Economic Organizations (*keidanren*), the Federation of Employers' Associations (*nikkeiren*), the Committee for Economic Development (*keizai-doyukai*), and the Japan Chamber of Commerce and Industry. *Keidanren* has a membership of more than 100 industry-wide associations and around 800 large corporations. *Keidanren* has had a powerful influence on government, with the most notable example being the merger of the Democratic Party and the Liberal Party to form the LDP in 1955. The power of *keidanren* is derived from massive financial contributions to the LDP.

The large industrial groups, or *keiretsus*, embrace various industrial sectors and account for nearly one-third of the total economy. The biggest are Mitsubishi, Mitsui, Sumitomo, Fuji, Dai-Ichi Kangyo, and Sanwa ("the Big Six"). The presidents of the member firms participate in presidents' clubs, which serve as an important channel for policy coordination, collaboration, and conflict resolution among members. At a lower level, the inter-firm group member is itself the center of a group of small and medium-sized companies (subcontractors and parts suppliers). Ninety-eight percent of the manufacturing companies in Japan have less than a hundred employees. The importance of *keiretsus* in the government–business relationship is manifested in *keiretsu* dependence on the "in-house" bank, which is influenced by the Bank of Japan (BOJ) in terms of monetary policy, credit, and loans rationing.

The LDP

The LDP has been until most recently very successful in winning elections. A simple majority (256 of the 511 seats in the House of Representatives) was regarded as a Party disaster, which could lead to the resignation of the incumbent prime minister. Its uninterrupted tenure of office for the past few decades was a necessary guarantee of the government–industry relationship in Japan (Reading 1992: 230–243). The vote is obtained by chains of personal connections that reach all the way to local influential figures. Traditionally, gift-giving is expected as a reward to those who can mobilize voters, thereby resulting in many scandals and vote-buying.

The Party is a coalition of various factions that are seeking higher representation and more seats in the Cabinet. The Japanese single, multi-member non-transferable electoral vote system gives the factions their chance. Factional competition is most heated in the biennial contest for presidency of the LDP, which virtually guarantees access to the premiership due to the LDP's majority in the Diet. As money plays an important role in getting votes, a successful LDP leader should be someone who is capable of raising the necessary funding. This ability is the single most important precondition for promotion as opposed to possessing a legislative track record. Big business is the main source of funding for both the Party and individual politicians.

The dynamics of the triangular relationships

There is frequent formal and informal consultation among the three players. Their communication is made easier by the fact that the majority of the elite members are recruited from Tokyo University. Policy clubs and advisory councils gather together officials, business tycoons and politicians on a regular basis. Trade and industry associations constitute another channel in the communication chain. *Keiretsu* groups embody the industrial constituency and channel ideas to and from key bureaucratic institutions. The LDP assumes a central position between the bureaucracy and business, coordinating their interests and playing the role of referee. It serves to hold the triangle together.

The bureaucracy maintains good access to the communication networks by practicing *amakudari* (descending from heaven), which moves retired bureaucrats from MITI, MOF, and other key institutions into the LDP, where some may become ministers, or into the Bank of Japan, public corporations, commercial banks, trade and industry associations, and private corporations. As bureaucracy is a major player in policy-making, private businesses are eager to employ the retired bureaucrats in order to benefit from the personal bonds these people have built up in their former ministries. In addition, key policy-deliberating councils, such as the Economic Council, the Industrial Structure Council, and the Foreign Capital Council, are set up by the Economic Planning Agency, MITI, and MOF, respectively, to communicate with business.

The relationship between these key players is characterized by interdependence (see Figure 11.1). The bureaucracy needs the approval of the Diet for its policies and is thereby compelled to maintain good ties with the LDP, which dominates the Diet. The business privileges that are distributed by the bureaucracy can help LDP politicians take care of the interests of certain businesses in return for electoral constituency and contributions from industries. The LDP politicians have to guarantee a closer fit between bureaucratic actions and popular expectations; getting involved in this triangle, the business reaps huge benefits but becomes heavily dependent.

Such a triangular relationship seems to benefit each party and is justified by the hundred-year-old imperative of catching up with the West, which has contributed to a sense of national mission and during the postwar period has protected successive governments from public supervision. Nevertheless, it would be simplistic to assume that such cooperation is always harmonious, as each side has its own interests. The United States'

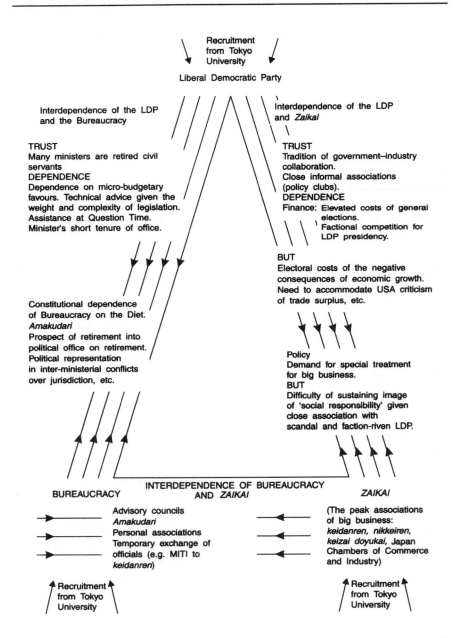

Figure 11.1 Triangular relationships among the leading players in government–industry relations
Source: Boyd, 1987, p. 69.

increasingly harsh demands for reducing the trade surplus, for example, have sharpened conflicts of interest among the three players and have increased the tensions on their traditional relationship. It is also a triangle of corruption, breeding one scandal after another. A recent National Tax Administration Agency survey revealed that $400 million in spending by the construction industry is unaccounted for each year. It has become common knowledge that most of this money goes into the pockets of politicians (TBT 1993: 28).

Industrial policy instruments

Industrial policy has received a consistently high priority in the postwar period in Japan, but the objectives and the instruments have changed. During the first period of reconstruction, which ran from the end of the Second World War to the mid-1960s, the government–industry relationship could be characterized as the "government industrial guidance model," in which the government controlled extensive subsidization, preferential capital, and license allocation. This was the prime period of MITI. The first period was replaced by a new "private sector industrial guidance model," in which MITI's role began to erode seriously (Johnson 1982). Pressures were building up for the liberalization of capital, the internationalization of Japan's economy, environmental protection, and the reduction of MITI's role in the economy. Mitsubishi's decision to form a joint venture with Chrysler against MITI's arrangement of a Mitsubishi–Isuzu venture was a milestone event demonstrating MITI's weakening position.

The government controlled a wide range of policy instruments. Once identified as being strategic, an industry became the candidate of both protective and nurturing instruments. The protective instruments mainly comprised trade tariffs, the restriction of imports and foreign capital, and a commodity tax system favoring home-produced goods. Nurturing policies covered below-market interest rates on loans from public and private financial institutions, special depreciation status and tax exemptions, subsidy grants, authorization of foreign currency to import necessary foreign technology, and exemptions from import duties on necessary machinery and equipment.

Public procurement has also been effectively used to enforce industrial policies. Although MITI itself does not have public procurement budgets, several governmental organs, such as the Defense Agency, the Ministry of Construction, and the Ministry of Transport have significant procurement budgets. Many public corporations, such as Nippon Telephone and Telegraph, also have substantial procurement capabilities. The procurement decisions of these organizations are heavily influenced by the governmental procurement policies based on the priorities of the governmental industrial policies.

Various cartels were also organized by MITI to control Japan's industrial output, market share, and investment (Magaziner and Hout 1980: 36). The industry associations collaborate closely with MITI in the organization of such cartels, which are designed to achieve a number of goals such as rationalization of production, promotion of vertical integration, short-term production allocation, reduction of excessive production, and export price floors during trade crises. Under growing public pressure to reduce the monopoly of cartels, the Fair Trade Commission passed a series of measures to limit the role and number of cartels. The number of cartels has decreased by half in a decade from 1,000 in the early 1970s down to about 500 in the early 1980s (Boyd 1987: 82). Moreover, the policy objectives have also changed in the remaining cartels, with more than 400 of them being designed to promote environmental protection or protect small and medium-sized enterprises from the *keiretsus*.

GOVERNMENT–BUSINESS RELATIONS IN SOUTH KOREA

Government domination

Business and government in Korea interact in diverse ways. The government plays a combination of roles, such as a competitor and customer, caretaker and regulator, and supporter and money extractor of business; the most prominent roles are of regulator and supporter. The Korean government has been heavily involved in business activities in the marketplace.

The government not only makes strategic plans to identify priority industries, but also places a substantial portion of investment funds under its budget to achieve the goals set by the plans. By controlling commercial banks and manipulating interest rates, the government also controls credit. The Korean government has also maintained a strong tax administration. Moreover, the government owns a large number of enterprises (when the government owns more than 50 percent of an enterprise, it is called a government enterprise) (Song 1990: 117), including the Korean Development Bank, the Korean Highway Corp., the Korean Trade Promotion Corp., the Korean Broadcasting Corp., the Korean Tourism Corp., the Korean Land Promotion Corp., the Korean Electric Power Corp., the Pohang Steel Corp., and the Korean Telecommunications Authority.

The Korean government also has considerable power in determining which company should enter specific sectors of the economy. In many industries, private companies need the approval of the government before they can start a new business. Meanwhile, the government also has the power to force some companies out of specific industrial sectors. The governmental power to manipulate entry or exit of private companies has been one of the most powerful instruments that it wields to influence private business. At the micro-level, the government's role has also been evident where, for example, it exercised strict control on labor movements prior to the mid-1980s. Product prices and wages in private firms were heavily regulated until the early 1980s.

For a long time the Korean government would choose a select group of companies in targeted industries and support those businesses by providing them with financial and tax incentives, plus information services. The "chosen" companies were typically large, export-orientated corporations and were awarded many privileges. Government favoritism toward these companies led to questionable business dealings and monopolistic tendencies. The government didn't try to end these practices until the early 1980s, when the Law of Monopoly Regulation and Fair Trade was finally passed.

In comparison to Japan, Korean government intervention seems to be much more widespread. Unlike the triangular structure of the Japanese bureaucracy, LDP and business, the Korean government has clearly played a dominant role in its relations with business. Since the Korean government had until most recently been very authoritarian, the role of the parliament and leading parties had been minimal. Korean businesses had to be much more subservient to the government. The history of Korean shipbuilding illustrates this point. Hyundai was virtually compelled by the Park government to venture into shipbuilding, even though it did not have the necessary skill or experience. By following the advice of the government, Hyundai successfully constructed supertankers within the shortest possible time and became one of the leading shipbuilders in the world.

Government and the birth of *chaebols*

From the end of the Korean War up until the mid-1970s, the Korean government helped *chaebols* reap huge profits in a number of ways. Based on chronology, *chaebols* can be classified into three groups: (1) the late 1950s; (2) the 1960s; (3) the 1970s (Lee and Yoo 1987: 96). *Chaebols* of the late 1950s, such as Hyundai, Samsung, and Lucky-Goldstar, were created by self-made founders who benefitted from the sale of government-owned properties, preference in taxation, and the preferential allotment of grants. The governmental sale of "enemy property," i.e. the factories left behind by the Japanese in 1945, was particularly significant for some *chaebols* formed in this period. *Chaebols* of the 1960s, such as Hanjin, Korea Explosive, Hyosung, Sangyong, and Dong-A, took shape with the help of foreign loans induced to implement five-year plans. *Chaebols* of the 1970s developed by taking advantage of the rapid growth in exports and domestic demand; these *chaebols* include Daewoo, Sunkyong, Lotte, Kolon and Doosan.

In short, the role played by the government was significant in the development of *chaebols*. This can be clearly illustrated by the government's control of commercial bank credit, where the government controlled both the price and quantity. Interest rates were kept very low, with real interest rates (bank's general loan rates minus inflation rates) averaging a negative number in the 1950s and 1970s; this has led to chronic excess demand for bank credit. *Chaebols*, the government-favored locomotives of rapid industrialization, naturally benefitted the most from subsidized bank credit as well as the government's own development funds. *Chaebols* can afford to lower their cost of capital by using the external source of capital made available by the government policies. Even in the late 1980s, when the Korean government began to push *chaebols* to lower their indebtedness, the debt-to-equity ratio averaged 5.1:1, with the seventh largest *chaebol*, Hanjin's, reaching a staggering 14:1 ratio (Kearney 1991: 51). Since *chaebols* have virtually been allowed by the government to indulge in over-dependence on these external sources of funds, *chaebol* owners have good reason to discount the risk of bankruptcy significantly.

It was estimated that the profit received by the *chaebols* from the distorted money market amounted to some $5.2 billion, which was more than half of the estimated total net value of the top fifty *chaebols* in 1980 (Jung 1989: 21). In addition, other types of government subsidies in the forms of tariff barriers, tax incentives, and wage/labor movement controls were also available. Although this estimate may be subject to a wide range of variations, the government did play a crucial role in the rapid expansion period of *chaebols*. As will be shown in the following section, *chaebols* have also contributed to the government's drive for rapid industrialization by venturing into many large and risky projects with relatively insufficient technological and financial capabilities.

The role of *chaebols*

While the Korean government's role in the development of the Korean economy is significant, the role played by *chaebol* founders should not be ignored. They consisted of a group of men with outstanding leadership, sharp vision, great determination, and unfailing devotion. The market distortions discussed earlier were not initially created by the Korean government solely for the sake of those *chaebol* founders, but the government's development strategies have resulted in generating new opportunities that the *chaebol* founders took quick and full advantage of.

The rapid industrialization and fast-changing industrial structure has forced *chaebols* to continuously look for new opportunities. If they do not constantly form new businesses they will suffer from lower growth rates and lose their relative share in the market. Therefore, *chaebols* tend to diversify into products and markets that are not related to their current lines of business. *Chaebols* include almost all large private corporations, and *chaebol* affiliates have grown faster than non-*chaebol* companies. Major *chaebols* are among the fastest-growing conglomerates in the world.

Chaebols have been widely criticized for their monopolistic power and also for their control of economic wealth. In the early 1980s, for example, 80 percent of major commodities were controlled at one point by a very limited number of *chaebols* (Kearney 1991: 39). Nevertheless, *chaebol* business structure also has positive effects on the Korean economy. It is much easier for these well-diversified and large business groups to undertake risky projects that normally require substantial investment. In comparison with large state enterprises, *chaebols* are much less bureaucratic and more dynamic. Large and diversified business groups can match up with the power of foreign MNCs in both the world and domestic markets. Also, they are in a better position to move into highly technological capital-intensive industries. *Chaebols* have indeed championed Korean industrialization within a short period of time.

SUMMARY/CONCLUSION

This chapter has reviewed and analyzed the historical evolution of government–business relationships in Japan and Korea. As discussed earlier, this relationship in both Japan and Korea has been distinguished by heavy governmental involvement. Encouraged by a catch-up mentality, both the Japanese and Korean governments felt obligated to take the lead in economic development, concentrating national resources and pushing the private sector to develop in targeted areas. Nevertheless, there are various differences in the ways and degrees in which they were involved in this development. For the Japanese, the three major players (i.e. the government, LDP, and business) deal with each other in a triangular framework, in which none would survive well without the others. In the case of Korea, government bureaucracy took charge in its relations with business, while the Korean parliament, until just recently, had very little power. In comparison with the Japanese government, the Korean government intervenes much more directly and extensively in the economy. In other words, "Japan Inc." symbolizes a government–business partnership in which the policy represents a consensus between equals. "Korea Inc.," meanwhile, connotes an unequal partnership in which the government sets the policies and businessmen tend to follow (Lee and Yoo 1987: 104).

By the 1980s, this kind of government–business relationship had been under growing pressure, both domestically and internationally. Various problems from heavy governmental involvement, such as built-in corruption, low efficiency, and a distorted market, had become better known to both government and business. Among the basic measures taken by both governments since the early 1980s are efforts to open the domestic market to foreign competition, more reliance on price and market mechanisms, and the promotion of small and medium-sized companies. On the other hand, many large business groups that had already accumulated substantial strength and experience by the 1980s and had been good at dealing with foreign competition, also began to realize the advantage of less governmental intervention, thereby pushing for less of it in the economy. The defeat of LDP in the 1993 election in Japan temporarily broke down the so-called golden triangle, while the current democratic reform in Korea has greatly weakened the government's ability to manipulate businesses. Nevertheless, in spite of these policy changes, big business groups in the two countries still have countless links to their respective governments; therefore, the process of disengaging government from business will be slow and involved.

QUESTIONS FOR DISCUSSION

1 Why have both Japan and Korea developed strong government–business relationships?
2 Who are the major players in the triangle of government–business relationships in Japan and how do they interact with each other?
3 How do you evaluate the role of MITI in Japan's industrial policy-making and implementation?
4 Why has the relationship between the Korean government and businesses been defined as an unequal partnership? Do you see this relationship changing?
5 After governmental reforms in both Korea and Japan in 1993, do you think that the government–business relationship will experience fundamental change in either country?

FURTHER READING

Boyd, Richard (1987) "Government–Industry Relations in Japan: Access, Communication, and Competitive Collaboration," in Stephen Wilks and Maurice Wright (eds), *Comparative Government-Industry Relations: Western Europe, the United States and Japan*, New York: Oxford University Press, pp. 61–89.

Johnson, Chalmers (1982) *MITI and the Japanese Miracle*, Stanford, Calif.: Stanford University Press.

Jones, L.P. and Il Sakong (1980) *Government, Business and Entrepreneurship in Economic Development: The Korean Case*, Boston: Harvard University Press.

Jung, Ku Hyuan (1987) *Growth Strategy and Managerial Structure of Korean Business*, Seoul: Korean Chamber of Commerce and Industry.

—— (1989) "Business–Government Relations in Korea," in Kae H. Chung and Hak Chong Lee (eds), *Korean Managerial Dynamics*, New York: Praeger, pp. 11–27.

Kearney, Robert P. (1991) *The Warrior Worker: The History and Challenge of South Korea's Economic Miracle*, New York: Henry Holt & Co.

Lee, Kyu-Uck and Sung-Soon Lee (1985) *Corporate Mergers and Concentration of Economic Power*, Seoul: Korea Development Institute.

Lee, S.M. and S.J. Yoo (1987) "Management Style and Practice of Korean Chaebols," *California Management Review* 95: 95–110.

Lincoln, Edward J. (1984) *Japan's Industrial Policies*, Washington, D.C.: Japan Economic Institute of America.

Lockwood, William (1955) *The Economic Development of Japan*, New York: Oxford University Press.

McMillan, Charles J. (1989) *The Japanese Industrial System*, New York: Walter de Gruyter.

Magaziner, Ira C. and Thomas M. Hout (1980) *Japanese Industrial Policy*, Berkeley, Calif.: University of California Press.

Masatsugu, M. (1985) *Management and Society – Lessons from Contemporary Japan*, Singapore: Federal Publications.

Morikawa, Hidemasa (1992) *Zaibatsu: The Rise and Fall of Family Enterprise Groups in Japan*, Tokyo: University of Tokyo Press.

Park, Byung-yoon (1982) *Chaebol and Politics*, Seoul: Hankook Yangseo.

Reading, Brian (1992) *Japan: The Coming Collapse*, New York: HarperCollins.

Sasaki, N. (1981) *Management and Industrial Structure in Japan*, Oxford: Pergamon Press Ltd.

Song, Byung-Nak (1990) *The Rise of the Korea Economy*, New York: Oxford University Press.

TBT (1993) "A Bad Case of the Japanese," *Tokyo Business Today* (January / February): 26–34.

Yanaga, Chitoshi (1968) *Big Business in Japanese Politics*, New Haven, Conn.: Yale University Press.

Chapter 12

Comparative large Japanese and Korean business groups

INTRODUCTION

One outstanding feature that both Japanese and Korean economies share is the dominance of large business groups – *keiretsu* in Japan and *chaebol* in Korea. By the mid-1980s, total sales of the six largest *keiretsus*, Mitsui, Mitsubishi, Sumitomo, Fuyo, Sanwa and Dai-Ichi Kangyo, accounted for 14.35 percent of Japan's corporate economy, with their total assets amounting to 12.96 percent and the number of employees to 4.14 percent. In the same period, the fifty largest *chaebols* accounted for about 20 percent of Korea's gross domestic product (GDP), with the five largest *chaebols*, i.e. Hyundai, Samsung, Lucky-Goldstar, Daewoo, and Sunkyong, occupying about 10 percent of GDP (TBT 1989: 14; Lee and Yoo 1987a: 96).

Their influence is not just restricted to the economy. Both *keiretsus* and *chaebols*, for example, have maintained very close relationships with their governments. They have benefitted from heavy governmental involvement in economic development and exerted various degrees of influence on governmental policy-making. By recruiting mainly from top universities, they also control first-rate human resources in their respective countries. However, they do have significant organizational and managerial differences. The main goal of this chapter is to compare the ownership, organization, and management of *keiretsus* and *chaebols*, and to analyze their differences.

DEFINITIONS OF LARGE BUSINESS GROUPS IN JAPAN AND KOREA

Japanese business groups are divided into two categories: *zaibatsus* and *keiretsus*. *Zaibatsus* began in the late 19th century and were dismantled by the Allied Forces Supreme Command after the Second World War. *Keiretsus* are horizontally linked business groups first formed in the 1950s. *Chaebols* are more similar to *zaibatsus* than to *keiretsus* in many ways. A *zaibatsu* can be defined as a large business group vertically controlled by family members which have diversified business operations and powerful influences in the national and regional economies of Japan (Morikawa 1992: xvii–xviii). This definition of *zaibatsu* can nominally be applied to *chaebol*, which is also a family-controlled and diversified business group. Large *chaebols* have oligopolistic influences in their respective industries. An owner-family of a *chaebol* controls 20–40 percent of the stock of its subsidiary companies either directly or indirectly.

Nevertheless, there is a fundamental difference in the concept of "family members" between the Japanese and Koreans (Lee and Yoo 1987a: 97). The Japanese concept of family consists of two meanings. One is the concept of family based strictly on blood relationship (consanguinity). The other is the concept of *ie* (household or clan), which is not only based on blood relationship but also on adoption. The Japanese hardly distinguish between the two meanings. But the succession of the property in Japan is often based on the concept of *ie*, according to which the heir of a property is not necessarily a family member by blood. A successor in *ie* can be described as a successor of the role. The main objective of *ie* succession is to protect and expand the wealth of the family led by a capable individual rather than to bequeath the wealth only to blood-related family members. Therefore, the family wealth can be bequeathed to an adopted son with no blood relationship.

The Korean concept of family is strictly based on a blood relationship. This difference in concept has an important implication to family inheritance and to the ownership structure of *zaibatsus* and *chaebols*. In Korea, the inheritance is carried out strictly on the basis of blood relationship, with the eldest son enjoying priority and other members of the family having their due shares. Under the Korean system of inheritance, those who are not related by blood are not entitled to the estate.

The difference in the concept of family is crucial to understanding the differences in ownership, organization and management of *zaibatsus* and *chaebols*. Since the family wealth in Japan is bequeathed to an individual on the basis of his ability to take care of it rather than on his blood relationship, it was not uncommon for *zaibatsu* family members not to be directly involved in management of the *zaibatsu*. Most of the *zaibatsu* family members in Mitsui and Mitsubishi, for example, did not participate in management. The separation of business ownership and management was designed to maintain the family wealth as an economic unit. In Korea, as the family wealth is bequeathed on the basis of blood relationship, the blood-related family members tend to take the managerial responsibility as well.

KEY FEATURES OF LARGE JAPANESE GROUPS

Zaibatsu played an important role in the rapid modernization of Japan from the late 19th century to the Second World War. The four largest *zaibatsu* groups, Mitsui, Mitsubishi, Sumitomo and Yasuda, accounted for about 25 percent of all Japanese business combined. The earliest *zaibatsu* groups benefitted greatly from the governmental auction of state enterprises in 1880. For example, the first *zaibatsu*, Mitsubishi, was formed in 1893. A large number of *zaibatsus* took shape during the first two decades of the 20th century. Mitsui and Sumitomo, for example, were formed in 1909 and 1921 respectively (Morikawa 1992: 26–92). With the support of the Japanese government, many *zaibatsus* evolved into large groups within three to four decades. Hattori (1989: 82) has provided a concise overview of the ownership and management of the three largest *zaibatsus* by the end of the Second World War.

Mitsubishi expanded from the shipping business into other areas by diversifying its products. By 1945 the Iwasaki family owned 55.5 percent of the Mitsubishi holding company, which in turn owned more than 52 percent of the subsidiary and affiliated companies. In contrast, the Iwasaki family owned only 0.4 percent of the subsidiary and affiliated companies. Mitsubishi practiced a system with a strong president, in which the Iwasaki brothers held the posts of president and vice-president; professional managers, however, were given a great deal of power, and all other executive positions in Mitsubishi parent and subsidiary companies were assumed by professional managers from non-Iwasaki families. While ownership and management were not completely separated due to the Iwasaki brothers' direct involvement in management, professional managers ran the day-to-day business.

Mitsui was initially concentrated on textile and money exchange businesses. By the end of the Second World War, the group consisted of twenty-two subsidiary and affiliated companies. With the ownership of 67 percent of the holding company stocks and more than 50 percent of the stocks of all the subsidiary and affiliated companies, the Mitsui family virtually owned the entire Mitsui group. But as the group grew, the owning family gradually dissociated itself from direct participation. The transformation of Mitsui from a thriving small business in the Edo era to a *zaibatsu* was largely led by professional managers from non-*zaibatsu* families. The Mitsui family imposed a strict rule against participation of family members in company management.

Sumitomo made wealth from copper refining and mining businesses. In comparison with Mitsui and Mitsubishi, the Sumitomo family commanded a lower ownership percentage in 1946, with 29 percent ownership of the group's holding company and 13 percent of the subsidiary and affiliated companies. However, the parent company had more financial and personnel control over the subsidiary companies than those of Mitsubishi and Mitsui. Like Mitsui, the Sumitomo family had gradually dissociated itself from direct management, with the exception of the head of the Sumitomo family, Domonari, who assumed the office of president; his role, however, was nominal, and the group was actually managed by professionals.

In short, the *zaibatsu* ownership structure resembled a pyramidal model (see Figure 12.1) in which *zaibatsu* families owned a large portion of the stock of the holding company, which in turn owned a large portion of the stocks of the subsidiary and affiliated companies. Although Mitsubishi and Sumitomo family members controlled the top positions of the groups, all of the big three left the management of the business operations to professional managers, who were not related to the families.

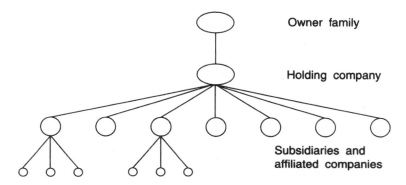

Owner family

Holding company

Subsidiaries and affiliated companies

Figure 12.1 Zaibatsu pyramidal structure
Source: Hattori, 1989, p. 85. Reprinted with permission of Greenwood Publishing Group, Inc., Westport, CT. © 1989

After the Second World War ended, *zaibatsus* became the target of the Allied Forces Supreme Command. Eighty-three *zaibatsu* holding companies were initially targeted. The dissolution of the *zaibatsu* was focused on depriving them of their ownership interest in banks, subsidiaries, and affiliated companies, freezing their assets and imposing a capital levy on their wealth (Bisson 1954). The four largest *zaibatsu* groups (Mitsui, Mitsubishi, Sumitomo, and Yasuda) voluntarily made dissolution proposals, with dissolution committees established to administer the dissolution process. To prevent their reestablishment, the Allied Forces Supreme Command instituted anti-monopoly laws.

In December 1947, the de-concentration of 1,200 companies was planned but quickly abandoned as Occupation policy shifted from reform to recovery. In 1951, the United States and forty-seven other countries signed a treaty with Japan by which Japan regained its independence. The post-Occupation Japanese government allowed the former *zaibatsus* to reestablish relations with the banks of their former groups; old familiar names like Mitsui, Mitsubishi, and Sumitomo began to reemerge. Around 1955, the presidential clubs for the reestablished groups such as *Kinyokai*, *Nimokukai* and *Hakusuikai* were organized. Nevertheless, the old families and holding companies that dominated the prewar *zaibatsu* groups never regained their original ownership and control. Some companies did not reestablish connections at all.

Postwar Japanese business groups, *keiretsu*, were different from prewar *zaibatsu* in many aspects (Okumura 1976: 20–25). To begin with, the pattern of ownership changed from a hierarchical system, in which the owning families controlled the stocks of the holding company which in turn owned the stocks of affiliated companies, to an interlocking ownership pattern with the member companies cross-owning the stocks of others within the group (see Figure 12.1). Next, the governing body is the Presidential Club, which consists of the presidents of member companies with mutual owner-ship of stocks. The Club makes decisions that affect the entire group, but does not, as a rule, interfere with the operations of a troubled member company. Last, each group is organized around a general trading company and a major bank that help finance the member companies, which consist of their own subsidiary and affiliated companies.

Large *keiretsu* groups (see Figure 12.2) are closely linked through capital and personnel. Cross-holding of stocks among the members of the group has become a common practice to guarantee "stable stockholders." In the late 1980s, the ratio of cross-holding of stocks among the six major corporate groups was around 24 percent (TBT 1989: 15). Ties among the group members can also be strengthened via exchanges of directors or the finan-cial priority given by the group bank to the members. Moreover, old *zaibatsu* families rarely get involved in management, as these large groups are almost entirely run by professional managers, who are internally promoted through the ranks in the same company they entered after graduation from college.

In 1989, *Tokyo Business Today* conducted detailed studies on the general situation of the six largest *keiretsus* (TBT 1989: 14–19). The largest among

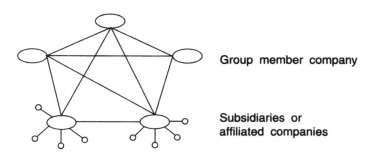

Group member company

Subsidiaries or
affiliated companies

Figure 12.2 Keiretsu star structure
Source: Hattori, 1989, p. 85. Reprinted with permission of Greenwood Publishing Group, Inc., Westport, CT. © 1989

these groups is the Mitsubishi group. The President Club is called *Kinyokai* or "The Friday Meeting," as the presidents of twenty-nine group companies hold an informal meeting on the second Friday of each month. Twenty-three are listed companies, with Mitsubishi Bank, Mitsubishi Corp., and Mitsubishi Heavy Industries, Ltd. among the leading members. The mutual stock-holding ratio is around 27 percent, but Mitsubishi Bank and three other financial companies held around 60 percent of the entire group-company shares. In terms of management, the twenty-nine group companies listed in the Kinyokai Club have several hundred executives, of whom about 70 percent are internally promoted, 20 percent transferred from other group companies, and less than 10 percent are hired from outside.

Mitsui Group is ranked second in terms of size. The Presidential Club of Mitsui is called *Nimokukai*, because the presidents of the twenty-four group-member companies meet on the second Thursday of every month. Twenty-two are listed companies and leading members include Mitsui & Co., Mitsui Real Estate Development Co., Mitsui Bank and Taisho Marine & Fire Insurance Co. The share of ownership held by the group companies stands at around 17.1 percent. Twenty-two listed group companies in the *Nimokukai* Club have around 78 percent of their managers internally promoted, 12 percent transferred from other group companies and only around 9 percent hired from nonmember companies.

Sumitomo Group, the third largest, is organized around its Presidential Club, named *Hakusuikai*, which meets once a month. The group consists of twenty companies, of which nineteen are listed companies. The mutual stock ownership ratio among group companies is around 24.2 percent. The leading members of the group are Sumitomo Bank, Sumitomo Metal Industries, Sumitomo Chemical Co., and Sumitomo Corp. About 73 percent of Sumitomo executives were internally promoted, 20 percent transferred from other group companies and only 7 percent hired from outside.

The other three groups are Fuyo, Sanwa and Dai-Ichi Kangyo. Fuyo, organized around *Fuyokai*, consists of 29 companies, including NKK Corp., Nihon Cement Co. and Nissan Motor Co., with Fuji bank playing the central role. The presidents of the group meet once a month over lunch. Group cross-owning stands at around 15.6 percent. Sanwa group, centered on *Sansuikai*, consists of 44 members, including Sanwa Bank, Hitachi, Kobe Steel and Nichimen Corp. Group cross-owning amounts to about 16.5 percent. The Dai-Ichi Kangyo group is organized around the Presidential Club of *Sankinkai* and consists of 47 members, including Dai-Ichi Kangyo Bank, C. Itoh & Co., Kawasaki Steel, and Shimizu Corp. The Club meets on the third Friday of each month and cross-owning within the group is around 12.5 percent.

In short, these large Japanese business groups resemble each other in terms of ownership, organization, and management. There are a number of comparative advantages in forming such large groups. First, the mutual stock holding among the group member companies enhances the stability of group companies. For publicly traded corporations, 20 percent of stock ownership can almost guarantee dominant ownership control. It is beyond a doubt that the cross-holding of stocks is conducive to the maintenance and development of large *keiretsu* groups. The group members are virtually protected from external takeover, though they still have to answer to the group as a whole for poor performance. The cross-holding also promotes mutual support of the member companies in times of difficulties.

Second, each *keiretsu* group is supported by a general trading company, or *sogo shosha*, and several financial firms. The general trading company plays a coordinating role over the group companies, and provides not only buying and selling services but also information services and builds information networks within the groups. Financial firms, such as in-house banks and insurance companies, serve to promote the growth of member companies through financial assistance and low-cost capital. In 1989, for example, it cost Japanese companies less than 0.5 percent per year to raise funds in the stock market. The fact that almost all large groups are organized around large banks is evidence the importance of financial firms.

Finally, joint business among the members within the group is an important means for promoting group cohesiveness and helps members to participate in large projects. Each *keiretsu* has an organized research group to promote joint development. While the cross-mobilization of talented managers among group companies is still limited in number, it helps build mutual trust, communication, and personnel development among the group member companies. Membership in a *keiretsu* guarantees to some extent the company's market for its products, as employees are encouraged to purchase consumer goods made by member companies.

KEY FEATURES OF LARGE KOREAN BUSINESS GROUPS

Like *keiretsu* groups, *chaebol* groups are comprised of many affiliated companies, though many of them are not listed on the Korean Stock Exchange. According to the Korean Productivity Center, the 100 largest *chaebol* groups in 1985 controlled 823 corporations. Each of the ten largest *chaebol* groups controlled an average of 18 corporations (Chang 1988: 52). *Chaebols* also take a higher percentage of the market share. In 1987, for example, the 335 products of the first 30 *chaebols* took 40 percent of the market (Jin 1991: 87). Compared with large Japanese business groups, *chaebol* groups are generally much younger, with the oldest, the Samsung group, established in 1938. The average size of *chaebol* groups is also much smaller than their Japanese counterparts. The Mitsubishi group is approximately twenty times larger than the Samsung group (Kang 1989: 73). The individual Japanese corporations are also substantially larger.

Another prominent feature of a *chaebol* is that many corporations are still owned by the founders' family members. Since most of the *chaebols* were established during or after the 1950s, such an ownership is understandable. The ratio of family ownership of *chaebol* groups is generally 30 percent of the listed corporations' stock, with larger *chaebol* groups having a relatively higher ratio of family ownership (Lee and Yoo 1987a: 98).

According to Hattori (1989: 87–88), the family ownership of Korean *chaebols* can be classified into three types (see Figure 12.3). The first is direct and sole ownership, where the founder or his family members own all the *chaebol* affiliated companies. The Hanjin group typifies this type of ownership. The second is the domination of a holding company in which the founder or his family members own the holding company, which in turn owns the affiliated companies. The Daewoo group is a suitable model of the second type. The third is interlocking mutual ownership, where the founder or his family members own the holding company and/or some kind of foundation, which in turn owns the affiliated companies. The Samsung group represents this type. The common trend seems to be a progression from the first type to the third as *chaebols* grow in size, though it may be a long-winded and difficult process.

According to a study of Lee and Yoo (1987b: 71), more than 30 percent of the executives of the top 20 *chaebol* groups are family members of the owners. Unlike *keiretsu* groups, the influence of the *chaebol* owner and his family on *chaebol* management can be assumed to be fairly high. Family members of the founders play very important roles in the management of most *chaebols*. Often, children of the founders hold key positions in *chaebols*, with one of them, often the eldest son, succeeding his father when he retires or dies. Fathers-in-law, sons-in-law, brothers, uncles and nephews are also involved in managing *chaebols*. The four largest *chaebol* groups clearly illustrate the family domination (Chang 1988: 52–53).

The Samsung group, which was founded by Byung Chul Lee, has one of the highest ratios of nonfamily member executives, who account for about 95 percent of the total executives. The founder is the first in Korea to use a competitive recruiting system, but family members still dominate the most important positions in the group. His third son, Kun Hee Lee, succeeded him as chairman after his death. Byung Chul Lee's second son and two sons-in-law also hold top positions in the Samsung group.

The founder of the Hyundai group is Ju Yung Chung, who has seven sons. While an extremely bureaucratic management system is established in the group, five of Ju Yung Chung's sons manage ten members of the Hyundai group, either as top executives or in top-executive-track positions. His sixth son, Mong Jun Chung, is expected to succeed his father upon his retirement. Sei Yung Chung, a brother of the founder, leads Hyundai Motors, which exports Hyundai cars to the West.

The Lucky-Goldstar group was founded by In Hoe Goo, who emphas-

a) Type I: Direct ownership structure

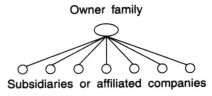

b) Type II: Holding company structure

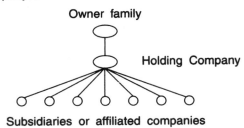

c) Type III: Mutual ownership structure

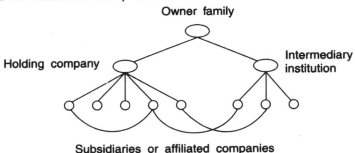

Figure 12.3 Ownership structure of *chaebols*
Source: Hattori, 1989, p. 88. Reprinted with permission of Greenwood Publishing Group, Inc., Westport, CT. © 1989

ized the importance of harmony in managing the group. He had six sons and five brothers. When he died, his eldest son, Ja Kyung Goo, succeeded him as the chairman of the group. Ja Kyung Goo's son, Bon Moo Goo, has already become a top executive and is anticipated to succeed his father. Two brothers of In Hoe Goo and two brothers of Ja Kyung Goo are holding key executive posts.

The Daewoo group, created and still led by Woo Chung Kim, has a somewhat different pattern of ownership and control. The shares directly owned by the founder and his family account for less than 2 percent of the total shares. Apart from Kim's wife, Kim is the only one from the owning family actively involved in management. Known as "the hardest-working man in Korea," Kim demands hard work from his employees, but also delivers high compensation. The Daewoo group was created as late as 1967 and Kim himself is still in his fifties. It is still in question whether his children will participate in management and succeed him as in other *chaebol* groups.

Interestingly, the influence of the owner or his family members seems to be in inverse relation to the share of family ownership (Hattori 1989: 89). As the size of the *chaebol* group grows larger, the share of family ownership seems to grow correspondingly, but management control of the owner or his family members is reduced. In the smaller *chaebol* groups, the owning family usually has a smaller share of ownership but retains stronger managerial control. The extent to which professional managers are hired, both from within and outside the groups, seems to be connected to the size of *chaebols*. The greater the size of the *chaebol*, the more professional managers are likely to be employed in comparison with the owner's family members.

For example, the Kumho group, which is not among the top twenty, belongs to the second type of ownership pattern. The owning family dominates the Kumho holding, which in turn owns the affiliates. The number of the owning family members involved in management in the Kumho group does not necessarily surpass those of Hyundai and Lucky-Goldstar, but the owning family in the Kumho group actually controls more power as a result of its small size. As the size of *chaebols* grows, they have to promote more managers from within the groups and hire more outside professional managers. Unlike *keiretsu* groups, about 40 percent of top *chaebol* executives are recruited from outside the group, while approximately 30 percent are internally promoted (Lee and Yoo 1987b: 71). One reason for the higher percentage of external recruitment is the high rate of expansion of most *chaebol* groups, which has made external recruitment a necessity. As a result, *chaebol* groups are more tolerant of heterogeneity and of employees switching companies compared to their Japanese counterparts.

Not only is family ownership critical to the understanding of management control and professionalization in *chaebols*, but also the form of control the ownership takes is just as important. Korean tradition allows the unequal distribution of family wealth with clear favor for the eldest son. As the Korean concept of family is defined strictly on the basis of blood relationship, family ownership of business provides for certain mechanisms to protect and continue *chaebol* groups. In contrast to the Japanese succession system, *chaebol* successors are generally restricted to those related by blood. Usually, priority of inheritance is given to the oldest son in Korea, since the Confucian tradition stresses hierarchical order within the family. According to one comprehensive study (Shin 1985: 246), the ratio of inheritance to the first son is 65 percent, to family members other than the first son 24.4 percent, and to nonfamily members 9.7 percent.

Interestingly, the mechanisms to restrict arbitrary disposition of ownership shares constitute a crucial factor that promotes professionalization of management structure, including promotion of managers from within the groups and external employment in *chaebol* groups (Hattori 1989: 92–93). Samsung, for example, has a rule for assigning business succession to a single successor, who has the responsibility for continuing and developing the group. Arbitrary disposition of ownership shares is firmly restricted. Therefore, many professional managers have been promoted internally or hired externally to support the central figure. In contrast, Lucky-Goldstar provides for joint ownership among family members and restricts arbitrary disposition of ownership shares. Consequently, family members are forced to become professionalized, while professional managers have been promoted internally and hired externally as business expands.

Family involvement in management also has an influence on the relationship between the owning family, or holding companies, and the affiliated companies. In contrast to the Presidential Clubs of the *keiretsu* groups, many *chaebols* have a powerful chairman's office which is not only in charge of the group's administration and planning but also functions as a watchdog for poor performance (Kang 1989: 75). The chairman's office of the Samsung group, for example, has an implementation committee responsible for correcting the poor performances of member companies. If the corrective action proposed by a troubled member company does not produce the expected result, the committee would swiftly come down on the company like paratroopers and participate in problem solving until new proposals are made. A *keiretsu* would seek to correct the situation by intervening at the company level, not the group level.

Unlike *keiretsus*, *chaebol* groups do not have powerful general trading companies (GTC) nor major in-house banks. The general trading companies of *chaebols* began to develop in 1975 as a result of dialogue between government and business leaders on how best to encourage exports. By the mid-1980s, there were already 9 GTCs in Korea: Hyundai Corp., Daewoo Corp., Samsung Co., Sangyong Corp., Kukje-ICC Corp., Hyosung Corp., Lucky-Goldstar International Corp., Sunkyong Ltd., and Korea Trading International Inc., which was established to export goods of smaller, independent Korean companies. However, these GTCs function more like export companies than like real general trading companies which are capable of performing financial, informational, and administrative services, as the general trading companies of *keiretsu* groups do. Moreover, *chaebols* historically produced for export to foreign buyers. The general trading companies of *chaebols* exported more than 50 percent of the total exports of Korea (Jin 1991: 70).

Financial firms within *chaebol* groups are in most cases controlled by the owning families or by holding companies. Unlike their counterparts in *keiretsu* groups, these financial firms do not own their own stocks nor the stocks of other group companies. The *chaebols'* financial capability to support affiliated companies is very limited. *Chaebols* have been heavily dependent on external finance, especially that of the government, to expand production and diversify business activities. However, many *chaebol* groups have been trying to build up this area. For example, as of the early 1980s, Daewoo owned three financial companies (i.e. Korea Capital Corp. Daewoo Securities and Orient Investment) and indirectly influenced a number of other financial companies through stock ownership and personal relationships with their management. When Korea's first joint venture, commercial bank KorAm Bank, was opened in 1983, Daewoo held the largest share with 9 percent of the 50.1 percent owned by Korean companies. Daewoo has also been actively involved in offshore financing (Aguilar and Cho 1984: 8).

SUMMARY/CONCLUSION

This chapter has compared the structure of ownership and management in large Japanese and Korean business groups, with specific discussions on a number of the major differences. One major difference is that ownership and management in *keiretsus* are separated while the owning families of *chaebols* still actively participate in management. Another major difference is that since the end of the Second World War the management of large Japanese groups has not been centralized, while the Korean groups still have a powerful management center which intervenes regularly when subsidiaries get into trouble. Also, the cross-holding of group members' stocks is a key feature of the ownership structure of *keiretsus* while owning families of *chaebols* still directly control a substantial share of the group's stocks. They are also different from each other in that 90 percent (or more) of Japanese executives are internally promoted while a large number of Korean professional managers (about 30 to 40 percent) are recruited from outside the organization, probably due to the rapid growth of the *chaebols*.

One major reason for these differences is their differing family emphasis. The Japanese family concept is based on the *ie* family which includes adopted sons and the importance of retaining and developing family assets. Therefore, the Japanese owner can adopt a son and bequeath to him the business if he feels his children are not capable of leading the family business. On the other hand, the Korean concept of family is strictly based on blood relationship and Koreans emphasize the importance of keeping their business in the hands of family members. Another reason may be derived from the age differences between these two large business groups. Many large Japanese business groups have much longer histories than their

Korean counterparts; many can be traced back to the late 19th century or the early 20th century, while most large Korean business groups were established during the 1950s. Finally, the dismantlement of the old *zaibatsu* groups and anti-trust measures have made the domination of family ownership in Japan virtually impossible, while this kind of reform has never taken place in Korea.

Since 1980, there has been growing pressure to reform large business groups in Korea, as the Korean government enacted a number of laws to restrict the monopolies of large business groups and encourage small enterprises. Many large Korean business groups are in the process of succession to the second generation owners, and many are experiencing business internationalization. These developments have put increased pressures on them to change. There is a trend among the *chaebols* that more management powers ought to be delegated to professional managers. It can be projected that with modernization and maturity, family domination in business group management will gradually erode. Meanwhile, large Japanese business groups are also in the process of change to cope with the impact of internationalization and heightened competition. Nevertheless, owing to their historical and cultural differences, both groups will remain significantly different from each other in ownership control, organizational structures, and management styles for many years to come.

QUESTIONS FOR DISCUSSION

1 What are the major structural differences between *zaibatsus* and *keiretsus*?
2 How is a *chaebol* structurally similar to a *zaibatsu*?
3 How does *ie* differentiate the Japanese from the Korean companies?
4 Compare the functions of the Presidential Club of a *keiretsu* with that of a chairman's office in a *chaebol*.
5 Describe the three ownership structures of *chaebols*.

FURTHER READING

Aguilar, Francis and Dong Sung Cho (1984) "Daewoo Group," *Harvard Business School Cases 385–014*, Cambridge, Mass.: Harvard Business School.

Bisson, Thomas Arthur (1954) *Zaibatsu Dissolution in Japan*, Berkeley, Calif.: University of California Press.

Chang, Chan Sup (1988) "Chaebol: The South Korean Conglomerates," *Business Horizons* (March–April): 51–57.

Hattori, Tamio (1984) "Ownership and Management in Modern Korean Enterprise," *Asian Economy* (May–June).

—— (1989) "Japanese Zaibatsu and Korean Chaebol," in Kae H. Chung and Hak Chong Lee (eds), *Korean Managerial Dynamics*, New York: Praeger, pp. 79–98.

Imai, Ken-ichi (1992) "Japan's Corporate Networks," in Shumpei Kumon and Henry Rosovsky (eds), *The Political Economy of Japan: Vol 3, Cultural and Social Dynamics*, Stanford, Calif.: Stanford University Press, pp. 198–230.

Jin, Ke-qi (1991) "Introduction to the Chaebols," *Industrial Finance (Taiwan)*, 86: 83–91.

Jung, Ku Hyun (1987) *Growth Strategy and Structure of Korean Firms*, Korea: Chamber of Commerce and Industry.

Kang, T.W. (1989) *Is Korea The Next Japan?*, New York: The Free Press.

Komiya, Ryutaro, Masahiro Okuno and Kotaro Suzumura (eds) (1988), *Industrial Policy of Japan*, San Diego: Harcourt Brace Jovanovich.

Korea Development Institute (1982) *Ownership Structure of Korean Chaebols*, Seoul: KDI.

Lee, S.M. and S.J. Yoo (1987a) "Management Style and Practice of Korean Chaebols," *California Management Review* 95: 95–110.

—— (1987b) "The K-type Management: A Driving Force of Korean Prosperity," *Management International Review* 27(4): 68–77.

Morikawa, Hidemasa (1980) *Managerial Analysis of Zaibatsu*, Tokyo: Oriental Economic News.

—— (1992) *Zaibatsu: The Rise and Fall of Family Enterprise Groups in Japan*, Tokyo: University of Tokyo Press.

Okumura, Hiroshi (1976) *Six Largest Business Groups in Japan*, Tokyo: Diamond Publishing.

Sato, Kazuo (1980) *Industry and Business in Japan*, White Plains, N.Y.: M.E. Sharpe.

Shin, Yookeun (1985) *Structure and Problems in Korean Enterprises*, Seoul: Seoul National University Publishing.

TBT (1989) "Intimate Links With Japan's Corporate Groups," *Tokyo Business Today* (January): 14–19.

Yasuoka, Shigeaki (1985) *Comparative Analysis of Zaibatsu*, Tokyo: Mineru Publishing.

Chapter 13

Japanese management style

INTRODUCTION

Nihonteki Keiei, or Japanese-style management, has become a popular phrase in the West. It refers to what people see as substantially different between Japanese management techniques and those widely practiced in the West. The differences often cited include group consensus in decision-making, career job security, a pay and promotion system heavily reliant upon seniority, and in-house unions enlisting all company employees. Later, focus is expanded to include aspects from quality control (QC) to *kanban.* There is now a fashion in the West to learn from the Japanese management system.

Part of the Western admiration is derived from the higher labor productivity growth rate of Japan. For example, from 1960 to 1980, Japan's labor productivity growth rate in manufacturing averaged a robust 9.3 percent annually while the United States averaged a meager 2.7 percent (Whitehill 1991: 231). Into the 1980s and 1990s, the Japanese have continued increasing productivity to higher rates, even though the U.S. still maintains its leading position in terms of productivity in many industries. Another aspect of Western admiration is the perceived devotion Japanese employees have to their companies and work. In spite of rising living standards, the Japanese workers still put in more hours than their counterparts in the West. In 1986, for example, the Japanese worked 2,192 hours, compared with 1,850 in the U.S. and an average 1,691 in fifteen Western industrialized countries (Whitehill 1991: 188). Days lost to industrial disputes are significantly fewer than in most other industrial nations. Absentee rates in Japan are lower than in other major countries. Suggestion systems for productivity improvements and quality control circles are found in most Japanese companies, with high rates of participation.

These are all true facts that help explain why the Japanese have successfully turned a war-wracked economy into the second most powerful economy in the world within three decades. Nevertheless, the Japanese management system is not flawless. In contrast to Western infatuation, it is the Japanese who have consistently sought to de-mystify and criticize their system. Akio Morita, Sony's Chairman, systematically criticized Japanese management in his "Nihon-teki keiei Shunju" (the Japanese Management in Trouble) (*Bungei Shunju*: February 1992), touching off a whole series of discussions in Japan (Hazama 1993: 462). Moreover, the Japanese management system is a product of Japanese society and any transplantation of this system must be handled with much discretion. Finally, some of the core elements of the Japanese management system, such as lifetime employment and seniority promotion, have been under growing pressure to change. Knowing only the positive sides of Japanese management, while slighting the negative ones, would leave American managers with an inaccurate picture of the system. This chapter is intended to present a balanced view.

MANAGERIAL AUTONOMY IN JAPANESE COMPANIES

Interestingly, one major advantage that Japanese executives have over their American counterparts in managing their companies lies in their relationship with shareholders. The Japanese corporate system is competitive because its managers can devote themselves to compete with other companies both at home and abroad, without having to worry too much about satisfying the parasitic interests of shareholders. Management also does not have to serve the passive interests of workers who have much less stake in the viability of the company. In addition, Japanese companies can greatly influence ownership of the company, which is in contrast to the West where there is little say about who the shareholders will be. In Matsumoto's words, "Managerial autonomy is necessary. . . . The superiority of the Japanese corporate system is that it keeps managerial autonomy, once the core of capitalism, intact" (Matsumoto 1991: 193–200).

In the West, the separation of ownership from company management necessitates a board of directors that represents the interests of the shareholder-owners. In American companies, directors are usually named to the board from outside the company; the board is supposed to monitor company affairs and intervene in cases of mismanagement. American shareholders expect to receive a substantial share of profits in the form of dividend payments. Most American companies regard a dividend payout rate of about 50 percent of earnings as proper. The rate and level of dividends paid symbolize how successful company operations are and how well the company is managed. Share price is closely related to the rate and level of dividends paid.

To provide management with more incentives to work in the interests of the shareholders, measures that link the interests of executives with those of the shareholders, such as stock options and other profit-related bonus plans rewarding senior executives for increased earnings, have been widely adopted. Since American stock markets are very sensitive to trends in earnings per share, the executives have been driven to ensure steady improvement in earnings. Dramatic fluctuation in earnings trends tends to lower share price, which in turn lowers the value of stock options and the relevant management bonus programs. Therefore, the American corporate system is best represented through a coalition of shareholders and senior executives which aims to optimize current company earnings. As shareholders depend heavily on the work of top management, they tend to reward those who succeed in promoting earnings. Some top American executives can earn as much as three to five million dollars per year.

According to Abegglen and Stalk (1985: 184–188), the situation in Japanese companies is quite different. Common stock shareholders of a Japanese company are similar to preferred shareholders in an American company. Having taken the capital to invest in the company, the Japanese shareholders also expect a decent return on their investment in the form of dividends. However, the dividends are paid not as a percent of earnings but as a percent of the par value of shares of the company. Consequently, dividend yields as a percentage of market value of Japanese shares are relatively low, averaging merely 1 to 2 percent. It is extremely important that the company, even though it has to borrow money, meets the investors' expectations of dividends in order to be able to continue raising equity funding.

As long as the Japanese shareholders are satisfied with a return on their investment they have very limited power in meddling in the company's affairs. The majority of the board of directors in a Japanese company is made up of inside board members, i.e. the members are selected from the senior executives of the company. As career employees, they become board members as they move up in the executive hierarchy and closely identify themselves with the company itself. Unlike their American counterparts, Japanese executives do not hold a substantial amount of shares nor do they enjoy stock option programs. In cases where the companies are either members of large business groups or heavily indebted to commercial banks, outside directors may be appointed to represent the solidarity of the group or protect the interests of the bank. Nevertheless, outside directors can neither function as real outsiders to the company nor can they constitute a majority.

The different approach toward dividend payment gives management another advantage. Since dividends are paid as a percent of the par value of shares, a highly profitable company can easily meet its dividend requirements with a small percentage of its total earnings. Therefore, the bulk of its earnings can be utilized for reinvestment in the company. In contrast, a less profitable company has to pay out a large share of its earnings in dividends if it wants to meet the dividend requirement. Such an approach to dividends payment tends to further strengthen successful companies while putting already unprofitable ones in an unfavorable position. The successful Japanese companies can expand rapidly.

About three-quarters of all shares in Japan are owned by legal entities that are business organizations. Contrary to the common practice in which the shareholder selects a company whose shares he wants to acquire, a Japanese company tends to select shareholders that it wants to acquire its shares. Usually, shares are mutually held among companies and financial institutions that have business relationships (Matsumoto 1991: 5–6). The top shareholders of Toyota Motors Corporation, for instance, include Mitsui Bank, the Tokai Bank and the Sanwa Bank, all of whom hold 4.8 percent, and Toyota Automatic Loom Works, Ltd., which hold 24.8 percent. On the other hand, Toyota holds 4.2 percent in Mitsui Bank, 5.2 percent in the Takai Bank, 2.2 percent in the Sanwa Bank and 24.8 percent in Toyota Automatic Loom Works, Ltd.

As a common practice, most institutional shareholders submit blank proxies to general shareholders' meetings and do not send representatives to board meetings to monitor the company's operations. Companies that hold each other's shares tend to mutually exchange blank proxies. If they interfere in the operation of the other company, they would incur similar treatment. The influence based on shareholding is balanced out. Therefore, unless the two companies which cross-own each other's shares intend to end their relationship, they show little interest in the management of the other company. This practice "is a de facto total separation of management from the wishes of the owners" (Matsumoto 1991: 6). The management does not have to worry about the interference of the shareholders, and thereby enjoys a high degree of autonomy.

In short, under such a pattern of shareholder and senior management relationship, Japanese executives are not subject to the pressures that their American counterparts have for steady improvement in earnings per share. Nor do they have to be concerned with the price of their company's shares. The well-cited preoccupation of American executives with short-term earnings has resulted from the fact that their job security and personal income depend on steady earnings improvements. Therefore, Japanese executives are able to plan well into the future for the company and worry less about any unfavorable short-term consequences. This long-term view is as much related to the cultural legacy of Japanese executives as it is to the relationship they enjoy with shareholders.

Managerial autonomy not only lies in the relationship between management and shareholders, but also in the relationship between management and employees. The Japanese system of employment has not only provided employees with more job security, but also ties them to the company for which they work. As will be shown later in the chapter, the lifetime employment system, combined with enterprise unionism and seniority wages, has contributed to less mobility among Japanese employees and a relatively higher labor commitment to their companies. The management can afford to make long-term plans for the employees enjoying a lifetime employment system. The major advantage of this system is a shift of "the burden of corporate risk to the side of labor" by restricting the ability of workers to move from one company to another (Matsumoto 1991: 12–26). Although the burden to keep employees working in an economic downturn can be heavy and costly, the management in a Japanese company has been largely freed from the restraints of the labor market, where the workers can strike or leave if their compensation is not satisfactory.

LEADERSHIP AND DECISION MAKING

As with Japanese society, Japanese corporations are rigidly organized and extremely hierarchical (see Figure 13.1). At the top of the organization is the *kaicho* (chairman), who is followed by the *shacho* (president). Within the organization, each department constitutes an independent power center. For this reason, the *bucho* (department manager) often commands the same level of respect as the president of a small company. In most companies, however, the groundwork is accomplished at the level of the section manager, *kacho*. Usually, the highest ranking executives in Japanese corporations are seldom the drivers of new projects. The main functions of the senior executives include theme establishment, strategy development, loyalty promotion within the corporation and high-level external relations management (Morgan and Morgan 1991: 54).

Decision-making is an important issue in Japanese-style management studies. The *ringi* system of decision-making was first interpreted as one of the most important features of Japanese management by a group of Japanese scholars during their visit to the U.S. in the late 1950s (Fukuda, 1988: 65). Two of the methods of the *ringi* system have been extensively discussed: *nemawashi* and *ringi seido*. There are certainly cultural roots for consensus decision-making, as the Japanese believe that *wa* or harmony, which constitutes the essence of Japanese life, can be best maintained in this way. Decisions thus reached can be carried out most efficiently. One tendency is to describe all Western companies' decision-making as an individual process while all decision-making in Japanese companies is a group process. Japan certainly has its own share of one-man companies, in which decisions are quickly made by one or two top leaders. Another tendency is to idealize the consensus process as truly democratic and optimal, though much evidence points to the opposite conclusion.

Nemawashi is an important Japanese business concept that literally refers to dealing with the roots of trees. In Japanese gardening, the transplanting of a tree requires much skill and meticulous effort. Business decision-making involves a similar process, with careful attention being given to the preliminary stages of the process. *Nemawashi* refers to the practice of

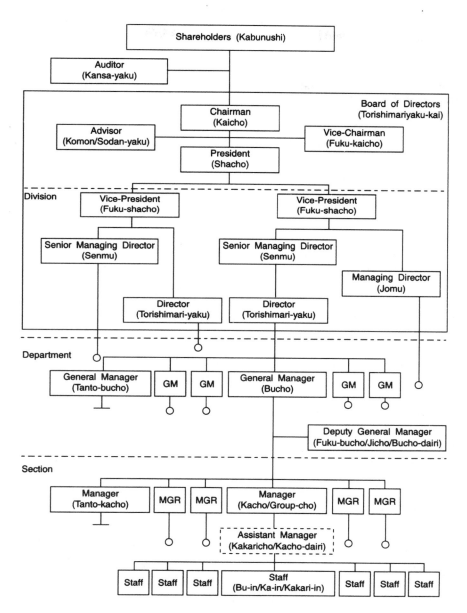

Figure 13.1 Japanese company structure
Source: Compiled with the assistance of Masatoshi Sato.

preliminary and informal sounding out of employees' ideas about a proposed course of action or project. *Nemawashi* also implies the activities that take place below ground-level and describes the nature of the sounding out, in which contacted persons remain anonymous and feel free to talk about their ideas.

Ringi seido, as opposed to *nemawashi*, is a commonly used formal procedure of management by group consensus (see Figure 13.2). A *ringisho* is a proposal that originates in one section, and is forwarded to all relevant sections on the same level, the section heads, the managers, the directors, and eventually the president of the company. Upon receiving the *ringisho*, each will make comments on a sheet attached to the back of the proposal. The decision will be made by top management based on the comments from all people involved in the process. The purpose of this roundabout way of making decisions is to eliminate dissension, as many are given a chance to change a decision before it is actually made.

There are many advantages to the Japanese form of decision-making. It has some elements of democracy in the sense that employees at lower levels

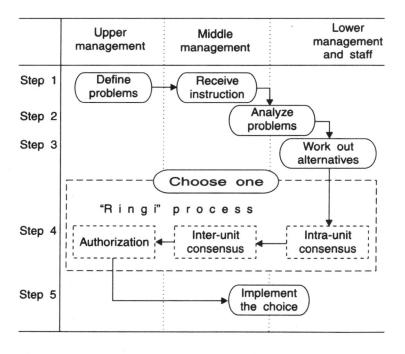

Figure 13.2 Ringi system of decision-making
Source: Fukuda, 1988, p. 64.

can initiate proposals or work out plans, which will be transferred upward to higher levels of management. Since many people are involved in the process and various meetings are held, there is a greater participation of decision-making in the company. Any decision adopted on the basis of such extensive discussions will more likely meet with general acceptance. Also, the inclusion of so many different individuals in the decision-making process tends to reduce the danger of a decision being manipulated by certain individuals, and because the decision is generally accepted, the implementation will be easier and more efficient.

There are, however, a number of flaws associated with this process. Often, too many people and sections get involved, even though a *ringisho* may only concern one section. Too many meetings are held, with many unnecessary questions and suggestions raised. To make things worse, many meetings are very long, as participants tend to follow all the proper motions and are not forthright with ideas that may upset their colleagues. According to a report of the Japan Management Association, managers spend around 40 percent of their time in conferences and meetings. These may significantly delay business decisions, which often require a swift response. By the time a decision is reached, the deal may have already been clinched by competitors.

Moreover, the final decision is often strongly influenced by the relationships between the participants. It is also simplistic in that participants believe that consensus decision-making means outright delegation to middle and lower level managers. It is true that *ringi* discussions do include most of the people who will be affected by the new decision, but the original idea is often initiated by top executives in the form of *nemawashi*. Many Japanese top executives can also be very autocratic and the process, therefore, may be viewed as "a confirmation-authorization process." The *ringi* process may often end up being nothing more than the record of a decision already made or an instrument of distributing responsibility for decisions throughout the entire company.

HUMAN RESOURCES MANAGEMENT

Many of the discussions on Japanese management have been devoted to its human resources management, which has been widely praised in the West as a major contribution to organizational integration and Japanese competitiveness. A great many scholars attribute this perceived Japanese advantage to their cultural influence. Pascale and Athos (1981: 25), for example, have argued that the Japanese "were generally more sophisticated than the West in utilizing social and spiritual forces for the organization's benefit, and in accepting the responsibilities to their employees that went with such broad influence." Without ignoring or slighting this well-quoted Japanese advantage, one should also pay attention to some of its inherent problems and the growing pressure on it for change.

Lifetime employment (*shushinkoyo*)

The lifetime employment system consists of several key components. First, most employees in this system are directly recruited from school rather than from an open job market. Second, they are expected to stay with the company for a lifelong period and can in turn expect lifelong job security. Third, the decision of recruitment is more focused on the general characteristics and abilities of potential employees than on a particular technical skill. The system, however, does not include part-time workers, women, and retirees. Quite a number of employees working in many large companies are on a part-time or seasonal basis. Many of them work up to 38 or 39 hours a week. They are not protected until they become regular employees. Many women stop working at marriage or on the birth of their first child, though some of them choose to reenter the labor force later. The many retirees who are virtually forced to leave between the ages of 55 and 60 find that they need to continue working (Woronoff 1992: 90). Millions of small companies that have limited resources often find it impossible to practice lifetime employment, even though they may feel the necessity to or are pressured to do so.

The concept of lifetime employment has far-reaching consequences for Japanese management. When recruiting a new employee, the company has to be extremely cautious because a mistake in recruitment can be very expensive and difficult to correct. Therefore, a complicated process is involved, ranging from academic examinations of the candidate, investigations of the family background, and an individual history, to detailed personal interviews. On the other hand, the potential employee also has to exercise a fair amount of care in determining which company he should apply to for employment. He is not simply looking for a job but rather a lifelong commitment. Usually, a graduate looks forward to a post in a company that has good long-term prospects.

In a sense, the process of recruitment is really a process of exchanging commitment. The candidate takes a significant risk in betting his future on a particular company. If a Japanese leaves mid-career or is fired from a large company, he will have a much harder time than his American counterpart in being hired by another large company. By recruiting someone, the company assumes the obligation of a family to take care of him for his entire career. This means that the company must be prepared to make sacrifices for its employees. Even when the company is experiencing a business downturn, it is still obliged to carry the burden of protecting the job security of its employees. The company's commitment to its employees in terms of job security is reciprocated by a higher degree of commitment from its employees as compared with that of American employees, despite the extraordinary sacrifice that must be made in their personal lives and by their families.

With this exchange of commitments, the Japanese company becomes an extension of an employee's own family. Nothing in Japanese society is more feared than to be excluded from the group. As the employee grows with the company, he becomes increasingly entrenched within the corporate family. The result is an employee being a part of the company as much as the company being a part of the employee. A substantive socialization process begins with the entry into a Japanese company. During the first few years, a new employee is constantly shifted between departments to learn job skills as well as the nature of the company's activities, its history, and its culture. He may live in a company dormitory, thus having extensive social exchanges with his colleagues and further deepening his understanding of the company. In this way, the Japanese company becomes a real family-type social organization.

Out of these various social exchanges, the Japanese *sempai-kohai* mentor system is often cited as something outstanding that not only provides new employees with on-the-job training and role models, but establishes a personal bond between superiors and subordinates (Clark 1979: 126). Those below know that those above them will protect them if something goes wrong, and are more willing to be fully devoted to the work. The relationship is not restricted to business, as the partners are expected to discuss their personal lives with each other as well. Therefore, the *sempai-kohai* relationship is characterized by tying the two together through both successes and failures. A *sempai-kohai* relationship with those who have good prospects to become top executives in the company will often bode well for the junior member.

Nevertheless, lifetime employment has some clear drawbacks and is under increasing pressure to change. In comparison with American companies, the Japanese companies cannot quickly adjust to an economic downturn. The system was instituted when Japan was in the midst of rapid economic growth and companies were competing for new employees for their expanding businesses. The pressure to retrench was first felt by declining industries. Yet under the pressures of slower economic growth in the 1990s, this problem is no longer limited to those in declining sectors. The trouble is that only after all possible methods are exhausted, and with full agreement of the union and workforce, can the company proceed with layoffs. In past slumps, many large firms avoided layoffs by paying smaller bonuses or getting rid of part-timers, but in the economic slump of the early 1990s, "unemployment within the company" has become too heavy a burden for many to carry much longer (*Asiaweek*, 31 March 1991: 41). The problem of carrying an immobile labor force is evident in many large

Japanese companies, where the redundant workforce is maintained while new recruitment is continued to cope with new competition.

As far as motivation is concerned, the Japanese lifetime employment system is a tradeoff of opportunity for security. Owing to cultural and historical factors, most Japanese prefer security. Until a fairly recent period, Japan was a relatively poor country. Deep-rooted feelings of insecurity exist among the Japanese due to their country's extreme lack of natural resources, very limited arable land, and exposure to constant environmental disasters such as earthquakes, volcanic eruptions, and tidal waves. In more recent history an extended period of war, the humiliation of total defeat, and the despairing situation of the late 1940s contributes to a strong preference for security over risk. Nevertheless, with the significant changes in these conditions, the security–risk tradeoff has also gradually changed, with young people more willing to take career chances that their parents would not have taken. The opportunity to move to better jobs may seem to be a reasonable exchange for the security of their current job. Job hopping is on the rise, especially among managers who have worked overseas. According to a *Wall Street Journal* report (18 November 1991: B1), about one in 10 Japanese managers jumped ship following a U.S. assignment, compared with one in 100 a decade earlier.

Seniority promotion (*nenko joretsu*)

Closely related to the system of lifetime employment is the importance of length of service in the Japanese company in determining promotion. If the Japanese company is committed to the lifetime employment of its employees, they are naturally entitled to promotion during their long period of service. The term used in relation to work compensation is *nenko* or the merit in the number of years an employee has provided his services. Since most employees are recruited directly from school, age and length of service parallel each other, and seniority becomes an appropriate standard for reward. The seniority promotion was another major motivation for employees to stay long in one company. Although the system never insured everyone a title, many did have a good chance to become a section head (*kacho*) or department head (*bucho*).

The seniority promotion system within the framework of lifetime employment has benefitted the fast-growing Japanese companies, which need to hire large numbers of new employees. As most of them are new recruits from school, a high level of hiring results in a lower average age of the workforce. As the average age of the company decreases, so does its average pay level. Thus, the fast growth of the company is further accelerated by pay advantage. In contrast, the slower growing company, which hires no, or only a few, new employees, suffers from a continual increase in the average age of its workforce. Its already unfavorable growth rate is worsened by rising pay levels.

Nevertheless, the seniority promotion system has come under increasing pressure from the mid-1980s onwards. With slower economic growth, the competitive advantages of the system have declined. Moreover, longer life expectancy has put increasing pressure to extend the retirement age from fifty-five to sixty. Automatic pay increases with each additional year of service have become increasingly burdensome as seniority grows. As fewer junior employees are entering at the bottom, there is less need for higher positions. According to the survey "Japan's Labor Market in the Year 2000," conducted by the Economic Planning Agency, only one out of every four male college graduates will have the chance to become *kacho* or *bucho* by the end of the century (Woronoff 1992: 89).

Like the lifetime employment system, this is very likely to undergo major changes in the near future. Its attractiveness to employees is wearing thin. The younger generation is becoming increasingly impatient with the seniority promotion system. As the possibilities of alternative employment have grown, job-hopping is becoming more acceptable. In various companies a variety of experiments, which seek to either even off the wage curve at the mid-forties or encourage early retirement with increasingly large bonuses for those who retire voluntarily, are already under way. By discarding those best handled by the seniority system, the companies have admitted that the system is no longer sustainable. This will also put greater strain on the lifetime employment system and weaken the emotional ties between employees and their companies.

The enterprise trade unions (*kigyo-betsu kumiai*)

The modern labor movement in Japan was largely a postwar phenomenon, after the Labor Union Law was enacted by the Occupation. The basic organizations in Japan's labor movement are the enterprise trade unions, which are now widely cited as a competitive advantage of the Japanese management system and comprise all employees of the company with no differentiation as to occupation and job status. Union members include all white-collar and blue-collar workers. In some companies, assistant section leaders (*kakaricho*) may participate in the union. As employees are promoted to management positions, they will have to quit the enterprise unions.

A leading position in a Japanese enterprise union often leads to a promising future within management. According to an investigation by one management association, almost one in six senior executives of major Japanese companies have been leaders of relevant enterprise unions (Whitehill 1991: 245–246). The enterprise union and the company have a unique interdependent relationship: the union does not exist as an entity separate from the company, while the company regards union experience as valuable training for efficient management rather than merely treating it as an adversary. The union automatically includes all regular company members; part-timers, temporary and subcontract workers are typically excluded. Company office space and facilities are often provided for the union. The future of the company and its union seems identical.

The competitive advantage of linking the fate of company and union effectively places limits on the extent to which the union is willing to risk hurting the overall economic conditions of the company. While the union is viewed as a protection against potential abuses of management, the members of the union are also keenly aware of the fact that damage to the company may also involve damage to their own interests. Therefore labor unrest often stops short of carrying out work stoppages that may damage the company. Vocal demonstrations are held during lunch breaks or after working hours. Labor unrest that does result in work stoppage is often symbolic of a total breakdown in trust between the management and the union.

In spite of the establishment of the National Federation of Private Sector Unions in the late 1980s to coordinate union activities, the influence of the trade union movement in Japan, as elsewhere, seems to be declining. The steam of the *Shunto*, or Labor Spring Offensive, seems to have diminished substantially in recent years. The *Shunto* is characterized by annual labor demonstrations for higher wages and shorter hours that take place in March and April. Top union federations and the major employers' associations negotiate a guideline for a certain percentage raise. All the companies are supposed to adhere as closely as possible to the guideline figure in deciding their "base-up" for the year. As in the United States, the unionization rates in Japan are declining. Between 1977 and 1987, the unionization rate in Japan decreased from 33.2 to 27.6 percent; this means that around two-thirds of Japanese workers, mainly in small and medium-sized companies, are not organized (Ohta 1993: 167). As more Japanese companies move into service sectors, this declining trend may continue to erode union influence.

The compensation system

The employees of the Japanese company share more equally in the cash pay available from the company than is the case in Western countries. Japanese executive pay levels are usually set within tolerable ranges in comparison with other levels of compensation in the company. According to *Fortune* (19 March 1984), the annual pay for Japanese top executives ranges from $50,000 to $250,000, depending on the size of the company. In comparison, at least 85 American CEOs made more than $1 million in the same period. The emphasis on egalitarianism and togetherness in Japanese ideology not only contributes to the relatively low degree of income distribution inequality in Japanese businesses but also in the Japanese society as a whole. This relative equity in distribution of benefits is often cited as a major factor enhancing degrees of integration and the sense of common destiny.

Another outstanding component of the Japanese compensation system that has often been cited as a competitive advantage of the Japanese management system is bonus payments. Generally, about one-third of the total annual compensation is paid in the form of a semiannual bonus during the traditional gift-giving seasons at mid-year and year-end (Whitehill 1991: 179). Larger companies tend to pay more generous bonuses that are paid to all employees.

The bonus has many advantages for the Japanese company. It is really a deferred payment that provides a good chunk of working capital for the company until the bonus is paid. Since retirement benefits are calculated on base pay, increasing bonus pay based on the performance of the company will not necessarily increase the burden of retirement benefits. The bonus is a flexible payment system, which is contingent on the performance of the company; it can be easily cut down during economic downturns without having to lay off employees and it can make up for deficiencies inherent in the seniority system by recognizing a junior employee's ability through boosting his bonus. For the employees, the bonus system is regarded as a kind of planned savings for them and provides extra money for gift-giving on New Year's Day and for vacation.

Still another competitive component of the Japanese compensation system serves to illustrate the nature of labor relations within the Japanese company. This is best reflected in wage-cut negotiations between the management and the union (Abegglen and Stalk 1985: 197). When a Japanese company falls into deep crisis, it can feel free to discharge its part-time and temporary employees because there are no rules against cutting down that part of labor cost. This will be followed by reducing bonus payments. If these measures are still not sufficient, wage reductions will have to be negotiated. As a general procedure, management will announce across-the-board cuts in executive compensation before approaching the union to begin negotiations on wage reductions for employees.

These components, together with other forms of compensation such as family allowances, housing assistance and separation pay, contribute to the sense of common destiny among all the employees whose personal well-being will share the success or failure of the company. Therefore, the prevalent Japanese company compensation system helps make the Japanese company a much more egalitarian and integrated organization than most of its Western counterparts. This is a tremendous competitive advantage, which, combined with the other advantages discussed earlier, has significantly promoted the productivity of Japanese companies. In comparison with the first two practices, this one seems to have more vitality and is under fewer challenges.

SUMMARY/CONCLUSION

This chapter has discussed several major aspects of the Japanese management system, including managerial autonomy in Japanese companies, leadership and decision-making styles such as the *ringi* system, human resources management, lifetime employment, seniority promotion, enterprise trade unions, and compensation systems. Although all these issues are widely discussed by many authors in the United States and Japan, serious confusion still prevails. Diametrically different opinions exist about how Western businesses should cope with or learn from Japanese-style management. Myths have been created that hinder a clear-minded and objective assessment of the Japanese management system.

The Japanese management system is the result of ever-evolving tradition, culture, and social conditions, as well as political and economic systems. From the early 1970s, Japanese management has attracted increasing interest among both management scholars and business executives in the West. There are already over a hundred books that specifically describe and analyze Japanese-style management, with more still to come. From earlier discussion, it is beyond doubt that the Japanese management system has provided some comparative advantages, notably management's autonomy vis-à-vis shareholders and employees. Others, such as consensus decision-making, lifetime employment, enterprise trade unionism and a fairly unique compensation system have contributed in varying degrees to corporate integration. Nevertheless, as has already been shown, it also has many flaws and will continue changing and adapting itself to the ever-changing operational environment.

Among the few elements of the Japanese management system discussed in this chapter, some of those related to personnel management are under the highest pressure to change. It is generally agreed that the seniority promotion system will be slowly supplemented by the merit and ability system, while more and more employees will voluntarily give up their lifetime employment benefits by jumping ship in mid-career. Specialized skills may receive more attention than the traditional emphasis on general ability. Even the long-cherished consensus decision-making process has been questioned by many who complain that the time-consuming process has cost Japanese companies many business opportunities. There are also growing complaints about the stressful aspects of Japanese human resources management, which is often blamed for *karoshi* (sudden death caused by overwork). Nevertheless, it is highly unlikely that the Japanese management system will ever become another version of the American management system and lose those component elements that have made Japanese companies such fierce competitors all around the world.

QUESTIONS FOR DISCUSSION

1 What is the unique relationship between stockholders and professional managers in Japanese companies that gives the managers a competitive advantage?
2 What is so important about *bucho dairi* in the hierarchy of Japanese companies?
3 Describe the dynamics of *nemawashi* and *ringi seido*.
4 What are the advantages and disadvantages of lifetime employment and seniority based promotions?
5 What is so unique about the Japanese union system?

FURTHER READING

Abegglen, James and George Stalk Jr. (1985) *Kaisha, the Japanese Corporation*, New York: Basic Books.

Ballon, Robert J. (1988) *The Financial Behavior of Japanese Corporations*, Tokyo: Kodansha International.

Clark, Rodney (1979) *The Japanese Company*, New Haven: Yale University Press.

Durlabhji, Subhash and Norton E. Marks (eds) (1993) *Japanese Business: Cultural Perspective*, Albany, N.Y.: Suny Press.

Fortune (1984) (19 March): 15–19.

Fukuda, K. John (1988) *Japanese-style Management Transferred, The Experience of East Asia*, New York: Routledge.

Hayashi, Shuji (1989) *Culture and Management in Japan*, Tokyo: Tokyo University Press.

Hazama, Hiroshi (1993) "Trends in International Business Thought and Literature: The Recent Literature of 'Japanese-style' Management," *The International Executive* (September–October) 35(5): 461–465.

Koike, Kazuo (1988) *Understanding Industrial Relations in Modern Japan*, New York: St Martin's Press.

Matsumoto, Koji (1991) *The Rise of the Japanese Corporate System* (trans. by Thomas I. Elliott), New York and London: Kegan Paul International.

Misawa, Mitsuru (1987) "New Japanese-style Management in a Changing Era," *Columbia Journal of World Business* (Winter): 9–17.

Modic, Stanley J. (1987) "Myths about Japanese Management," *Industry Week* (5 October) 235(1): 49–53.

Morgan, James C. and J. Jeffrey Morgan (1991) *Cracking the Japanese Market: Strategies for Success in the New Global Market*, New York: The Free Press.

Odaka, Junio (1986) *Japanese Management – A Forward-Looking Analysis*, Tokyo: Asian Productivity Organization.

Ohta, Toshiaki (1993) "Works Rules in Japan," in Subhash Durlabhji and Norton E. Marks (eds), *Japanese Business: Cultural Perspective*, Albany, N.Y.: Suny Press, pp. 153–168.

Pascale, Richard and Anthony Athos (1981) *The Art of Japanese Management*, New York: Warner Books.

Sato, Kazuo (1984) *The Anatomy of Japanese Business*, Armonk, N.Y.: M.E. Sharpe.

Whitehill, Arthur M. (1991) *Japanese Management: Tradition and Transition*, New York: Routledge.

Woronoff, Jon (1992) *The Japanese Management Mystique*, Chicago: Probus Publishing Co.

Chapter 14

Developing competitive advantages of Japanese companies

INTRODUCTION

Since the late 1950s, Japanese manufacturers have become some of the fiercest competitors in the world. Initially, Japanese companies made textile goods and cheap mass-assembly products, then they made cars, electronic goods, and other high-quality and high-tech products that swamped Western markets. Japanese companies have consistently underpriced their Western competitors by 20 to 30 percent for equivalent products. The result has been the collapse and closing of many Western industries, such as the British motorcycle industry, which used to be the best in the world. Western businesses, panting under these throat-cutting pricing strategies, have universally directed various charges against the Japanese companies, such as "kamikaze bidding," and "predatory tactics." To some extent, these charges seem to be supported by Japanese strategies, as evidenced by a 1985 Hitachi sales presentation that stressed the "win at any cost" spirit by saying "Quote 10 percent below competition; if they requote, bid 10 percent under again; the bidding stops when Hitachi wins" (Fallows 1993: 100).

Nevertheless, behind these emotional charges is also a painful recognition that many Japanese factories have tended to be more competitive than their Western counterparts. Japanese superiority has also been lavishly attributed to the Japanese management style, which includes managerial autonomy, a lifetime employment system, seniority promotion, consensus decision-making, enterprise unionism, a more egalitarian compensation system, etc. As noted in Chapter 13, there are certainly some elements of truth in these analyses of Japanese competitive advantages, but there is also a negative side to some aspects of the Japanese management style. Moreover, many authors have ignored other relevant sources of the Japanese competitive advantage. The lack of a comprehensive understanding has hampered an effective response in the West. This chapter is intended to identify some additional sources of competitive advantage of successful Japanese companies.

STRATEGIC PLANNING AND THE JAPANESE COMPETITIVE ADVANTAGES

One often-quoted Japanese advantage is their process of strategic planning. Many books and papers have been published that discuss how Japanese strategic planning has helped their companies win in worldwide competition. On the basis of observing many cases of effective planning processes in successful companies in Japan, Toyohiro Kono (1984: 256–258) has arrived at a model which is divided into five basic phases:

1 Establishing premises: the corporate goals and philosophy are constructed and revised by taking into consideration the opinions of stakeholders who control the key resources. Then information is widely collected on the general business environment, the trends of industry and the situations of competitors. Past performance is evaluated so as to reveal the problems, thus providing information that is useful for forecasting future problems. Comparisons with the competitors are made to identify the strengths and weaknesses of the company. The future competitive positions of the company are projected. With a detailed analysis of various forecasts, opportunities and threats are clearly identified.

2 Clarifying issues: levels of aspiration, such as the growth rate, are determined on the basis of the clarification of the above premises. Then the future performance in the key results area under present policy is forecast. A comparison between the forecast future performance and the aspiration level is made to discover if any significant gaps exist. Then new strategies are sought to close these gaps.

3 Long-range strategy: new product-market strategies are pursued for closing the gaps between forecast and aspiration. This is an extremely important process, in which issues like the development of new business, multinational management, vertical integration, joint ventures, etc. are studied. Cost reduction of existing products and business expansion is researched. If either of the above two strategies is carried out, the future performance is forecasted. Investigations will be conducted to see if the future gap can be closed. If the future gap is not closed, the above process will have to be repeated and new research will be conducted. The long-range strategy mainly consists of three parts: the long-range goals, the long-range strategy projects that support the goals, and the long-range policies in key areas.

4 Medium-range planning: after the long-range strategy is decided, medium-range goals and guidelines are established and medium-range plans are made. The medium-range plans also consist of three parts: first, medium-range project planning, which includes such items as schedules and resources allocation; second, planning by product groups, which includes the change of product mix and the competition strategy for each product group (usually conducted by the relevant product division); and

third, corporate functional planning, which is worked out by the corporate functional department and composed of facilities plans, personnel plans and profit plans.
5   Short-range planning: following the medium-range planning is short-range planning as well as implementation and control.

According to Kono, this model (see Figure 14.1) represents a successful planning process in many Japanese companies. The process has a number of characteristics: the gap is first clearly identified, and then relevant measures to close the gaps are adopted. The process is focused on achieving satisfactory performance rather than on maximizing the performance. A long-range strategy receives the first priority, the guidelines for medium-range plans come next and the short-range plans are last. The process starts from general decisions and moves down to detailed decisions.

The development of Sony's Hit Bit personal computer shows that good long-term strategic planning can significantly improve a company's competitive position (Katzenstein 1991: 50). When Sony entered the extremely competitive PC market in the mid-1980s, it lagged way behind the leading market manufacturers. The product was viewed by many in the field as a perfect candidate for money loss. Nevertheless, Sony's strategic planning identified the importance of the Hit Bit's digital technology in developing the products of the 1990s. Therefore, a long-range strategy was developed and the relevant medium-range and short-range plans were made toward realizing the long-term goals of the company. The short-term losses were made up by the development of its long-term market winner. The result is that Sony has become a leader in the field.

As mentioned in Chapter 13, the managerial autonomy in most Japanese companies gives the management a free hand to think long term and enables them to sacrifice short-term profits for long-term development. If Japanese shareholders had the same kind of power as their American counterparts in interfering in the company's management, this model would have been significantly modified. Moreover, detailed strategic planning is not a guarantee for business success, nor can it totally avoid strategic mistakes. The time-based strategic surge that will be discussed later in the chapter will clearly demonstrate this point.

DEVELOPING COMPETITIVE ADVANTAGES IN THE WORLD MARKET

Manufactured goods have been and still are the leading export of the Japanese. The successful Japanese manufacturers have dexterously developed and exploited their comparative advantages in carving out a position in the world market. From the 1950s to the first half of the 1970s, their competitive edge was mainly in low-cost manufacturing. Major export

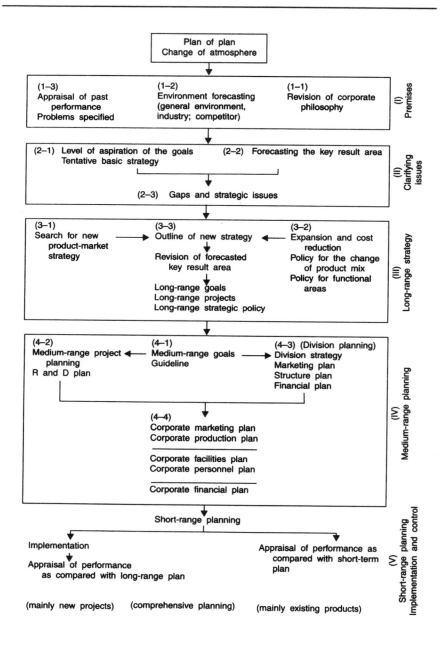

Figure 14.1 Long-range planning process model
Source: Toyohiro Kono, 1984, p. 257. Reprinted by permission of M.E. Sharpe Inc.,
Armonk, NY 10504

businesses of textiles, steel and shipbuilding were developed on the basis of this advantage. With the continued increase of wages, the Japanese have had to develop a variety of comparative advantages, ranging from the diversity of their production line to the development of high-technology products. The Japanese companies that are the most successful overseas have often experienced the toughest competition at home, have been the survivors of cut-throat domestic competition, and have strong international competitiveness.

Many Japanese companies that began exporting to Western markets in the 1960s and 1970s were faced with powerful Western competitors, who had broader product lines and were solidly established in their home markets. Head-on competition was both difficult and costly. The only feasible alternatives were either to locate market niches for which there were no Western products or to concentrate all their resources on the products that had the greatest market demand and provided the easiest access to customers (Abegglen and Stalk 1985: 79–80). By adopting either of these two alternatives, Japanese companies could achieve competitive costs relative to those of their Western competitors, resulting in the ability to undercut the prices of their Western competitors while maintaining very high quality.

Therefore, many Japanese companies began to enter the world market with products having either tremendous market demand or easy access, such as textiles or simple engineered products like machine tools and bearings. The Japanese companies provided low-cost, high-quality products, not only by taking advantage of relatively cheap labor but also by focusing on narrow lines of products. With a focused strategy, a smaller manufacturer producing a narrow line of products can achieve much lower costs than a larger manufacturer producing a wide line of products. The Japanese companies quickly penetrated many Western markets with their low prices, forcing many Western competitors either to close down or to follow the Japanese example by paring down their line of products. Meanwhile, the Japanese companies continue to expand the scale of their production lines and to lower unit costs.

In the course of their rapid expansion, Japanese companies have actively sought to promote their manufacturing advantages. One revolutionary manufacturing process, commonly called the Just-In-Time system (JIT), was widely adopted by Japanese companies in the 1960s and 1970s. It was the need to produce many models of Toyotas in small batches that induced the company to introduce the JIT system. The concept is that one should supply parts as they are needed. The process starts from the final stage of production and works backwards. Instead of "push out," the system uses "pull out," as workers in the final stage dictate the flow of parts needed from the prior stage. The creator of the system, Tai-ichi Ohno, Vice-President at Toyota, drew the original inspiration from the operational logic of the American supermarket, where empty shelf space or gaps constitute the "trigger mechanism" for shop assistants to replace products (McMillan 1989: 211–218).

The technique greatly improves inventory control, because materials, parts, and components are produced and delivered just before they are needed. A small card, or *kanban* in Japanese, is attached to each part, which describes the part's origin and destination. The operation is based on multi-machine manning (see Figure 14.2), whose goal is not high utilization of the machine, but high utilization of the worker. By streamlining the production flow and enhancing flexibility in scheduling, the costs associated with a varied product mix and changeover time can be significantly reduced. The increased automation, robotization, and computerization further contribute to efficiency.

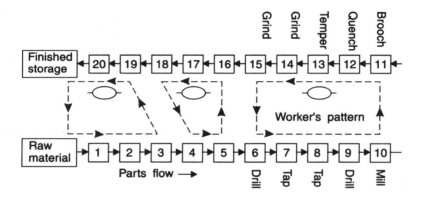

Figure 14.2 Large multi-machine manning crankshaft line
Source: Abegglen and Stalk, 1985, p. 100.

The JIT system is a good example of an area in which the Japanese management system can facilitate productivity experiments; redundant workers, for example, can be transferred to other factories. The same attempt to maximize the utilization of the worker's potential may meet with strong resistance from trade unions in the West. The close relationship between the Japanese company and its trade union has clearly made such efforts easier. The JIT system is also not possible without the sacrifices of small contractors, who bear the cost of warehousing and carrying parts until large companies need them. A similar system with the same efficiency would be hard to institute in the United States.

Japanese companies have also consistently sought to develop technology-based advantages. Historically, Japanese companies have been labeled as skilled adapters of existing inventions rather than as creators of their own innovation. The massive postwar transfer of technology from the United States and Western Europe laid the technological foundation for almost all of Japan's modern industries. On the other hand, Japanese open-mindedness and the ability to adapt to existing technology have facilitated their absorption through the course of development, allowing them to challenge the originators of technology in their home base within a very short time. Into the 1990s, an increasing number of Japanese companies are rapidly changing their image from being adaptive copiers to innovative creators.

The reasons explaining how the high rate of technological absorption has been possible are complex, ranging from close government-business co-operation to a highly competitive education system and a good-quality workforce. One outstanding feature of Japanese companies has been their increasing commitment to research and development (R&D). Investment by Japanese companies in the R&D of key technologies has substantially increased since the early 1980s. There has been a myth in the West that the reason for Japan's dynamic growth in innovative R&D is that the Japanese government has paid the bill. The facts, however, are that about half of all research funds are contributed by the West European and American governments, while only one-quarter of these funds are provided by the Japanese government, and only half of that is allocated directly to private industry (Whitehill 1991: 256). The implication is that Japanese companies have financed nearly all of the R&D projects that they conduct.

BREATHTAKING GROWTH AND AGGRESSIVE FINANCIAL STRATEGIES

Over the past four decades, Japanese companies have steadfastly pursued the use of time as a source of competitive advantage, and many of them have seemed to follow the same strategy for the same industry at the same time (Stalk and Webber 1993: 98). Subsequently, in one industry after another, Japanese companies have overwhelmed their foreign competitors with a strategic surge that many from outside Japan have criticized as a well-orchestrated Japanese conspiracy, but which, in reality, represents only a group of Japanese companies from the same industry flocking to the same strategy. When the world economy boomed, Japanese companies quickly seized market opportunities and rose with extreme speed to dominate a whole set of industries. Within a relatively short period of time, Japan owned the world's largest shipbuilding, steel-making and textile-manufacturing industries. The Japanese speed of growth was unparalleled.

This phenomenal growth could not have been achieved without very aggressive corporate financial policies. Japanese companies depend much more on debt financing than do their Western counterparts. Although a highly leveraged company may be too exposed to financial risks, it can aggressively use debt to fund growth at significantly higher rates, even though profitability may be relatively low. In contrast, a more conservatively financed company may achieve higher profits and suffer from slower growth. By sacrificing "profits," a company with aggressive financial policies may be able to cut prices, make critical investments in R&D, and attain greater market share.

Such aggressive financial policies would inevitably impose competitive pressures on those having more conservative policies. In the late 1970s and 1980s, many American semiconductor manufacturers, for example, felt the effects of the aggressive financial policies of their Japanese competitors on their ability to compete (Abegglen and Stalk 1985: 160). The Japanese companies typically borrowed more, spent more, made less as a percentage of revenues, paid less in dividends, and grew faster than their American competitors. Some of the leading Japanese companies in semiconductor manufacturing had debt-to-equity ratios surpassing 2:1. In contrast, the debt-to-equity ratio for the major American semiconductor manufacturers stayed around 0.2:1. Nevertheless, few American companies changed their financial policies to match those of the Japanese, as American shareholders normally expected high dividends and high profits while traditional American financial institutions were unwilling to indulge in the pursuit of aggressive financial policies.

It is self-evident that financial risks grow with the growth of leverage. Nevertheless, the inability to match the aggressive financial policies of rapidly expanding competitors can be much more risky. If the aggressive financial policies of the competitors are not duly met, there will be growing pressure for higher prices and greater profits. This tends to push companies into manufacturing products that have higher gross margins but lower sales volumes. This often leads to a vicious cycle in which those forced to manufacture higher margin products at higher selling prices will gradually lose their market share and will have to be compensated by another round of chasing higher margin products and prices, with the eventual result being loss of market share. Many Japanese companies have failed to grow as quickly and as a result have shrunk or collapsed. For instance, there were 50 motorcycle makers in Japan in the 1950s, but only four of them had grown big enough to survive by the 1980s (Abegglen and Stalk 1985: 44).

Despite all these advantages, it is difficult for American companies to embrace aggressive financial policies similar to those adopted by successful Japanese companies. For one thing, the attitudes and roles of the Japanese stockholders are significantly different from those in the United States. Japanese stockholders can benefit more if their company grows than they can if given more dividends. In Japan, dividends are taxed as ordinary income, but no taxes are paid on capital gains. Consequently, Japanese shareholders are less interested in the profits of a company than its growth potential. As analyzed in Chapter 13, the role of Japanese shareholders in the management of their company resembles that of preferred shareholders in an American company; they have few rights except for the right to receive dividends.

Japanese financial institutions' willingness to support aggressive financial policies derived mainly from one of two factors: first, in-house financial institutions of large *keiretsu* groups are more committed to helping group members and thus are more willing to lend money for their development. Second, compared with their American counterparts, Japanese financial institutions had, until most recently, only lent money against collateral. Many Japanese companies had collateral assets that were substantially undervalued on their balance sheets, including land, long-term receivables and market securities. The availability of these assets reduced the financial risks of many Japanese companies, which borrowed aggressively to finance their rapid growth.

The downside of such a time-based strategy and breathtaking growth is a repeated cycle of boom and bust, as every major Japanese company follows the exact same strategy in each industry at the same time. In each cycle in the past few decades, Japanese companies created a considerable overcapacity in these industries, causing prices to drop and profits to dwindle; then these companies were forced to pull out of the industries, leaving behind an industrial mess. The rise and fall of the Japanese shipping, textile and steel industries have evidenced the downside of these strategic surges. By the early 1990s, it appeared that the Japanese auto industry would follow suit. In the words of Stalk and Webber (1993: 98–99), "Like passengers on a ferry, they have swamped the vessel by all simultaneously running to the same side of the boat for the best view."

Another obvious drawback of such a time-based strategy is that even under a high growth period the profit levels are much lower in Japan than in the United States and Western Europe. In fact, the average profitability of the listed manufacturing companies (measured as a ratio of operating profit to sales) has been continually declining for over 30 years. Beginning at more than 8 percent in the 1960s, it dropped to 6.4 percent in the 1970s and to 5.1 percent in the 1980s. There are no signs of a reversal in the 1990s. This trend shows that while the Japanese corporate system has done a lot to establish a competitive position and has grown at astonishing speed, it has made Japanese companies less and less profitable (Shimizu 1993: 12).

As for the aggressive financial policy to fuel this growth, it is most viable in the rapidly growing industrial sectors and least effective in the stagnant and declining sectors. Slow growth can make the financial burden of expanding and upgrading production intolerable. The cost of expanding with high leverage is justified by lower unit prices and larger market share. If the market is saturated, companies will be stuck with excessive capacity and high leverage. The collapse of the bubble economy in the early 1990s has drawn increasing attention to this problem, as many faltering companies struggled to pay the interest on their loans. In this situation, for banks to continue aggressive loan policies would be tantamount to suicide. Therefore, many banks were forced to turn to a "safety first" strategy (*Tokyo Business Review*, Jan/Feb. 1993: 29–30).

ENDLESS DRIVE FOR HIGH QUALITY AND LOW COST

Total Quality Control (TQC) has been one of the most cited competitive advantages of Japanese companies. The method was developed by Professor William Deming of New York University, but was not popularized in the United States. The Japanese adopted it as a way to revive their war-torn economy and considered quality and productivity as one and the same. In the TQC concept, quality by inspection, scrap, and rework are unacceptable. The corrective measures must be built into the entire productive process. What has distinguished the Japanese most is their emphasis on the participation of all the employees, not just specialists. For the Japanese, quality is too integral to the survival of the company to be dealt with only by supervisors and specialists. Each individual employee is exhorted to try his utmost to guarantee the quality of his own products and also to help to improve the overall quality of the company's products.

A core element of the Total Quality Control concept is the use of quality circles, which are small groups of employees who do similar or related work. They meet regularly to examine, identify, analyze and solve product-quality problems and to improve overall production. There is no unified formula for scheduling and for payment of participants. If the meetings take place during normal working hours, no additional payment is offered; otherwise some form of overtime payment can be expected. Often, the zeal for participation is so high that even long meetings after work do not provide overtime pay.

The quality circles also deal with issues like personal training, job enrichment, and leadership development. Participating employees are encouraged to make suggestions, which are put into a handy box and examined by specialists. If these suggestions prove to be appropriate, they will be put into practice and the originators of the accepted proposals will receive some sort of reward.

The activities of quality circles are also merged into broader productivity campaigns, with the various factory quality circle groups competing for who will make the best suggestions. Those selected are awarded a Deming Prize. There are now more than 100,000 circles in Japan, with a total membership of over 10 million workers (Whitehill 1991: 239). The QC is a continuously improving process or *kaizen*, which would demand progressively reduced defects. A rate of four defects per one thousand, for example, is expected to be lowered to two or one per thousand as a part of continuous improvement, though it may be extremely difficult to do this.

Paralleling QC is a cost control concept, which is also often cited as a competitive advantage of the Japanese. Those who are responsible for cost control are cost engineers rather than accountants. Unlike accountants in American enterprises, who know little about products, the cost engineers in Japan have already worked in other departments, such as purchasing, design, or production, and have acquired an ability to identify a great variety of ways to reduce cost.

One notable feature of the Japanese cost control system is that the cost from manufacturing to management is already estimated at the stage of planning and design. Called "target cost," it is obtained according to the price that customers are willing to pay and serves as the basis for calculating the prices of other component parts, ranging from designing and manufacturing to sale. Each of these parts can be itemized on the basis of its own "target price." For example, the price of a car that a customer is willing to pay is first estimated, which is then followed by itemized estimates of windshield, trunk, etc. This involves a complicated process of bargaining among the various departments of the enterprise and between the enterprise and its suppliers.

In contrast, the typical method in the United States and Western Europe is to design first, then estimate cost based on a series of standard costs, such as labor cost, material cost, and manufacturing cost. Each item is calculated according to the standard costs and is then put together by the accountant. If the cost is too high, they will scrap the design and start again.

The Japanese method of cost control is not only applied to the development of new products, but also to the cost reduction of existing products (Zhou 1991: 79–80). TDK's Ideal Production System (IPS) is a typical example. By "ideal," it is meant the best efficiency that can be achieved, assuming equipment and employees make no mistakes. Stages are set up toward achieving this ideal goal in the *kaizen* process. The cost of production can be divided into the cost of processing and the cost of materials. Through the IPS, TDK has changed the proportion of processing cost to material cost from 6:4 to 4:6. Thus, the cost of TDK video tapes was reduced by 75 percent within six short years.

Both high quality and low cost have relentlessly been pursued. The Japanese workers are exhorted to follow the spirit of *gambare*, or endure and persevere. Nevertheless, there is a limit to this, and the built-up pressure may undermine harmony in the workplace. Although the initial QC activities were mostly spontaneous, the endless drive for high quality and low cost has changed the voluntary basis, with many workers virtually pressured into participating in imposed quota programs. Those who do not actively participate or do not make enough good suggestions will eventually encounter trouble (Woronoff 1992: 28).

COMPARATIVE ADVANTAGE AND THE ECONOMIC DUAL STRUCTURE

The unique subcontracting system in Japan has also often been cited as a significant comparative advantage of large Japanese companies. The hierarchical business structure in Japan is organized as follows. Every big Japanese company resembles the top of a giant pyramid. These are the companies whose stocks are traded on the Tokyo Stock Exchange and have well-known trademarks. Many are members of the large *keiretsu* groups. One level below these companies are a few dozen direct subsidiaries. The parent is a majority stockholder in these companies and often assigns directors to their boards. One more level down consists of 100 or more *kanren* (affiliated) companies that may or may not share the parent company's name. Some of them may be spun-off divisions of some subsidiaries, others may be companies the parent has investment in, and still others may have even asked the parent for "adoption" – meaning the right to use the parent's name in exchange for stock in their companies.

Under all these levels are millions of small companies, which are the subcontractors for the big companies. Large Japanese companies usually have thousands of subcontractors, which form this group. The companies in a manufacturing group are like the parts of a machine. Subcontractors are expected to produce goods for the company one level above them. They are required to produce what big companies want, when they want it, and at the price they desire. Therefore, some critics argue that this large group of subcontractors "represents the source of flexibility and entrepreneurial creativity for big firms" (McMillan 1989: 61). Once a small subcontractor firm joins the group, it is supposed to deal almost exclusively with companies inside the group. As a member of a parent manufacturer's business group, a small subcontractor is automatically accepted as a member of its *keiretsu* business group. Therefore, a small subcontractor is also expected to do business with other companies within the *keiretsu*.

Such a widespread subcontracting network has largely resulted from what Sasaki (1990: 19–24) has called the "dual structure" of the Japanese economy, in which a few big companies with high productivity and high wage rates exist side by side with numerous small and medium-sized companies with low productivity and low wages. According to his research, around 70 percent of the workers hired by small and medium-sized companies get only 60 percent or less of the wages of the workers employed by big companies. These small and medium-sized companies have been left behind. The dual structure in the Japanese economy has given big companies substantial power to control small and medium-sized companies, as approximately 70 percent of them depend on subcontracting to big companies. A typical pattern of this relationship is reflected in the automobile industry. The ratio of products to be used for assembling a car that is produced by the parent companies constitutes about 30 to 35 percent, with the rest made by small and medium-sized subcontractors.

Therefore, many have argued that large Japanese companies have relied heavily on small companies for maintaining their competitive edge. The predominant reason that larger parent companies use subcontractors has been the cost reduction they provide. Generally speaking, work conducted by subcontractors is cheaper than work conducted by the parent in the dual structure of the Japanese economy. Subcontractors have smaller plants with lower operating costs, pay lower wages, and enjoy lower taxes. In addition, since the big companies are in a dominant position to deal with their subcontractors, they can afford to shift their costs to the smaller subcontractors, whether through JIT systems or through outright threat and pressure.

One outstanding feature of the relationship between the larger companies and their smaller subcontractors lies in their ability to command complete control over a subcontractor's operations, even to the extent of asking him to sustain huge losses in order to allow the larger parent company to set a more competitive price. How parent companies use their subcontractors to cope with economic downturns is illustrated by the lowered unit prices paid to subcontractors during the yen's dramatic appreciation in the mid-1980s (see Figure 14.3) as a result of the Plaza Accord of September 1985 (Russell 1990: 26). Larger Japanese companies, confronted with export price hikes for their goods, were forced to slash production costs by 50 percent in order to maintain their overseas market share.

How could they slash costs by 50 percent within a short time? The management system of large companies does not allow them to lay off staff at will, nor could they drastically reduce the processing cost. The best

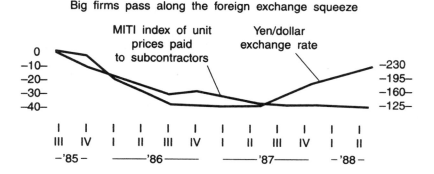

Figure 14.3 Cost passing chart
Source: Russell, 1990, p. 26.

solution seemed to lie in the cost reduction of their input of material and parts used in manufacturing. By forcing subcontractors to cut their prices, the parent companies survived the sudden shock of yen appreciation and gained time for further readjustment. As the smaller subcontractors were so dependent on the bigger parent companies for business, they had no other choice. What might have deeply embittered some smaller subcontractors was that some parent companies were reluctant to share the consequences of a bad economic situation by slashing cost on their side. Although big companies do care about a good relationship with these subcontractors and provide various forms of assistance to their subcontractors, as they are dependent on the quality of the finished parts supplied by the subcontractors they have a tendency to treat them as the shock absorbers of a recession (Sasaki 1990: 24).

SUMMARY/CONCLUSION

The chapter has reviewed the expansion strategies of Japanese companies. With rapid growth and deep penetration of the world market, Japanese companies have proved to be some of the fiercest competitors of American and West European companies. Successful Japanese companies have had a number of competitive advantages in the course of business growth, including long-term strategic planning, a competitive manufacturing capability, an aggressive expansion of market share, and the ability to swiftly shift strategies, as well as the support of a large subcontracting system. The introduction of the Just-in-Time system, a process of continual cost-cutting and quality promotion, and creative copy of foreign technology have greatly enhanced Japanese competitiveness within a short period of time. As a group, they have been very successful in expanding into the world market and overwhelming their foreign competitors.

Nevertheless, by the 1990s, the successful Japanese companies are facing the serious challenge of globalization and some of their traditional competitive advantages are becoming passing phenomena. With the collapse of the bubble economy, the Japanese companies can no longer continue their aggressive financial policies. The strategic surge has not only ruined many Japanese competitors but also deeply hurt Japanese companies themselves. Instead of continued expansion, many Japanese companies have to retrench and pare down their operations. Foreign advanced technology can no longer be easily upgraded unless the Japanese companies rapidly improve their capability for basic research. In order to stay in the black in the current economic downturn, some Japanese companies are even lowering their long-cherished standards of quality (*Wall Street Journal*, 29 September 1993). Therefore, it is important for Western companies to choose eclectically what is to be learned from the Japanese. It would be dangerous to pick up ideas that the Japanese themselves are eager to dump. Thus, a Japanese scholar, Kunio Odaka's, warning may serve as a concluding remark:

> The myth claims that Japanese management will work well in other countries just as it has worked well in Japan. Although foreign business-men are certainly free to try to learn all they can from Japanese management, the disadvantages of Japanese management are coming to outweigh the advantages even in Japan. How can a system which is not even performing as expected at home be able to perform as expected elsewhere?
>
> (Odaka 1986:4)

QUESTIONS FOR DISCUSSION

1 According to Kono what is a typical process of the strategical planning in a successful Japanese company?
2 Describe the JIT system. Can an American company follow the same system?
3 Assess the R&D practices of Japanese businesses.
4 Analyze the advantages and disadvantages of aggressive financial policies.
5 How do you view the economic dual structure and its advantages to large Japanese companies?

FURTHER READING

Abegglen, James C. and George Stalk, Jr. (1985) *Kaisha: The Japanese Corporation*, New York: Basic Books.

Ballon, Robert J. and Iwao Tomita (1988) *The Financial Behavior of Japanese Corporations*, Tokyo: Kodansha International.

Fallows, James (1993) "Looking at the Sun," *The Atlantic Monthly* (November): 69–100.

Gerlach, Michael (1987) "Business Alliances and the Strategy of the Japanese Firm", *California Management Review* (Fall), 30(1): 126–142.

Imai, Masaaki (1986) *The Key to Japan's Competitive Success*, New York: McGraw-Hill.

Katzenstein, Gary (1991) "Japanese Management Style: Beyond the Hype: What to Try, What to Toss," *Working Women* (February): 49–101.

Kester, W. Carl (1990) *Japanese Takeovers*, Boston: Harvard Business School Press.

Kono, Toyohiro (1984) *Strategy & Structure of Japanese Enterprises*, London: Macmillan.

Lillrank, P. and N. Kano (1989) *Continuous Improvement*, Ann Arbor, Mich.: Center for Japanese Studies, University of Michigan.

McMillan, Charles J. (1989) *The Japanese Industrial System*, New York: Walter de Gruyter.

Moritani, M. (1982) *Japanese Technology: Getting the Best for the Least*, Tokyo: The Simul Press Inc.

Odaka, Kunio (1986) *Japanese Management – A Forward Looking Analysis*, Tokyo: Asian Productivity Organization.

Russell, David (1990) "The Truth About Big Business in Japan," *Business Tokyo* (April): 22–28.

Sasaki, Naoto (1990) *Management and Industrial Structure in Japan*, New York: Pergamon Press.

Shimizu, Norihiko (1993) "In Japan, Don't Do as the Japanese Do," *Tokyo Business Today* (January–February): 12–13.

Smitka, Michael J. (1991) *Competitive Ties, Subcontracting in the Japanese Automotive Industry*, Princeton, Princeton University Press.

Smothers, Norman P. (1990) "Patterns of Japanese Strategy: Strategic Combinations of Strategies," *Strategic Management Journal* 11: 521–533.

Stalk Jr., George and Alan M. Webber (1993) "Japan's Dark Side of Time," *Harvard Business Review* (July–August): 93–102.

Wall Street Journal (1993) (29 September): 1.

Whitehill, Arthur M. (1991) *Japanese Management: Tradition and Transition*, London and New York: Routledge.

Woronoff, Jon (1992) *The Japanese Management Mystique*, Chicago: Probus.

Zhou, Hui-qing (1991) "Cost Management: The Secret Weapons of Japanese Enterprises," *Commonwealth (Taiwan)* (1 September): 78–82.

Chapter 15

Managerial styles of Korean companies

INTRODUCTION

The spectacular economic success of Korea can be traced to a number of factors, one of which is the competitiveness of Korean companies. The Korean management system has three major sources of influence. The first is Confucianism, which was the state philosophy of Korea for more than five hundred years, beginning in the Yi Dynasty in 1392, and ending in 1910 when Korea was annexed by Japan. The profound influence of Confucianism on the values, attitudes, and behavioral patterns of Koreans has apparently spilled over to the Korean management system. The second and third sources, i.e. Japanese and American influences, are more recent. Comparatively speaking, Japanese influence on the Korean management style came earlier than the American influence, as Korea was a Japanese colony from 1910 to 1945. After 1945, American influences outweighed the Japanese until 1965, when Korean–Japanese relations were normalized. Since then, American and Japanese influences have been equal in importance, as many Korean companies have close business ties with both nations. They depend on the United States as the key market for their exports while relying on Japan as a source of intermediary products needed to manufacture those exports.

Based on these three sources of influence and Korea's own historical traditions and experiences, Korean companies have developed their own management system, known by some as K-type management, which includes top-down decision-making, paternalistic leadership, clan management, *inhwa* (harmony-orientated cultural values), flexible lifetime employment, personal loyalty, compensation based on seniority and merit rating, high mobility of workers, expansion through conglomeration, etc. (Lee and Yoo 1987b: 75). In spite of various inherent problems and a constant pressure for change, the Korean management system has maintained its own uniqueness. This chapter will concentrate on a discussion of the organizational structure of Korean companies, their common managerial processes, their competitive corporate strategies, as well as their trend of development and change.

ORGANIZATIONAL STRUCTURE

Organizational structure is an important aspect in helping to understand the Korean management system, as structure refers to relatively stable relationships between individuals and subunits within a given organization. In many ways, organizational structure reflects the managerial values of Korean culture.

Formal structure

The organizational structure of many Korean companies is characterized by a high degree of centralization and formalization. Authority is concentrated in senior levels of managerial hierarchies, with major decisions – especially financial decisions – entailing *kyul-jae*, a formal procedure of approval from top levels of management which involves taking many *chops* (personal stamps of approval). The Samsung group in the past used a process of twenty-one *chops*, which took several months to get a project approved. After Kun Hee Lee took over the group, he demanded that these twenty-one *chops* be cut down to three (Paisley 1993: 64). The hierarchic structure starts with the chairman, followed by the president, vice-president (*busajang*), senior managing director (*junmu*), managing director (*sangmu*), department manager (*bujang*), section manager (*kwajang*), and continues down to the foreman and blue collar workers.

Korean companies usually have a "tall" hierarchical structure of organization. One outstanding organizational feature of Korean companies is that they normally do not employ personal staff, with the exception of assistants for the group chairman. Other executives tend to be supported by deputies and assistants as line positions rather than as personal staff. This increases the layers of vertical hierarchies conducive to a centralized and tall organizational structure. Another outstanding organizational feature of Korean companies is that their vertical and hierarchical control is supported by strong functional control from staff departments like planning, finance and personnel. Korean companies attach great importance to functional specialization, allowing the planning and finance departments to exercise significant functional control under the leadership of the chief executive. Many *chaebols* have a planning and coordination office under the group chairman, which is responsible for allocating major internal resources within the group (Aguilar and Cho 1984: 12). Therefore, many Korean companies have a combined organizational structure placing a vertical concentration of decision-making power at the senior levels of management and a horizontal concentration of functional control in staff departments.

In contrast to the centralized organizational structure and formalized functions, individual jobs are not clearly structured in many Korean companies and usually do not have clear-cut job descriptions. The responsibilities of individual employees tend to be decided by the supervisor according to the needs of the occasion. Although poorly defined job assignments can bring about low efficiency from ill-distributed workloads and work redundancy, the managers may enjoy a high degree of flexibility in adjusting to changing conditions. As the high degree of centralization and formalization is combined with poorly defined job assignments, the individual's or supervisor's ability to obtain the support of others becomes crucial to work performance.

Generally speaking, the organizational performance of Korean companies is closely related to how effectively the company can overcome the centralized and functionalized structure. This can be achieved in a number of ways. Many companies depend heavily on autonomous or temporary organizations like task teams and special committees. Others take advantage of informal interaction. Highly successful Korean companies tend to use fewer top executives and staff personnel in order to increase delegation of authority while decreasing central control (Lee 1989: 154). Task forces and informal interactions help overcome departmental divisions and enhance organizational flexibility. Authority delegation helps simplify the organizational structure.

Informal structure

The concentration of authority results partly from the fact that ownership and management are not separated in most Korean companies. The owner family actively participates in the management of most Korean companies, as family or clan members together dominate the management power (see Table 15.1). Many Koreans value blood relationship so highly that they have an extended clan, or *chiban*, which provides broad-based security for the family members. The larger the *chiban*, the broader based the security would be for members of the clan (Song 1990: 194). Business founders are expected not only to take care of their own immediate family members but of other relatives also. The relationship with the owner based on kinship is called *hyul-yun* (literally meaning "blood-related").

Professional executives and managers also form an important power group in Korean companies (see Table 15.1). In some Korean companies, the career managers, who have been promoted during their extended service in the company, can also exert powerful influence on company management through the creation of personal networks within the company and foster them over the years. Many of these managers are initially recruited through open competition from an elite group (*gong-chae*); most Korean companies have been using the *gong-chae* system since the early

1960s (Jung 1987). With the passage of time, internally promoted career executives and managers will grow in number and power.

Common geographical and school ties also play a strong role in the formation of management power groups. A common practice is for owners

Table 15.1 Backgrounds of *chaebol* executives

	The Founder and his family members	Professional career managers	Others	Total
Hyundai	7	42	8	57
Samsung	2	28	11	41
Lucky-Goldstar	7	26	11	44
Daewoo	2	25	25	52
Sungung	3	21	2	26
Sangyong	2	11	8	21
Hankuk Hwayak	1	9	11	21
Total	24	162	76	262

Source: Chang, 1988, p. 55.

to bring their school and hometown friends into management (Chang 1988: 53–54). In some Korean companies, top management positions are predominantly filled by those who are from the same geographical area, such as Seoul, Honam (a southwestern province), or Yeongnam (a southeastern province). In other Korean companies, graduates from elite universities, like Seoul National or Yonsei, dominate top management. In the past, one who had a "K-S Mark" (or a degree from Kyunggi High School and Seoul National University) would automatically enjoy a better chance to get into top management. The relationship with the owner based on geographical ties is called *ji-yun* (region-related) while the relationship with the owner based on school ties is *hahk-yun* (school-related). Both *ji-yun* and *hahk-yun* tend to constitute a very strong factor in informal relationships, giving common identities, backgrounds and a sense of belonging.

Hyul-yun (blood-related) internally promotes career managers, while *ji-yun* and *hahk-yun* are not only important in senior-level power group formation, but also in the formation of informal cliques or groups at all levels within a Korean company. All of them affect the power structure and informal groupings in Korean companies. The family ownership based on *hyul-yun* has been the most important factor affecting the power structure of Korean companies whose ownership and management are not separated. While the power of internally promoted career managers has been increasing with continued management professionalization, power based on *hyul-yun* remains predominant in Korean companies. *Ji-yun* and *hahk-yun* also significantly influence informal groupings and social interactions in Korean companies.

MANAGERIAL PROCESSES

Managerial processes – which comprise planning, directing, organizing and controlling the entire range of management activities from setting organizational goals to completing them – also exemplify the influence of Korean culture. The following analysis focuses on the influential role of Korean culture on such managerial processes as leadership, motivation, and communication.

Leadership and decision-making

Owing to the strong influence of family traditions, there is a tendency for Korean corporate leaders, especially founders, to manage on the basis of principles governing the family or clan system. In the traditional Korean family, the father is the unquestioned and respected head. He has almost absolute power to wield if he so wishes. The traditional Korean father also had full responsibility to feed the family and to decide the future of his children. One legacy of such a family tradition for business leadership in Korean companies is the strong authoritarian style of superiors in the managerial process. A top-down decision-making style is fairly typical among Korean companies. Usually, 80 percent of the authority lies in the upper management level, with middle or lower level management having very limited authority (Lee and Yoo 1987a: 106). Authoritarian leadership has been a well-accepted managerial norm under the centralized structure of Korean companies. The passive attitude of the subordinates is further conducive to the authoritarian style. The traditional decision-making *pummi* style (proposal submitted for deliberations) was used more to diffuse responsibility than to reach consensus (De Mente 1991: 92).

Nevertheless, the authoritarian style is not despotic. Corporate leadership in Korean companies is also heavily influenced by a key value of Korean behavior, *inhwa*, which is defined as harmony and is similar to the Japanese *wa*. However, *inhwa* does not emphasize the group element as in *wa*. *Inhwa* emphasizes harmony between unequals in rank, power and prestige (Alston 1989: 29). Korean managers cherish good interpersonal relationships with their subordinates and try to keep the needs and feelings of the subordinates in mind. Another aspect of *inhwa* is that each party has responsibility to support the other.

The harmony-orientated leadership is evidenced in the decision-making pattern of Korean managers, who try to maintain good relationships with subordinates, even though they may sometimes have to compromise group performance. Korean managers tend to make decisions with the consultation of subordinates. The Korean process of informal consensus formation, or *sajeonhyupui*, is similar to Japanese *nemawashi* (Song 1990: 29), but Korean subordinates are usually reluctant to express their opinions. Subsequently, managers are often expected to understand the feelings of the subordinates before making appropriate decisions. Managers maintain various interactions on an informal basis with the subordinates as an important way to achieve harmony-orientated leadership, which is based on mutual trust and benevolent authoritarianism.

Motivation

Koreans are highly motivated workers and are well known for enduring long work days. The motivation of Korean employees is influenced by traditional values as well as realistic needs. The key Confucian values of diligence and harmony have contributed to a relatively high work ethic. The instinct for survival has also been an important driving force among Koreans, who have been haunted by instability and poverty throughout most of their recent history. Therefore, a strong work ethic and harmony have become the most cherished values of Korean employees.

While the specific motivations of Korean employees vary depending on the size of the company and the level of seniority, high wages and job security tend to be the most important motivational factors. According to a study conducted in 1984 by the Korean Chamber of Commerce and Industry, executives of large companies tended to cite "environment for voluntary participation" as the most effective incentive, while the CEOs of small companies regarded the management-by-objectives system as the best way to heighten the spirit of workers. It was also reported that older employees over sixty cited wages as the most important incentive for hard work, while new management staff under thirty viewed "environment for voluntary participation" as the most effective means to motivate employees and promote productivity (Kim and Kim 1989: 214).

Apparently, Korean employees as a group tend to put a somewhat heavier emphasis on extrinsic factors (i.e. wages, working conditions, and job security) than on intrinsic factors (i.e. creativity and achievement) for high motivation (Lee 1989: 161). Moreover, the need for achievement and recognition tends to be satisfied within the framework of the harmony of a given group. Since harmony is a dominant value in interpersonal relationships within a group, the external factors are even more important motivating factors to Korean employees. Nevertheless, the trend is that more Korean companies are shifting their emphasis to intrinsic motivating factors such as *changjo* (creativity), achievement and recognition.

Communication

One outstanding feature of organizational communication in Korean businesses is that formal communication is mainly achieved along vertical hierarchies (Lee 1989: 158–159). The organizational communication process depends heavily on hierarchical relations, which are determined by a combination of factors, ranging from formal authority and informal social status to length of employment and age. In the vertical communication process, the superiors are expected to give directives while the subordinates are expected to understand and implement those directives. The superiors tend to prefer issuing general directives, as opposed to specific and detailed directives. On the other hand, the subordinates prefer using their own judgments instead of asking the superiors for explanation, when the latter's directives are not clear-cut or detailed.

Another notable feature of communication in Korean companies is that Korean employees usually attach much greater importance to upward formal communication on hierarchical lines rather than to communication on horizontal interdepartmental lines. This may have resulted from the high centralization of authority in Korean companies. The strictly hierarchical structures of Korean companies tend to determine the nature of vertical and horizontal communication. For employees, vertical communication is more work-related than horizontal communication, and thus more important. Poor horizontal communication between vertically structured departments has become a major barrier of many large Korean companies to efficient organizational performance (De Mente 1991: 94).

The superiors' preference of communicating in general terms, combined with a relatively large power distance, comprises a major source of misunderstanding in Korean companies. It is very important for subordinates to develop the ability to decipher the intentions of the superior from general directives. Good personal relations with superiors tend to help overcome hierarchical barriers to the subordinates' communication with them. Blood relationship as well as school and regional ties may further enhance mutual understanding and trust, thereby contributing to straightforward and clear-cut communication. Those who share better communication tend to develop an informal management clique within the company.

Many Korean employees are not good at open communication in formal meetings and have difficulty in airing their views, especially the opposing ones. An openly different opinion may embarrass or antagonize one's superior, or provoke a colleague. Besides, Koreans are not culturally encouraged to share information openly with others except within close personal relationships. However, many Koreans are very good at free communication on informal occasions, especially on a one-to-one basis with a superior. There are many opportunities for informal communication between superiors and subordinates; sophisticated superiors will constantly make such opportunities available. Superiors, for example, may invite their subordinates to dinner either at a restaurant or at their home. Subordinates, on the other hand, may visit their superiors at home for a private talk. The use of informal occasions or settings for open communication is very important for mutual understanding and trust between superiors and employees.

HUMAN RESOURCE MANAGEMENT

Korea has a large pool of well-educated and devoted human resources. About 98 percent of the populace can read and write. More than 80 percent of Korean teenagers finish high school studies while most high school graduates attend colleges or professional training schools. The priorities of Korean companies' human resources management include recruiting the best candidates, operating on-the-job training programs, and instituting a reward and appraisal system.

Recruiting and training

In a general survey (Shin 1985: 245), it was found that most large Korean corporations classify employees into three categories: core (top management), basic (permanent employees), and temporary. Most Korean companies hire employees through reference check, a test for knowledge in the special field (and/or common sense), a test of English proficiency, a personal interview, and a physical examination. They prefer new college graduates or experienced professionals. Large Korean companies recruit twice a year, in June and November, and prefer to recruit their management trainees from reputable universities, such as Seoul National University, Yonsei University, and Korean University. Mid-sized and small Korean companies recruit once a year. The recruitment of large Korean companies is very competitive.

Once they hire new people, they tend to assign the elite group to such core departments as planning and finance after an in-house training of 7–10 days. Employee development in Korean companies is normally conducted through in-house training programs. Korean companies place great emphasis on employee development. Many large *chaebols* have their own employee-training centers and set aside as much as 5 percent of regular work hours for formal training. The emphasis on employee development is in conformity with traditional Korean cultural values, which attach great importance to education. The traditional Korean society was ruled by the *yangban* class or literati (Song 1990: 34). The biggest ambition of promising sons of *yangban* families was to pass the civil service exam and attain a high rank in the government.

Reward and promotion system

The reward and promotion system in Korean companies is traditionally based on seniority, but performance is becoming an increasingly important factor (Lee 1989: 157). Korean companies have gradually combined seniority with performance in distributing their rewards. Wages are generally based on seniority, but bonuses may be awarded based on performance in many Korean companies. Although a growing number of companies utilize the performance criterion in reward decisions, seniority remains a dominant factor in most company decisions. Generally speaking, high-growth companies tend to attach greater importance to performance than low-growth companies do. Promotion is regarded as an extremely important matter to employees and employers as well. In many Korean companies, top management is actively involved in promotion decisions. Promotion is based on a number of criteria: seniority, performance, personality, family ties, school, and region.

In appraisal systems, many Korean companies consider not only performance, but also job attitude and special ability. Subjective judgments may hamper an objective evaluation of job attitude and special ability. Many Korean managers are unwilling to give their subordinates too negative an evaluation. *Inhwa*, which can be defined as harmony between the unequal, emphasizes the importance of harmony among individuals who are not equal in prestige, rank and power. Subordinates are required to be loyal to their superiors and superiors are required to care for the well-being of subordinates. A negative evaluation may undermine harmonious relations; consequently, most managers evaluate their subordinates leniently. Another Korean value *koenchanayo*, or "that's good enough," also hampers critical evaluation, as it urges tolerance and appreciation of other people's efforts. The key part of *koenchanayo* is that one should not be excessively picky in assessing someone else's sincere efforts (Kang 1989: 12).

Severance and retirement

Layoffs are a common practice in Korean companies. Whenever they encounter a business downturn, they feel free to lay off employees at all levels. On the other hand, Korean employees change jobs fairly freely, even though many of them work in one company till retirement. While Korean employees attach great importance to their companies, they would not normally feel embarrassed to accept better offers from other companies. The skilled employees tend to have a higher rate of job-hopping than those who are not skilled. As the concept of loyalty in Korea is based on individual relationships, the loyalty of Korean employees is often devoted to a specific superior (Song 1990: 195). When a manager moves to another company for a better job, often he may bring many of his subordinates with him.

Korean companies do not have a uniform retirement age, though many require their employees to retire at fifty-five to sixty. Retirement age is also determined by rank, and senior executives and managers usually have an extended retirement age. Korean companies do not make a distinction between resignation and retirement in calculating severance or retirement pay. Most Korean companies set aside one month's salary per year for severance or retirement (Chang 1989: 202). Some companies put in an additional two or three months per year in calculating the total period of service.

Trade unions

After the Korean War, American-style labor-related legislation guaranteeing the worker's rights to organize and to bargain collectively was enacted. Nevertheless, this right did not materialize as the government had not developed enforcement measures. The government-dominated Federation of Korean Trade Unions (FKTU) helped employers control workers. In 1960, embittered workers joined radical students in overthrowing Syngman Rhee's government.

Throughout the 1960s and 1970s, the Park Chung Hee government upheld a policy of growth first and distribution later, and suppressed the labor movement. The Special Act on National Security of 1971 required workers to obtain government approval prior to any labor confrontation. Although it was lifted in 1981, new restrictions were instituted. In order to control the power of trade unions, the government banned industry-wide national unions in 1980 and initiated "enterprise unions," which were managed by labor–management councils (Chung and Lie 1989: 218). This was designed to promote common interests between management and labor. Labor–management councils, composed of managers and labor representatives, were required to meet on a quarterly basis to coordinate the conflicts between productivity and welfare. However, the labor–management councils tended to favor the interests of management, with many labor representatives being appointed by management.

The political reform of 1987 has removed government intervention in labor–management relations and granted workers the right to unionize. Industry-based national unions are also allowed to be established. The newly amended Trade Union Act protects workers from unfair labor practices by employers, allowing them to organize, negotiate and take collective action. Trade unions have since been growing, actively promoting increased wages and improved working conditions.

COMPETITIVE STRATEGIES

Competitive strategies have significant influence over organizational structure and managerial efficiency. An analysis of competitive strategies commonly adopted by Korean companies is conducive to a better understanding of the rapid growth and development of Korean businesses. As many Korean companies have achieved rapid development by improving manufacturing capabilities and diversifying their business, the focus of analysis will be placed on manufacturing development and diversification strategies.

Manufacturing development strategies

In the early period of development, many Korean companies followed the strategy of choosing the growth/maturity stages of products (Hahn 1989: 138). By taking advantage of the governmental import-substitution policy, many companies selected growth/maturity-stage consumer goods, mostly in light manufacturing industries. Apart from the cement and fertilizer industries that were very important for the Korean reconstruction and agricultural development, most manufacturing companies were concentrated on labor-intensive light manufacturing industries. For Korean companies, the strategy of selecting maturity-stage products significantly decreased potential market risks. From the viewpoint of the government, the development of labor-intensive and consumer product industries would save badly needed foreign exchange and absorb the large pool of cheap and unskilled workers. With the protection of governmental policies, Korean manufacturing industries quickly developed into strong competitors for cheap labor-intensive products in the international market.

There have been two basic modes of technology transfer. The large intermediate goods manufacturers of chemicals, cement and fertilizers, etc. adopted an apprenticing strategy and relied heavily on foreign assistance in the form of turnkey plants, consultants, and licensing. On-the-job training under foreign suppliers' direction and off-job training at both foreign suppliers' and recipients' sites provided the groundwork for production expertise to Korean engineers and technicians. Smaller manufacturing companies that did not have financial resources to negotiate with suppliers of foreign technology, upgraded their products and production technologies through reverse engineering of locally available foreign products (Kim and Kim 1989: 126). This informal approach was prevalent in the early period of technology transfer. Korean Steel Pipe, for example, successfully duplicated and improved the Japanese model through imitation.

Other commonly used manufacturing strategies were concerned with the project implementation process, during which many Korean companies tried to minimize the total project completion period. There are a number of competitive advantages to this: cash flow can be generated much earlier; interest and overhead costs can be reduced significantly; and huge profits and large market share can be achieved through early entry into the growth market. Samsung, for example, completed its first 64K DRAM chip manufacturing facility in just six months, as compared to an average of eighteen months for a similar project in the United States (Hahn 1989: 140).

Diversification strategies

Diversification strategies are important for growth in any business. Large business groups, *chaebols*, have pursued diversification strategies in the past three decades. In fact, diversification strategies have been widely advocated by the Korean government as a part of the national economic policy. The Korean government has also favored the development of world-class big businesses that can compete powerfully in the international market. With the support of the government, *chaebols* have successfully implemented an "octopus-arm" diversification strategy and expanded their share in the Korean economy. Major *chaebols*, such as Samsung, Hyundai, Lucky-Goldstar and Daewoo, have developed as the mainstays of the Korean economy. Diversification has also been facilitated by strong Korean entrepreneurship. Many Korean business leaders had the attitude of "get the order first and figure out how to do it later" (Kang 1989: 67).

Generally speaking, diversification can be classified into seven categories: single, vertical, dominant-constrained, dominant-linked, related-constrained, related-linked, and unrelated. The largest *chaebols* have tended to follow the strategy of unrelated product diversification. Samsung, for example, entered into sugar and wood textiles in the 1950s; electronics, fertilizer and paper production started in the 1960s; construction, electronic components, heavy industry, synthetic textiles, petrochemicals, and shipbuilding were entered in the 1970s; aircrafts, bioengineering, and semiconductors were introduced in the 1980s. Smaller companies generally pursued the strategy of having a single or dominant product structure. Medium-sized companies have tended to adopt strategies in between these two extremes, typically the strategy of related product diversification (Cho 1989: 99–112). In terms of number, related product diversification seems to have been the most prevalent form of diversification (see Table 15.2). Since the ten largest *chaebols* own more than 200 companies, unrelated product diversification has been an important strategy and has greatly facilitated the rapid growth of Korean business.

The types and degrees of diversification strategies vary substantially from industry to industry mirroring the differences in their nature. Vertical diversification, for example, is most often used by manufacturers in the textile and apparel industries, because a continuous supply of raw materials and market outlets is critical to the maintenance of a company's competitive edge. A related-constrained strategy is more prevalent among companies in the food and beverage industry, which tend to produce products closely related to each other in the use of raw materials and

Table 15.2 Growth strategies of *chaebols*

Business group	Single	Dominant	Related	Unrelated	Total
10 largest (213)	0	1(10%)	1(10%)	8(80%)	10(100%)
11–20 largest (123)	0	2(20%)	3(30%)	5(50%)	10(100%)
21–50 largest (206)	0	9(30%)	14(47%)	7(23%)	30(100%)
51–108 largest (246)	12(21%)	21(36%)	19(33%)	6(10%)	58(100%)
108 largest (788)	12(11%)	33(31%)	37(34%)	26(24%)	108(100%)

Source: Jung, 1987, p. 85. Reprinted with permission of Greenwood Publishing Group, Inc., Westport, CT. © 1989

distribution channels. In the metal and nonmetallic industries, the dominant-constrained strategy seems to be popular, as it enables management to focus on a few dominant product lines while using the same organizational resources.

SUMMARY/CONCLUSION

This chapter has discussed the key characteristics of the organization and management of Korean companies, with a focus on formal and informal organizational structures (i.e. leadership style, motivation and organizational communication), various aspects of human resources management (i.e. training, reward, promotion, severance, retirement and trade union), and manufacturing and diversification strategies. Specific topics include top-down decision-making, paternalistic leadership, clan management, *inhwa* (harmony-orientated cultural value), flexible lifetime employment, personal loyalty, relation-based interactions, compensation based on seniority and merit rating, high mobility of workers, expansion through conglomeration, etc.

The business environment in Korea is experiencing rapid change. Traditional managerial values and organizational systems are under growing pressure to change accordingly. Some changes have already taken place in many companies, including a shift from mostly seniority-based to a more balanced reward-system combining seniority and performance, a shift from strict family control to an increased role played by career managers at the senior level, a shift from over-centralized functional control to decentralized horizontal cooperation, a shift of cultural emphasis on *inhwa* to the

encouragement of *changjo,* and a shift from emphasis on nonmaterial rewards to balancing nonmaterial with material rewards. The Samsung
Group, for example, is now trying to change its top-heavy and often
unwieldy management structure, which often hinders productivity and
competition. Chairman Kun Hee Lee hopes to graft modern Western management practices onto the group's Confucian hierarchy and give more
autonomy to middle and lower level management (Paisley 1993: 64–69).
With the continued internationalization of Korean companies, professionalization will gather dynamics, though Korean management will maintain
its uniqueness based on its general cultural and social environment.

QUESTION FOR DISCUSSION

1   What are the unique points in the organizational structure of a
    Korean company?
2   Can you identify the four manager groups in Korean com-
    panies?
3   Can you briefly describe the decision-making style of Korean
    companies?
4   What changes have taken place in the union system in Korea?
5   Can you assess some of the manufacturing development
    strategies of Korean companies discussed in this chapter?

FURTHER READING

Aguilar, Francis and Dong Sung Cho (1984) "*Daewoo* Group," *Harvard
    Business School Cases 385–014*: Cambridge, Mass.: Harvard Business
    School.
Alston, Jon P. (1989) "*Wa, Guanxi* and *Inhwa*: Managerial Principles in Japan,
    China and Korea," *Business Horizons* (March–April): 26–31.
Chang, Chan Sup (1988) "*Chaebol*: The South Korean Conglomerates,"
    Business Horizons (March–April): 51–57.
—— (1989) "Human Resource Management," in Kae H. Chung and Hak
    Chong Lee (eds), *Korean Managerial Dynamics*, New York: Praeger, pp.
    195–205.
Cho, Dong Sung (1989) "Diversification Strategy of Korean Firms," in Kae
    H. Chung and Hak Chong Lee (eds), *Korean Managerial Dynamics*, New
    York: Praeger, pp. 99–112.
Chung, Kae H. and Hak Chong Lee (eds) (1989) *Korean Managerial Dynamics*,
    New York: Praeger.
—— and Harry K. Lie (1989) "Labor–Management Relations in Korea," in

Kae H. Chung and Hak Chong Lee (eds), *Korean Managerial Dynamics*, New York: Praeger, pp. 217–231.

De Mente, Boye (1991) *Korean Etiquette and Ethics in Business*, Lincolnwood, Ill.: NTC.

Hahn, Chan K. (1989) "Korean Manufacturing Strategy," in Kae H. Chung and Hak Chong Lee (eds), *Korean Managerial Dynamics*, New York: Praeger, pp. 131–144.

Jung, Ku Hyun (1987) *Growth Strategy and Management Structure of Korean Business*, Seoul: Korea Chamber of Commerce.

Kang, T.W. (1989) *Is Korea the Next Japan?*, New York: The Free Press.

Kim, Dong Ki and Chong W. Kim (1989) "Korean Value Systems and Managerial Practices," in Kae H. Chung and Hak Chong Lee (eds), *Korean Managerial Dynamics*, New York: Praeger, pp. 207–31.

Lee, Hak Chong (1987) "Characteristics of Successful Korean Business Firms," in Kae H. Chung and Hak Chong Lee (eds), *In Structure and Strategy of Korean Business*, Seoul: Beupmunsa, pp. 87–109.

—— (1989) "Managerial Characteristics of Korean Firms," in Kae H. Chung and Hak Chong Lee (eds), *Korean Managerial Dynamics*, New York: Praeger, pp. 147–162.

Lee, Sang M. and Sangjin Yoo (1987a) "Management Style and Practice of Korean *Chaebols*," *California Management Review* (Summer) 29(4): 95–110.

—— (1987b) "The K-type Management: A Driving Force of Korean Prosperity," *Management International Review* 27(4): 68–77.

Paisley, Ed (1993) "Innovate, Not Imitate," *Far Eastern Economic Review* (13 May): 64–69.

Shin, Yookeun (1985) *Characteristics and Problems in Korean Enterprise*, Seoul: Seoul National University Press.

Song, Byung-Nak (1990) *The Rise of the Korean Economy*, New York: Oxford University Press.

Chapter 16

Comparative Japanese and Korean management systems

GENERAL

Despite various differences, Japanese and Koreans embrace similar cultural traditions that have together influenced the development of Japanese and Korean management systems. Both countries practice Confucianism and Buddhism, though Japan's official religion is Shintoism, while many Koreans are dedicated followers of Christianity. Some key values of Confucianism and Buddhism are still evident in both the Japanese and Korean societies, such as the emphasis of family, hierarchical order, interpersonal relations, the importance of education, hard work, and tolerance. More than three decades of Japanese colonial rule also left a deep imprint on the development of the Korean management system.

Nevertheless, significant cultural differences do exist. The Japanese are much more group-orientated (*amae*, or a need for a sense of belonging) than Koreans, as evidenced in the differences between wa (group-orientated harmony) and *inhwa* (harmony between unequal individuals). Koreans seem to have a much lower degree of indebtedness to a group or their colleagues. The concept of loyalty is important in both Japan and Korea, but the loyalty ideal in Korea further emphasizes subservience to superiors, rather than the more reciprocal relationship in Japan. In addition, the concept of family in Korea is generally restricted to blood relationships, while the Japanese family may include sons adopted to protect the overall family interests.

Although government–business relations in both Japan and Korea have been characterized by heavy governmental involvement, there are various differences in the ways and degrees of involvement. In the case of the Japanese, the three major players (i.e. the government, LDP, and business) deal with each other in a triangular framework, in which none could survive well without the others. In the case of Korea, the government took charge in its relations with business, while the Korean parliament did not play a major role for a long time. In comparison to the Japanese government, the Korean government intervenes in the economy much more directly and extensively.

COMPARATIVE ORGANIZATIONAL STRUCTURES

In terms of the structure of ownership and management in large Japanese and Korean business groups, one major difference is that ownership and management in large Japanese business groups are separated while owning families of large Korean business groups still actively participate in management. Another major difference is that the Japanese *keiretsus* have not had centralized management, while the Korean *chaebols* still have a powerful management center which is free to intervene in any troubled subsidiary. Third, the cross-holding of group members' stocks is a key feature of the ownership structure of large Japanese business groups, while owning families of large Korean business groups still directly control a large share of group stocks. Another difference is that *keiretsus* generally have powerful in-house banks, while *chaebols* have been heavily dependent on outside financial sources. Finally, the Japanese group trading companies have multiple functions, while the Korean group trading companies have served mainly as exporting agencies.

In terms of the internal organizational structure of Japanese and Korean companies, they do share some noteworthy similarities. Individual employees belong to sections, which in turn belong to departments. On top of the departments are directors. Section managers in Japanese are called *kacho* and department managers are called *bucho*; the Koreans use the exact same Chinese characters for these two titles, i.e. *kwajang* and *bujang*. At higher levels, the Japanese and Koreans also use the same Chinese characters to describe various titles. For the managing director, the Japanese use *joumu* while the Koreans used *junmu*; and the Japanese term for senior managing director is *senmu* while the Koreans use *sangmu*. At the highest levels, Chinese characters are again used for the titles of president (pronounced *sha-cho* in Japanese and *shajang* in Korean) and chairman (*kai-cho* in Japanese and *huijang* in Korean).

Nevertheless, the authority of Korean companies is much more centralized than that of their Japanese counterparts. Korean companies normally have "taller" organizational structure and are also much more functionally formalized. A similar part of the formal structure seems to lie in individual jobs, which are not quite formally structured. Both the Japanese and Koreans prefer some flexibility in job description and specifications. In terms of informal structure, professional managers in Japanese companies generally enjoy more authority than their Korean counterparts with regard to the members of the owning family. Also, they seem to be more cohesive as a group due to the fact that over 90 percent of Japanese executives are internally promoted. In contrast, a substantial number of

Korean professional managers (about 30 to 40 percent) are recruited from outside to meet the need for rapid growth in large Korean business groups.

COMPARATIVE MANAGERIAL PROCESSES

Both Japanese and Korean companies have powerful CEOs, but Korean business leaders are more authoritarian. The Korean managerial system is more top-down than the combined top-down and bottom-up style of the Japanese system. The mutual sense of obligation in Japanese companies is strong while the obligation in Korean companies is more from employees to employers. The loyalty of Korean employees is directed more toward an individual than to an organization. Even for the similar process of informal consensus formation (Korean *sajeonhyupui*, Japanese *nemawashi*), the Korean bosses seem to be more authoritarian than the Japanese, whereas Japanese managers actively seek consultations from various groups within their organizations before making decisions. Relatively speaking, they also spend more time in collecting and disseminating information.

In terms of motivation, both Japanese and Korean employees seem to put more emphasis on extrinsic factors such as job security, work conditions, and wages than on intrinsic factors like creativity and achievement. Often, creativity and achievement are accomplished in the form of group efforts and accredited to the group. They are also very responsive to non-monetary rewards, which often help consolidate and promote their overall positions within the group. Furthermore, there is a shift in both countries toward combining extrinsic and intrinsic factors. In general, Korean employees are more geared toward individual creativity and achievement, as Koreans are much more individualistic than the Japanese.

Japanese and Koreans are good at informal communication, but tend to be reluctant in expressing their views openly on formal occasions, especially when their opinions conflict with those of their superiors or colleagues. Both the Japanese and Koreans are reluctant to convey bad news in a direct manner and carefully avoid open interpersonal conflicts. Japanese and Korean managers and employees pay careful attention to developing informal channels for communication. Business communication in Korea is more along vertical hierarchies and horizontal interdepartmental communication is relatively poor; horizontal interdepartmental communication in Japan is well developed.

COMPARATIVE HUMAN RESOURCES MANAGEMENT

In the area of human resource management, the Japanese and Koreans again have some notable similarities and differences. Age and sex, for example, are very important factors in human resource management of both Japanese and Korean companies. Seniority has considerably influenced the consideration of promotion and reward, though both are experiencing similar pressures to increase the weight of performance in promotion. There are also similar discriminatory attitudes toward female employees in both Japanese and Korean companies. Performance appraisal, which is often compromised by the need to save face and keep harmony, also hampers the implementation of promotion based on ability and contributions.

Owing to Confucian influences, both Japanese and Korean companies have attached great importance to human resources development and employee training. Both make their recruitment of managerial trainees from prestigious universities. New recruits in both Japanese and Korean companies must go through intensive training, which not only includes technical cultivation but also the inculcating of company history, corporate spirit, and physical exercise. There is also a strong military influence in managing employee training.

One notable difference in the area of human resource management is the employment system. For those Japanese employees who are recruited on a lifetime employment system, their companies are generally committed to guaranteeing their job security, though this means that the companies have to carry on heavy economic burdens in a business downturn. On the other hand, mid-career job-hopping is rare and morally criticized. These employees are generally obliged or willingly devoted to their companies. Korean companies generally implement a sort of semi-life-employment system. In a business downturn, they feel free to lay off their employees at various levels, while job-hopping, even at senior levels, is not uncommon. Korean employees, though loyal to their companies, nevertheless feel little pressure from society, their companies, colleagues, or themselves to stay when they are offered better jobs in other companies.

Another notable difference lies in trade unionism. The Japanese trade unions are mostly in-house trade unions, which not only represent the interests of the employees but also have the responsibility to protect the interests of the company. Many Japanese executives used to be trade union executives and many Japanese companies provide offices for trade unions. Except for extreme situations, trade union protesting activities are not intended to hurt the interests of the company. On the whole, the influence of the trade union is decreasing in Japan. On the other hand, the Korean version of trade unions has been more militant. Traditionally, the government and management colluded in suppressing trade union activities. In-house trade unions have not become viable in Korea. Since trade unions were allowed to organize their activities freely in the early 1980s, they have been increasingly active in demanding higher wages for Korean workers.

COMPARATIVE COMPETITIVE STRATEGIES

Both Japanese and Korean companies have attached great importance to developing their manufacturing capabilities. Both have started from developing maturity/growth industries and increasing market share and have gradually moved to high-tech industries, though Japanese companies developed much earlier than Korean companies. Japanese and Korean companies are committed to long-term strategic planning and have followed rapid diversification in the course of development. Both have taken advantage of highly financially leveraged strategies to grow, though Japanese companies have been more dependent on in-house banks while many Korean companies have been dependent on outside sources, especially government-related sources. Many Japanese and Korean companies have followed the strategy of creative imitation as a way to absorb foreign technologies, though many of them frequently infringed on intellectual rights.

The Korean concept of *koenchanayo* ("that's good enough") forms a sharp contrast to Japanese *kaizen*, a continually improving process. In Japan, continuous improvement is a way of life and nothing is good enough. Quality can be raised and cost continually reduced. Japanese thoroughness is reflected in the whole process of production from planning to finishing. Good Japanese factories can often trace their product faults back to the design phase and maintain very small rework areas. In contrast, Koreans are much less thorough in the whole process. Korean long-term planning is usually shorter and more general than those of their Japanese counterparts. Many Korean companies prefer quick actions to detailed planning and are dominated by the "go for it first and fix it later" mentality.

SUMMARY

In short, the Japanese and Korean management systems are two of the most dynamic management systems in the world. They have contributed to the development of two of the strongest economies in the world. East Asian cultural traditions, such as Confucianism, and unique historical experiences have exerted powerful influence on the formation of these two management systems. Of the two, the Japanese management is much older and can be traced back to the beginning of the Meiji Restoration in 1868, while the Korean management system has only been developed since the end of the Korean war in 1953. As discussed earlier, the two management systems share many commonalities, but also have significant differences.

By the 1980s, both of them were under increasing pressure for radical change. For example, various problems of heavy governmental involvement, such as corruption, low efficiency and a distorted market, have become targets of criticism. Various measures have been taken by both

Japanese and Korean governments to reform government–business relations. Also, some long-established management practices, such as lifetime employment, seniority promotion and reward, and discrimination toward female employees are under growing pressure to change in order to meet the needs of modernization and internationalization. Nevertheless, the two management styles will retain many of their respective unique practices, which have made tremendous contributions to their competitiveness in the world.

Coping with different management systems

Part IV

Coping with different
management systems

Chapter 17

Understanding Chinese and Japanese negotiating styles

INTRODUCTION

The Chinese and the Japanese both have a well-deserved reputation for being tough negotiators. It has been estimated that for every successful Japanese–American negotiation, there are twenty-five failures, with "cultural differences" often cited as a major responsible factor (Tung 1984: 62–77). Lucian Pye has argued that "for centuries [the Chinese] have known few peers in the subtle art of negotiating" (Pye 1992: 11). They employ many strategies and tactics, and often push relentlessly for further concessions after agreements have been concluded. Although culturally the Chinese and Japanese are quite different, they do share many similar negotiating methods. However, it should be remembered that despite the obvious difficulties involved, their negotiating tactics are neither unpredictable nor insurmountable.

UNIQUE PERCEPTIONS ON NEGOTIATIONS

The success of doing business in both China and Japan depends heavily on the quality and sometimes quantity of personal relationships. Confucianism left a strong mark on much of East Asian life but it also left a system more in tune with rule by a sagacious man than by dependence on a system of laws. For the Chinese, in particular, contracts are expected to change and promises may be broken; only a strong personal relationship is reliable and often indispensable for the implementation of a contract.

The Chinese believe that as business dealings will always involve unforeseen and possibly difficult problems, the most comprehensive plan is to expect to work out answers for some of the trouble and for the rest one must rely on a network of relationships to find satisfactory solutions. Therefore, the Chinese are more interested in a long-standing sincere commitment to working together than they are in seemingly perfect contract packages that appear to contain no loopholes. A signed contract merely marks the end of the first stage in business dealings, not the final agreement, since who knows what troubles may lie ahead and further efforts may be necessary for a "win–win" outcome. A co-signatory to any contract, therefore, has automatically established himself or herself as a "friend" and one of the fundamental responsibilities of this position is to help troubled friends out (Seligman 1989: 166–167). It is considered not only a matter of face and reputation but of business necessity.

The Japanese are similar in that they too do not like to sign detailed and restrictive contracts. They also view business parameters as changeable and want some degree of flexibility in order to cope with unexpected problems or issues. The concept of *naniwabushi*, in which one is entitled to explain the reasons as to why one cannot implement the contract, allows even the most honorable man in Japan to dishonor a contract if his circumstances change for the worst (March 1988: 22–32). As a rule, the Japanese prefer an arrangement based on sincerity and goodwill, with the strength of this type of contract being based on a greater share of "mutual understanding" and sincerity demonstrated by both sides.

The result, then, necessarily means a much longer process of negotiation than is common in the West, with matters often continuing after the agreement seems final. In fact, since the contract is viewed as more of a preliminary stage, any of the more important and often stickier issues are brought up and presented for negotiation as business progresses. Western businessmen are often unpleasantly surprised to find that after they have signed contracts, their Chinese or Japanese counterparts freely interject matters that require additional negotiation.

This process serves not only as a function of the attitude discussed above, but may also serve as a test of the durability and serious intentions on behalf of the other side. It would be a mistake to view this tactic as malicious or capricious, because for the Chinese and Japanese it is not only a way of doing business but also a way of establishing "friends."

One must also not assume that the Chinese and Japanese do not keep their word. Once the bargain is sealed, they can be expected to uphold their end like anyone else. While the Chinese, for example, may haggle over a technical term or condition here or there they will not, as a rule, simply tear up a contract or refuse to adhere to it. The Japanese always keep a bit of leeway for dealing with unforeseeable changes, but they too honor contracts. The goal is to establish areas of mutual interest and to determine commitment. If the unforeseen should arise, "good faith" comes into play, and judgments based on prior negotiations can be changed. It is at this point where "flexibility" must exist, not merely legal guidelines and contractual obligations.

NEGOTIATING TEAMS

The members of a Chinese negotiating team in investment and trade dealings usually outnumber their foreign counterparts (Pye 1992: 53). Typically, the position of team leader is filled by a general manager or deputy general manager of the Chinese corporation. It is the team leader who coordinates the interests of the Chinese side. Other participants will usually include representatives from the relevant bureaucracies or corporations as well as engineers or technicians specializing in the area under discussion. In the past, it was quite common for a Party official to be available as a supervisor. Increasingly, however, corporate leaders have greater autonomy in carrying out their duties. Chinese negotiating teams always include interpreters, and Chinese lawyers are becoming more involved in negotiating sessions.

The confusion and possibly greatest difficulty in negotiating lies in the fact that very often the real "authorities" on the Chinese side are the officials "behind the negotiators." These people represent different bureaucratic interests that may be tough to analyze. The front-line negotiators are expected to gather information, send out trial balloons and then report results to the authorities who then examine the material and give them more questions. Since there may be a number of these "behind the scenes" authorities, this process can take some time. Therefore, it is important to know who the negotiators are and how they fit into the scheme of authority.

The Japanese also tend to have large negotiating teams, though for somewhat different reasons. The obvious psychological advantage of overwhelming the other side with a sizable team is perhaps one reason. More importantly, however, the Japanese require wider participation within their companies in making important decisions. Representatives from a variety of levels and departments are involved throughout the negotiating process. The Japanese realize that while this method may take a little more time initially, later on, as decisions are implemented, the level of consensus and cooperation is more satisfactory within their system (Otsubo 1986: 29–30). Like the Chinese, the Japanese count heavily on personal relationships and a less legalistic approach, and they do not usually include lawyers on their negotiating teams.

Initial stages of contact will include preparatory discussions. These preliminary discussions, while not of any decision-making importance, none the less, serve an important function in setting the tone for the real work to follow. Both the Chinese and the Japanese are very rank conscious. If the officer sent is of fairly low rank, both the Chinese and Japanese may assume there is a lack of sincerity on the part of the foreign firm or, worse yet, they may be insulted. They could then in turn send a low-ranking official from their side. Not only does this start negotiations badly but it will likely result in a waste of time, as low-ranking officials have very little authority to make decisions.

While there can be no strict rule on the size of a negotiating team, it is advisable to keep the same team members throughout the negotiations. The

Chinese and Japanese tend to resent a constant rotation of people involved in the negotiating process, finding it both disruptive and confusing. As they approach negotiations from the somewhat different perspective discussed earlier, it is not surprising that a change of players can often provide an opportunity for their side to "reinterpret" previous understandings and it may also allow them a position of greater strength based on their own continuity in the proceedings.

Considering the potential length and complexity of a negotiation, as well as the sometimes contradictory style of the Chinese and Japanese, it is helpful to position someone as team leader who has a high degree of patience and an ability to function in an atmosphere of apparent confusion. Both the Chinese and Japanese do not respond well to a gruff or abrupt manner and view a show of temper or the use of abusive language as signs of weakness and lack of control. A team leader should also have an unflappable character, as both the Chinese and Japanese are used to over-whelming their counterparts with flattery. Specialists in the technical areas under discussion should be available as well, and if possible some consultants who know how to get things done in the country. A good interpreter will help to facilitate both language and cultural differences. In addition, once negotiations are under way, arguments often occur about how to phrase contract clauses and language. It is well advised to have an expert understanding in these cases (Seligman 1989: 132–34).

NEGOTIATING PROCESS

In any bargaining situation, and especially one where a good deal of investment is at stake, it is always better to know as much about the Chinese or Japanese partners as possible. Therefore, the time prior to actual negotiations should include as much research as possible on all relevant aspects of the deal. The Asian counterparts will certainly do their homework using, among other sources, their own business networks. This is part of the personal approach mentioned earlier and it would be helpful to note that while they will try to prepare for the strengths and weaknesses coming from the foreign side of the bargaining table, the foreign firm should make the same preparations. Japanese companies, for instance, do a lot of note sharing on the foreign companies they work with and the time put in evaluating these notes can be considerable.

When negotiations actually begin, the Chinese first look to establish areas of agreement and explanations of general principles. This tendency is partly a cultural one since in the East one always tries to avoid or hold off confrontational issues. Beyond cultural formalities, and what may seem to Westerners as a waste of time, the Chinese also hope to achieve other goals during this phase. First, if agreements on basic principles are reached they can later criticize the other side for any perceived transgressions

(Frankenstein 1986: 148–160). Another reason is to have a chance to observe the personalities and negotiating strategies of their foreign counterparts. This is also common for the Japanese, who generally open first meetings with long non-task interactions. This may help provide an environment for developing personal relationship or positive *shinyo* (gut feelings). For many Japanese, this *shinyo* constitutes what makes the business deals go or not (Graham and Sano 1993: 548).

Many negotiation books emphasize the importance of focusing more on what unites the parties than on what divides them. Therefore, a sophisticated negotiator should try to expand upon common ground with his counterparts until full agreement is reached. Negotiation is also a process of reaching an agreement somewhere between two resistance points within a possible settlement range. A key part of the preparatory process is to clearly and appropriately define an objective (target point) and a bottom line (resistance point) (Kuhn 1988).

The Chinese obsession with general principles in the initial stage of negotiation, and their willingness to use compromise as a major conflict solution channel, contribute to their ability to focus on areas of potential agreement. However, the Chinese perception of compromise is somewhat different from that in the West. For a Westerner, compromise is generally regarded as horse-trading; it is not a win–win but a half win–half lose solution. The Chinese, however, tend to set high opening positions, then move to a compromise position, playing up the idea that when all is said and done the common interests of both sides will have been recognized. Thus, compromise in the Chinese view is represented by shared goals and is thereby an optimal solution. A common mistake that Western negotiators make is to set the resistance point too close to the target point, thus retaining very little maneuverability (Kirkbride and Tang 1990: 2–3).

Interestingly, the Japanese are quite different from the Chinese in their approach on compromise. The Japanese place great stock on the appearance of harmony. Therefore, an aggressive unwillingness to compromise would not be appreciated. However, there is also the Japanese perception that the party which makes the first concession is the weaker one, since it appears to be an admittance that that side needs the deal more. When the Japanese realize that they are in a position where compromise or concession is necessary, they will "apparently" sacrifice graciously in order to promote goodwill. In other words, there may be more in these maneuvers than the surface harmony would indicate, but in any case perception of one's position in the deal is always an issue.

As a rule, the Japanese do not like to make padded offers, or *banana no tataki uri* (the banana sale approach), as they regard this practice as insincere. In fact, one of the most common Japanese complaints against the Americans and the Chinese is that they can adjust their offers closer to reality after having spent hours to justify these offers. Although the

Japanese occasionally make padded offers overseas, they tend not to do so among themselves (March 1988: 135).

It is always difficult to tell exactly when negotiations have passed from the discussion stage into the finalizing stage. The East Asians, generally speaking, are quite adept at switching from one stage to the other. As this takes place there are some implicit signs. The East Asians usually begin to specify very concrete issues at this stage, some of which were previously postponed. Hard bargains on prices are struck. In spite of earlier harping on the goals of negotiations, some compromise is usually worked out at this stage. Earlier discussed problems that had appeared unsolvable may take an unexpected turn. In general, the East Asians prefer to make concessions at the end of a negotiation, while Westerners are used to dealing with a complex negotiation sequentially, solving issues one by one (Graham and Herberger 1983: 164).

In spite of the differences between the Chinese and the Japanese approach on compromises, both like to include informal discussions as part of the substantive negotiations. This means that bargaining may well extend outside the immediate negotiating room. Social activities are used to cultivate relationships. Casual talks may be purposefully pursued with the goal of figuring out whether and how much concession should be made. Third parties may be actively involved and inside information vigorously explored. These social functions can sometimes greatly contribute to the success or failure of a negotiation (Bond 1991: 87–88).

COMPARATIVE CHINESE AND JAPANESE NEGOTIATING TACTICS

The Chinese and Japanese use a variety of negotiating tactics. While they share some tactics, they do have some notable differences. It is important for a Westerner to know these similarities and differences, many of which have been widely discussed by Lucian Pye and other authors. Scott D. Seligman (1989: 141–147) has summarized several major tactics the Chinese often use during negotiations including, among others:

1 *Controlling the location and schedule*: the Chinese prefer to have major negotiating sessions take place in China for several reasons. The Chinese have a long tradition of making "foreign devils" look like supplicants, hoping for favor and concessions from the Middle Kingdom. In this way, they not only feel psychologically superior, but are also in a very advantageous position. Time is on their side, since every day a Westerner spends in China is both costly and stressful. They can test whether their counterpart's position is as firm as it appears and determine where the bottom line really is.

2 *Utilizing vulnerabilities*: one strategy that the Chinese often employ is to

identify areas of vulnerability either in a Westerner's position or in his personality. Any of his traits can be fair game for manipulation. For example, if a Westerner is susceptible to flattery, they will lavish all sorts of praise on him or, to use a Chinese phrase, "give him a big hat to wear," before manipulating him into accepting their terms. If they feel that a Westerner is under strong pressure to return home with a signed agreement, they will accordingly raise the terms that are often difficult to accept, as they know that he will not want to be responsible for failure. Good Chinese negotiators will not only use the vulnerabilities of the foreign side, but also their own. They may try to get a Westerner to understand their problems first and then push him for a concession.

3 *Creating shame*: brought up in a "shame culture," the Chinese are dexterous in digging up historical or political topics to put their counterparts to shame. The Chinese are also meticulous note-takers. Anything discussed in or out of the negotiating room will be recorded. They think it is fair to use somebody's own words to shame him. If they caught something their counterpart once said that is in conflict with his current position, they will relentlessly put him to shame. If a foreign counterpart has used an "unfriendly remark" or violated the principles established in the initial stage, the Chinese will try to utilize the obvious transgression to embarrass him into doing things their way.

4 *Exhuming old issues*: foreign negotiators often complain about the Chinese attempt to revisit problems that have supposedly been settled. When Chinese negotiators mention these issues, the immediate impression of their foreign partners is that the Chinese must have made a mistake as the problems have clearly been settled. In fact, they themselves are more likely to be mistaken in believing so. The Chinese will not hesitate to readdress issues in which they did not get all they wanted. This may occur at any time, even after negotiations are officially over. Like many of the other ploys, this one is sometimes used for getting additional concessions. When a foreign company finally sees the hope of success after protracted negotiations, they will, in the Chinese view, be more flexible with some old issues.

5 *Manipulating expectations*: negotiations may take months and years. When the Chinese finally decide to push for a project, they often express a strong sense of urgency. This ploy frequently proves useful for them, as it raises expectations to such a level that foreign negotiators will be willing to make concessions in order to take advantage of the opportunity. To be more effective, the Chinese deliberately lower others' expectations or keep their expectations low. When it is time for a deal, they can make foreign counterparts grateful by showing them how much effort they have contributed to the success of the deal, and the foreigners are expected to do the same.

It should be mentioned that some of the tactics discussed above are also used by the Japanese to varying degrees. The Japanese, for example, are very capable of manipulating place and time to their advantage. If a deadline is revealed, they will, when necessary, manipulate the time to strike a good deal. The Japanese, also brought up in a shame culture, do not hesitate to instill shame or give high-sounding moral preaching (Graham and Yoshihiro 1984: 68–78).

However, there are some distinctive Japanese tactics that the Chinese would not feel comfortable using. For example, once a firm position is achieved, the Japanese strongly commit themselves to it and give little room for bargaining and making concessions. Such a persistent tactic is characterized by Michael Blaker as "push, push, and push," just like "bulldozing." The Japanese can continually reiterate the same offer, with hardly any variation. This has a lot to do with their strong sense of self-respect and the belief that they are correct, and is also related to their views on negotiating discussed earlier (Blaker 1977).

Another major difference is that the Japanese utilize long moments of silence during meetings, silence that sometimes unnerves Americans. For the Japanese, "silence is golden," which can keep one out of trouble. When there is a dilemma, the Japanese do not feel uncomfortable remaining silent for a long time (Hall 1987: 118). This conforms to the Japanese concepts on *tatemae* and *honne*. *Tatemae* means "front face" which refers to the principles of polite behavior; *honne* means substance involving one's personal feelings which are rarely divulged. In most cases, Japanese negotiators will try their utmost to avoid open conflict in order to save face. In contrast, the Chinese, who also care about face and showing a smooth surface, may occasionally pretend anger in order to obtain the deal (Seligman 1989: 145–146).

It should be noted that many of the tactics discussed above are not exclusively Oriental. Many of them occur frequently during negotiations among Westerners. The differences are that the Orientals are particularly adept and natural in using them, and one can surmise that many of these tactics are used routinely in day-to-day dealings in Oriental societies and are not considered so much devious or dishonest as they are considered clever and admirable. The bluntness, particularly of Americans, is quite unlike the subtle use of mind games by the Chinese, for instance. As Sun Tzu, the most famous Chinese strategist once said, "Know yourself, know your enemy; one hundred battles, one hundred victories." This maxim is not only quoted, it is the way the Chinese have lived, along with Confucian ethics and other non-Western modes of thought, for thousands of years. Curiously, many of these attitudes lend themselves very well to the art of business negotiations (Chu 1991).

CONFLICT MANAGEMENT

The Confucian tradition in East Asian society is both historical as well as a basis for the rules of conduct today. A major goal of Confucianism is to achieve and maintain social harmony, and one way of accomplishing this is to consider the position of others and learn how to compromise. The ideas of "appearance is more important than truth" and "keep a smooth surface on the sea of life" are guidelines for behavior that extend from home and family to international business and politics (Reeder 1987: 69–75). It is, therefore, a custom and value that social interaction should be conducted in such a manner that nobody loses "face" and aggressive confrontation is generally avoided (Hofstede and Bond 1988: 8). In the West, an argumentative style may be admired, but in China and Japan this would be viewed as a loss of control and bad manners. Heated disputes and impatience are ineffective in negotiation with East Asians, as these behaviors show a high degree of weakness. Even in negotiations carried out between two Western parties, unnecessary confrontations tend to hinder rather than help achieve goals (Pruitt 1981). This confrontational attitude is even less useful in China or Japan.

If a confrontational situation does arise, Western businessmen, especially Americans, tend to look to legal solutions. The Chinese and, perhaps more so, the Japanese prefer not to use this course of action when serious differences come up. This is due much less to any fear of material loss that might result than it is due to the loss of face and reputation that such actions signify. If both sides are forced to settle problems in the courts or through arbitration, it indicates to everyone that they were unable to deal with each other in a civilized manner, which is considered a gross failure in the East. Both sides would be blamed for the breakdown in the relationship and any future business could be endangered if one's reputation is characterized by an inability to deal civilly with one's East Asian counterparts (Becker 1986: 75–92). To facilitate a private solution to their conflicts, a mutually respected third party is often used to mediate between the two parties.

If disputes cannot be solved or if for some other reason both sides agree to terminate negotiations, care should be taken to allow the termination to be smooth and blame-free. A Western businessman who has had negotiation problems in the past with his Asian partners can hardly hope to do future business with them. Also, as mentioned earlier, reputation is terribly important to both the Chinese and Japanese and, as there are few secrets among "old friends," entrance into the East Asian market may be blocked due to a poorly executed exit in the past. Of course, then, part of the graceful finish to end negotiation should be the effort to keep disputes private and not allow them to contribute to a loss of "face," either one's own or one's counterparts. Sometimes failed negotiations are described as a temporary halt in the proceedings that may later resume when circumstances allow.

SUMMARY/CONCLUSION

This chapter has reviewed the unique negotiation perceptions of the Chinese and Japanese as relations-orientated rather than contract-orientated. While their negotiating teams are normally larger than their Western partners, the negotiating processes of the Chinese and Japanese are quite different from each other. Where the Chinese expect to start high and work down, the Japanese are more like Westerners and begin at a point closer to where they expect to settle. Therefore, the Japanese are less likely than the Chinese to compromise (which is seen by the Japanese as a defeat), while the Chinese see compromise as both necessary and expected. The Japanese also have a somewhat different decision-making process than the Chinese; both tend to involve lots of people, but the Chinese have more of a hierarchical approach while the Japanese tend to look for consensus. Perhaps partly as a reflection of this, the Japanese are more inclined to set a very polite tone to the proceedings whereas the Chinese are not likely to be quite so formal.

Although East Asians are quite adept at business negotiation, their tactics can backfire. There is a fine line, for instance, between a solid outcome due to time-consuming tactics meant to build trust and under-standing, and a sheer waste of time that can result in the loss of business due to the unwillingness of their counterparts to delay any longer. More-over, an emphasis on saving "face" can lead to confusion and disputes due to an inability to express clearly an opinion or position.

It is always more difficult to understand or estimate one's counterpart when there are language and cultural barriers to overcome. The advantages that the East Asians have in negotiating tactics are largely based on the fact that Westerners are inclined bluntly to lay their cards on the table, or are unable to camouflage their personal quirks or desires. East Asians, on the other hand, practice self-control and patience every day. At the negotiating table, these practices often help the Chinese and Japanese, while they serve to confuse and frustrate Western negotiators. However, if the basic rules are kept in mind, the pitfalls can be counteracted.

The basic rules for negotiating successfully with the Chinese and Japanese are these. (1) Expect that negotiations will take time and be patient. Generally the East Asians will not be rushed and the foreign position will be weakened by attempting to do otherwise. (2) Prepare ahead of time by knowing as much about the other party as possible, including who are the key decision-makers and who are the "old friends" that are capable of influencing decisions. (3) Understand the need for flexibility in both the signing of a contract and the implementation of the contract. This can mutually benefit both parties. (4) Leave room to maneuver and expect, particularly with the Chinese, that compromise is the rule rather than the exception. (5) Expect East Asian negotiators to use a variety of tactics in order to accomplish a successful deal. The East Asians usually look for long-term relationships as much as they hope to maximize their profit, and the definition of profit is seldom seen as a one-time outcome. (6) Avoid anger or the display of temper and avoid the use of litigation to settle disputes. Rather than appearing tough and in charge there is the risk of jeopardizing both company reputation and future business in East Asia as well. (7) If negotiations fail, leave open the possibility of future negotiation. If this deal doesn't make it, at least contacts have been established and, when other opportunities arise, those with whom the East Asians are familiar will have an advantage over unknown competitors. There is an old saying in China, which is equally applicable in the West, which states "from an exchange of blows, friendship grows." Perhaps another piece of advice could be: when old friends get together everyone benefits.

QUESTIONS FOR DISCUSSION

1 What are the unique Chinese and Japanese negotiation tactics and their implications to the negotiating process?
2 Why do the Japanese tend to have larger negotiation teams than their Western counterparts?
3 In what way do the Japanese views on concessions differ from those of the Chinese?
4 Of the Japanese and Chinese negotiating tactics discussed in this chapter, which ones do you think would be the most difficult to deal with based on your experiences?
5 In the case of a failed negotiation, what would be the best way to terminate the process?

FURTHER READING

Becker, Carl B. (1986) "Reasons for the Lack of Argumentation and Debate in the Far East," *International Journal of Inter-Cultural Relations*: 10.
Blaker, Michael (1977) "Probe, Push and Panic: The Japanese Tactical Style in International Negotiations," in Robert Scalapino (ed.), *The Foreign Policy of Modern Japan*, Berkeley, Calif.: University of California Press, pp. 55–103.
Bond, Michael Harris (1991) *Beyond The Chinese Face: Insights from Psychology*, Hong Kong: Oxford University Press.
Chu, Chin-ning (1991) *The Asian Mind Game*, New York: Maxwell Macmillan International.
Frankenstein, John (1986) "Trends in Chinese Business Practice: Changes in the Beijing Wind," *California Management Review*, 29(1): 148–160.

Graham, John L. and Roy Herberger (1983) "Negotiators Abroad – Don't Shoot from the Hip," *Harvard Business Review* (July–August): 160–168.

Graham, John L. and Yoshihiro Sano (1984) *Smart Bargaining: Doing Business with the Japanese*, Cambridge, Mass.: Ballinger.

—— (1993) "The Japanese Negotiation Style," in Roy J. Lewicki *et al.* (eds), *Negotiation: Readings, Exercises and Cases*, Homewood, Ill.: Irwin, pp. 541–552.

Hall, Edward T. (1987) *Hidden Differences: Doing Business*, New York: Doubleday.

Hofstede, Geert and Michael Harris Bond (1988) "The Confucian Connections: From Cultural Roots to Economic Growth," *Organizational Dynamics* 16(4) (Spring): 5–21.

Kirkbride, Paul S. and Sara F.Y. Tang (1990) "Negotiation: Lessons from Behind the Bamboo Curtain," *Journal of General Management* 16(1) (Autumn): 1–13.

Kuhn, Robert (1988) *Deal Maker: All the Negotiating Skills and Secrets You Need*, New York: Wiley.

March, Robert M. (1988) *The Japanese Negotiator: Subtlety and Strategy Beyond Western Logic*, New York: Kodansha International.

Otsubo, Mayumi (1986) "A Guide to Japanese Business Practice," *California Management Review* 28(3) (Spring): 28–42.

Pruitt, Dean (1981) *Negotiating Behavior*, New York: Academic Press.

Pye, Lucian (1982) *Chinese Commercial Negotiating Style*, New York: Oelgeschleger, Gunn and Hain.

Reeder, John A. (1987) "When West Meets East: Cultural Aspects of Doing Business in Asia," *Business Horizon* (January–February): 69–75.

Seligman, Scott D. (1989) *Dealing with the Chinese*, New York: Warner Books.

Tung, Rosalie L. (1984) "How to Negotiate with the Japanese," *California Management Review* 26(4) (Summer): 62–77.

Chapter 18

Comparing Japanese general trading companies and Chinese foreign trade companies

INTRODUCTION

Japanese general trading companies (GTCs or *sogo shosha*) have received much attention in the postwar period because since the Meiji Reform they are considered to have greatly contributed to the rapid industrialization of the Japanese economy. Moreover, the world cannot overlook the contribution that the Japanese GTCs made in the construction of Japan's postwar economy, as well as in the development of its international competitiveness. The fact that the Japanese GTCs have served as an engine of Japan's rapid economic growth throughout its history has led many to wonder if this economic mechanism could be successfully developed elsewhere. A number of developing countries, such as Korea, Brazil, Mexico and the Philippines, have tried to start their own GTCs, though only Korea has been successful.

On the other hand, China's reform and open-door policy since 1979 have greatly enhanced the role of foreign trade in its national economy. The Maoist legacy of economic self-reliance has already largely been forsaken. In the ten years from 1979 to 1989, the ratio of China's foreign trade to its GNP tripled from less than 10 percent in the pre-reform years to nearly 30 percent of the GNP in 1989. By the early 1990s, China's trade volume was larger than all but a dozen advanced industrial nations. Throughout the 1980s, the Chinese government vigorously pushed for the reform of its trade system, which used to be monopolized by a dozen or so national foreign trade corporations (FTCs). As a result, these trade dinosaurs have been forced to transform themselves, with many advocating the Japanese GTCs as their role model.

The Japanese GTCs and Chinese FTCs do share some notable similarities but also have remarkable differences in their courses of development and business operations. Since the early 1980s, both have been under growing pressure to adjust to the changes in their business environment. A comparative study of their historical evolution and current trends of development would be conducive to a better understanding of the changing comparative advantages of these two large foreign trade organizations and their positions in the years to come. Another thrust of this study will be focused on the analysis of the feasibility of the Japanese GTCs as a potential role model for Chinese FTCs in the course of transformation.

HISTORICAL COMPARISONS

Both the Japanese GTCs and the Chinese FTCs are large trading organizations which are involved in a great variety of investments and businesses. In their initial formation both had close relationships with their respective governments, which wanted to put foreign trade back into the hands of their own nationals; this has led to their rapid growth and monopolistic tendencies. Nevertheless, as Japan has been a market-orientated economy and China had been, until recently, a planned economy, the Japanese GTCs and Chinese FTCs, from the very beginning, were also fundamentally different from each other.

The historical evolutions of the Japanese GTCs and their functions

There are now approximately 4,000 trading companies in Japan, with over 9,000 branch offices around the world. There are four categories of trading companies in Japan: the first includes the big multinational trading companies that handle a great variety of products and materials and provide a wide range of services. Though not monopolies, they each have monopolistic influences in certain businesses. This group mainly includes the nine largest general trading companies, which account for some 60 percent of the country's imports, 50 percent of the exports, and 20 percent of the domestic wholesale trade. They are Mitsubishi Shoji, Mitsui Bussan, Marubeni-Iida, Itochu, Nossho-Iwai, Sumitomo Shoji, Tomen, Nichimen, and Kanematsu-Gosho. If the next 20 largest trading companies are added, these 29 firms together control about 80 percent of the country's importing and 70 percent of its exporting.

The following three categories are much smaller and narrower in their businesses, and accordingly do not have any monopolistic influences in their areas. The second category is the large-scale specialized trade company, which is not very different from the import–export company in the West. These special trading companies are typically much smaller than the GTCs and are specialized in one area. For example, Chori, Itoman, Shinko Sangyo, Ichida, Sankyo Seiko, and Takashima are focused on textiles; Toshoku, Meiji Shoji, and Nozaki Sangyo are focused on food; Osaka Kozai, Toyoda Tsusho, Shinko Shoji, Okura Shoji, Seiko Sangyo, Tokyo Sangyo, Yuasa Kanamano, Kano Tekko, and Kobayashi Sangyo are specialized in machinery and metals. The third type is the window trading company, which mainly serve specific manufacturers such as Nissan Motor's Nissan

Sales Company. The last group consists of the wholesale companies, which are very important in the domestic market (De Mente, 1991: 56–58).

The GTCs originally were started during the post-Meiji Restoration period, when the government acted to recover the rights of trade from foreigners. They were developed as offshoots of the major industrial groups, such as Mitsui and Mitsubishi, and provided invaluable service as the marketing arm of the manufacturing companies that formed the groups. The member manufacturing companies relied on the trading companies with which they were affiliated, not only to develop markets but also to purchase goods from them. By representing these member companies, the GTCs took on all the risks and financial responsibilities related to the businesses. In the traditional Japanese business concept, marketing was an entirely separate function from the really important manufacturing role of a Japanese company (Yonekawa 1990: 92–169).

Before 1945, all the large general trading companies, with the exception of Mitsui and Mitsubishi, tended to specialize in certain lines. In prewar years, the general trading companies had a fairly high profit margin and accumulated great wealth. After the Second World War, the GTCs were forced to dissolve under the anti-*zaibatsu* policy of the American Occupation. However, the prohibitive policies against monopolies began to relax after the signing of the Peace Treaty in 1951. Japan revised its anti-monopoly laws in 1953, thus opening the way for the reformation of the GTCs and *keiretsu* groups under the names of the old *zaibatsus* – though such groups were less organized, with no holding companies controlling stocks.

The postwar period of rapid economic growth in Japan coincided with the golden era of the GTCs. First, the export-expansion policy of Japan provided a solid base for the development of the GTCs, which became the key beneficiaries of favorite Japanese governmental policies. Second, the structural changes of Japanese industries and exports also facilitated the growth of the GTCs. The development of the heavy and chemical industries in the 1950s and the 1960s required the import of large quantities of energy and raw materials and export of the products of these industries. As these products were either labor-intensive or capital-intensive with relatively low technology, the GTCs could handle their export with relative ease. Third, the continued high growth of Japan's economy from 1956 to 1973, combined with the low interest rates, low exchange rates, and low oil prices during the same period, provided a very propitious environment for the development of the FTCs.

Unlike their prewar predecessors, the postwar GTCs were diversified and traded with a much lower margin. Together, they had a number of general functions (Yoshino and Lifson 1986: 57–78). The first one was trade – especially the import of raw materials and energy, as well as the export of manufactured products of the heavy and chemical industries. They also actively operated in third country trade. As mentioned earlier the nine largest GTCs had dominated Japan's export and import in the early 1980s.

The second one was to finance trade, with their own money or the money they borrowed from banks at low interest rates. The GTCs had close relationships both with in-house banks and other commercial banks. They provided finance for manufacturers in return for an export agency and for importers' access to the market. By so doing, they assumed a great deal of financial risk. In a sense, the GTCs could be considered finance companies.

The third was information collection. GTCs had offices all over the world, which transmitted information equivalent to 6,000 pages of the *New York Times* daily. Marubeni, for example, had more than 150 offices around the world, linked by leased channels to three switching centers in Tokyo, New York and Brussels. Competitive bids for large public tenders could be offered in a matter of hours. Exchange rate variations could be accommodated almost as soon as they take place.

The fourth general function was overseas investment. By the early 1980s, the GTC's overseas investment constituted one-third of Japan's overseas investment. For investment in the developing countries, the GTCs basically channeled funds from domestic sources. For investment in the developed countries, the GTCs actively sought international sources, such as borrowing from international banks, issuing bonds, etc. Major investments were in the development of natural resources, infrastructure construction, and manufacturing industries. However, those investments tended to be made more as a supplement to trade activities than as an effort for direct profits.

The development of the Chinese FTCs and their functions

China's trading system was modeled after the Soviet system in the early 1950s (Hsiao 1977: 71–90). The communist regime took over the foreign trade corporations, which had played a significant role in the foreign trade of nationalist China. The Ministry of Foreign Trade, created in 1952, exercised control of foreign trade through a dozen Chinese national foreign trade companies (FTCs) that specialized in trade in defined product areas. The number rose and fell over the following two decades before reform was introduced in the late 1970s. These huge foreign trade monopolies had branches throughout the whole country.

These companies included ARTCHINA (China National Arts and Crafts Import and Export Corp.), CEROILFOOD (China National Cereals, Oils, and Foodstuffs Import and Export Corp.), CHINAPACK (China National Commodities Packaging Import and Export Corp.), CHINATEX (China National Textile Import and Export Corp.), CHINATUSHU (China National Native Produce and Animal By-Products Import and Export Corp.), COMPLANT (China National Complete Plant Export Corp.), EQUIPEX (China National Machinery and Equipment Import and Export Corp.),

INDUSTRY (China National Light Industrial Products Import and Export Corp.), INSTRIMIX (China National Instruments Import and Export Corp.), MACHIMPEX (China National Machinery Import and Export Corp.), MINMETALS (China National Metals and Minerals Import and Export Corp.), PUBIPORT (China National Publications Import Corp.), SINOCHEM (China National Chemicals Import and Export Corp.), and TECHIMPORT (China National Technical Import Corp.) (Wik 1984: 105–144).

All trade transactions with China were conducted by these national FTCs. They were responsible for implementing the state's foreign trade plan. They were put in an absolute trade monopoly position, acting as agents for manufacturing units and end-user organizations in China. The structure of the FTCs generally paralleled China's industrial production ministries. For example, the SINOCHEM was authorized to handle goods produced by the Ministry of Chemical Industry. The CHINATEX monopolized the import and export of goods produced by the Ministry of Textile Industry. Neither import nor export transactions could be concluded without the participation of the FTCs.

The FTCs did not operate on the basis of "profit motive," but were directed by the foreign trade plan co-developed by the Ministry of Foreign Trade and the State Planning Commission. This plan was based on the surpluses and shortfalls identified in the formulation of the national Five-Year Plans, though the FTCs furnished specific planning inputs for imports and exports within their respective areas of responsibility. While some trade was undertaken to achieve specific foreign policy objectives, the basic motivation was to fulfill the requirement of generating sufficient foreign exchange to finance imports of strategic and technological goods indispensable for the implementation of key projects laid out in the national economic plans.

By world standards, the national FTCs were colossal trading bureaucracies with an average annual turnover of almost $2 billion each in the 1970s. Based on the volume of import and export of specific commodities, China National Cereals, Oils, and Foodstuffs Import and Export Corporation had for a long time maintained the dominant position among all the national FTCs with a turnover of approximately $3 billion per year throughout the 1970s. The national FTCs conducted all negotiations with foreign trading partners; contracts were signed in the name of the FTCs or one of their branches involved in the transaction. Technical specialists, suppliers and end-users were also involved, but they only played secondary roles in the negotiations. Prior to trade reform, these national FTCs did not own any assets outside China nor did they maintain any offices abroad, though they did utilize agents in Hong Kong and Macao.

Theoretically, a foreign trade corporation was not a consuming or producing organization, but an official middleman in the planned economy.

Therefore, it did not possess fixed production-related assets, like factories or machines. The only asset related to its trading activities was working capital that was allocated by the state according to a plan. As with all other state-owned enterprises at that time, this working capital was controlled by the People's Bank of China. In trade with socialist countries, all payments, clearing accounts, and exchange quotations were managed by the People's Bank of China. In business with non-socialist countries, the Bank of China served as the principal foreign exchange agent.

The trade activities of the FTCs were also supported by the Chinese People's Insurance Company, the China Council for the Promotion of International Trade (CCPIT), and the semiannual Guangdong Export Commodities Fair. The Chinese People's Insurance Company was a super-monopoly that provided all the insurance needed for China's international trade. The CCPIT performed duties similar to those of the Chamber of International Commerce in other countries and was directed by officials from the Ministry of Foreign Trade, Ministry of Foreign Affairs, and from the FTCs. The Guangzhou Export Commodities Fair, co-sponsored by all the FTCs, was the main channel for China's exports and was held in the Spring and Fall every year. Except for some very minor readjustments, this organizational and managerial structure underwent no major changes from 1956 to 1978.

Comparative assessments of GTCs and FTCs

Both Japanese GTCs and Chinese FTCs were the products of specific historical conditions and the governmental policies of their countries that tried to wrench control of trade from the hands of foreign companies. This goal was achieved quickly and efficiently in both countries. With the support of the state, the GTCs and FTCs also achieved different degrees of monopoly in trade. However, the two countries followed very different trade policies and trade practices, which had far-reaching influences on the development of the GTCs and the FTCs. The postwar Japanese government had pushed for export expansion while China, until the early 1980s, mainly exercised import substitution. The two countries had also operated in entirely different economic systems. Japan followed a market economy while China practiced a rigidly planned economic system. Therefore, the two types of trade dinosaurs performed very different roles in their respective national economies and maintained different business operations.

With their size, financial strength, information network, and large pool of talent, the GTCs quickly emerged as fierce competitors in the world market. In spite of their monopolistic role in Japan's foreign trade, the GTCs made major contributions to the rapid economic development of the postwar Japanese economy. First, they helped insure the steady supply of grain, raw materials and energy, and facilitated the import of various kinds of production equipment. Second, they developed overseas resources and supported the development of the heavy and chemical industries in Japan. Third, they opened up overseas markets for export-orientated Japanese enterprises, thereby helping to maintain continued high economic growth. Fourth, they improved Japan's balance of imports and exports. Fifth, they served as middlemen for large enterprises and financial institutions and provided technical and financial support for mid and small-sized enterprises. Finally, as pioneers of internationalization, they provided many useful experiences and created favorable conditions for the internationalization of many manufacturing enterprises.

In contrast, the FTCs in China were much less dynamic and their roles in the development of the Chinese national economy were much less positive. First, as bureaucratic institutions, the FTCs were protected monopolies of China's foreign trade. They did not have to compete with any companies either domestically or internationally for business. With the mandate to trade from the government, they virtually suffocated any trade-promoting initiatives and competition. Second, the FTCs were over-centralized, with their headquarters dominating specialized businesses assigned by the government. Their business was not diversified and was restricted only to trade in their specialized areas, which resulted in their lack of vitality. Third, the FTCs were not created to promote China's foreign trade, but rather to secure governmental control over China's foreign trade. Therefore, they served to seal China off from international competition instead of encouraging and facilitating Chinese exports.

NEW TRENDS IN COMPARISON

The 1980s witnessed major changes in the business strategies and operations of both the Japanese GTCs and the Chinese FTCs. These changes were necessitated by the changing environment in which they operated. For the GTCs, the structural change of the related industries was the main factor, such as the rise in importance of service and technology-intensive industries and the slowdown of Japanese economic development. For the FTCs, the driving force for change was the economic reform beginning in 1979, which has significantly weakened the foundation of the FTCs as China's foreign trade monopoly. The new challenges have not only exerted pressure for change but also provided new opportunities for changes to develop.

Challenges and changes of the Japanese GTCs in the 1980s

As shown earlier, the GTCs' worldwide operations are deeply rooted in the Japanese economy. In fact, the GTCs have served as primary marketers, purchasing agents, and financiers for a number of Japan's industries in domestic as well as international markets. By the early 1970s, these industries had already begun to show signs of maturity when the domestic demand for their products became saturated. In addition, a dramatic rise in energy prices in the 1970s put Japan in an unfavorably competitive position in these industries, enhancing the necessity to restructure the Japanese economy away from the smokestack industries to more knowledge-based industries.

Also during the 1970s, Japan began to encounter competitive challenges in labor and capital-intensive industries, including steel and chemicals. These have traditionally been the areas in which the GTCs have had considerable strength. The slowdown in the domestic economic growth in the 1970s put additional pressure on the GTCs because the economic logic of the GTCs has been built around a high rate of capacity utilization, such as a fast turnover of traded products and an ever-increasing volume of traded goods. The slow economic growth has significantly weakened the operational strength of the GTCs in these fields. Even worse, a growing number of large manufacturers that had traditionally left their overseas marketing to the GTCs were beginning to develop their own overseas operations.

Therefore, by the early 1980s, all the GTCs were compelled to make major readjustments in their strategies and operations (Yoshino and Lifson 1986: 244–268). The defensive measures they took were to rationalize their operations. These included withdrawing financial support from marginal suppliers, divesting poorly conceived new ventures, and downsizing the company by encouraging early retirement and restricting the number of new managerial recruits. These were followed by the restructuring of nonprofitable businesses and reforming them into independent subsidiaries. This was designed to reduce the burden of the company and thereby force a problem company to become accountable for its performance.

Meanwhile, the GTCs have also begun to adopt a series of more positive steps. First, the GTCs have begun to shift their emphasis to large-scale foreign direct investment in major industries in key countries, such as oil refineries, in an attempt to improve their profitability. This represents a major departure from the long-held investment strategy, in which investment was usually relatively small and regarded only as a supplement to trading activity. Supported by their extensive international networks and their ease of access to financial sources, the GTCs are capable of undertaking large-scale investments to strengthen their leverage in the existing product line or to diversify their sources of income.

Another strategic step is to stress third-country trade, a type of business that does not involve Japan. In the past, third-country trade was usually limited to impromptu responses to opportunistic market situations. Throughout the high-growth period, the GTCs were busy with trade to and from Japan, and hardly had the energy to develop third-country trade. As

Japanese trade has slowed, third-country trade has become increasingly important. It has already accounted for about 15 percent of the GTCs' total sales. The third-country-related ventures have also become popular. The competitive advantage that the GTCs have in third-country trade lies in the fact that they can trade on an incremental cost basis, given their worldwide fixed investment and market coverage.

Other hopeful areas include construction projects, some high-technology products, such as biotechnology, computers and telecommunications, countertrade or barter arrangements, and financial services, such as fund raising in foreign markets, marketing of securities and equipment leasing. Some GTCs are also actively involved in investment in downstream activities like fast-food franchises. Mitsubishi, for example, has taken the lead by becoming partners with the Kentucky Fried Chicken business in Japan. Yojei Mimura, the president of the Mitsubishi Corporation, once said of the functions of a GTC: "the *shosha* locates, buys, ships, insures, finances and helps coordinate all the steps required to bring everything together." The recent diversification of the GTCs has further expanded his definition of the functions of a GTC (Zimmerman 1985: 173).

In spite of these innovations, the main competitive advantage of the GTC remains its close affiliation with a *keiretsu*. Being an integrated member of a large industrial grouping, a GTC can serve the manufacturing companies within the group on the basis of the *giri/on* (duty / obligation) relationship. The member manufacturers are not supposed to violate the *giri* maintained with the GTC that has been promoting their business abroad. The GTC is normally reluctant to give up its control over the overseas business of a member company in the *keiretsu* group. The separation would not occur until after the Presidential Club of the group decides that the relevant company is sufficiently mature to handle its own overseas operation. With such a dogged adherence to outdated prerogatives, the GTCs hope to get the badly needed respite to develop and diversify their operations.

The trade reform of the 1980s and the FTCs

From the early 1980s, the Chinese government fervently advocated foreign trade and pushed for the reform of its foreign trade system. Not only did China's foreign trade rise from 10 percent of GNP before the reform to around 30 percent of GNP by the early 1990s, but also its traditional composition of exports and imports changed. In the late 1980s manufactured goods replaced raw materials as the top export, accounting for two-thirds of the total. Also increasing in prominence in China's exports is merchandise like garments, consumer electronics, office and telecommunication equipment, toys and machinery. With regard to imports, the proportion of capital goods rose rapidly during the 1980s, accounting for more than one-third of the total.

Beginning in 1979, the major Foreign Trade Corporations were directed to decentralize their authorities, turning over much of the import and export operations to the provinces, autonomous regions, and municipalities. In other words, the local FTCs could now conduct direct transactions with foreign firms in the operation of foreign trade, which was never the case before 1979. The new system allowed the FTCs, under the local governments, to retain part of their foreign exchange earnings. The general orientation was to change the old way of doing foreign trade by government departments through bureaucratic directives into market-regulated business operations.

In the early 1980s, new product-centered FTCs were set up under the administration of relevant ministries producing specialized products rather than under the then Ministry of Foreign Trade. For example, the Ministry of Metallurgical Industry established its own foreign trade corporation in 1980 – the China National Metallurgical Import and Export Corporation – which enabled it to bypass MINMETALS. All the industrial ministries established their own trade corporations, including, among the most well-known, the China National Machinery and Equipment Import and Export Corp., the China Electronics Technology Import and Export Corp., the China North Industries Corp., the China Great Wall Industries Corp., and the Xinshidai Co. of China (Lardy 1992: 39–41).

Meanwhile, provincial and big municipality governments were allowed to establish hundreds of foreign trade corporations to handle trade in their own regions. For example, Guangdong, Beijing, and Shanghai established their own foreign trade corporations in 1980. Some major production companies were also granted the right to conduct foreign trade. Among the first group of such companies were Wuhan Iron and Steel Corp., Anshan Iron and Steel Corp., Shoudu Iron and Steel Corp., and the Shanghai Toy Company.

To coordinate the increasingly complicated system, in 1982 the Chinese government established a new Ministry, known as the Ministry of Foreign Economic Relations and Trade (MOFERT), which was a merger of the Ministry of Foreign Trade, the Ministry of Economic Relations with Foreign Countries, the newly established China's Foreign Investment Control Commission and the Import–Export Control Commission. Meanwhile, the scope of the national foreign trade plan was significantly reduced, with the share of planned exports and imports falling to 45 percent and 40 percent respectively by 1988 (Kleinberg 1990: 103–158).

Gradually, the Chinese government reduced the varieties of import and export goods monopolized by the FTCs. In 1984, the FTCs began to implement an import-export agency system, under which they provided services and accepted imports and exports on a commission basis, while the state only played a guiding role (Jian et al. 1991: 40). To retain their share of trade through a new agency system, the FTCs rapidly expanded their network overseas by establishing branch offices in the key trade centers of the world. Under the agency system, domestic prices of both imported and exported commodities were linked to international prices via the exchange rate.

To survive the impact of the radical reform of their monopoly, the FTCs were compelled to diversify their businesses into manufacturing, real estate, and natural resource development while trying to hold on to their traditional domestic and international clients by expanding the scope of trade services. MINMETALS, for example, got heavily involved in large hotel development in China and purchased large-scale commercial real estate in the United States. By the early 1990s they had together invested US$710 million both domestically and overseas and created over 1,000 enterprises.

During the same period, the number of newly emerged trading companies had soared to more than five thousand in 1990, with many of them gaining experience in international trade and establishing their own overseas offices or channels. By the early 1990s, the government became very interested in joining GATT in order to further expand China's export, and therefore to continue liberalizing the Chinese foreign trade system and reduce the remaining monopolies of the national FTCs. The FTCs have already been given clear signals to consolidate and develop their businesses on their own or perish in a much less controlled foreign trade system.

The GTCs, the role model of the FTCs in their reform?

As the FTCs' monopoly over China's foreign trade rapidly fades away, the only way out for them seems to be both diversification and internationalization. There are two major competitive advantages for the Chinese FTCs: first, they are relatively more sophisticated in international dealings, with years of experience and a large pool of talent; second, they have accumulated substantial financial resources in the course of development and have easier access to credit from both domestic and international banks. There are ongoing debates currently in China with regard to which model the FTCs should follow to diversify and internationalize their businesses: one is American multinational corporations (MNCs), the other is Japanese GTCs (Sarathy 1985: 102).

The American MNCs and Japanese GTCs have major differences. American MNCs enjoy relatively strong technological advantages and abundant financial resources, while the Japanese GTCs are relatively weak in technology and financial resources. American MNCs have concentrated their overseas investment mainly on the manufacturing industries of developed countries characterized by sole ownership, majority-stock ownership, and/or large-scale investment. By contrast, the Japanese GTCs have mainly invested in natural resources development and trade-orientated projects in underdeveloped countries with relatively smaller-scale investments characterized by joint ventures, minority stock control or even non-stock control.

In comparison, the Japanese GTCs seem to be a better model for the Chinese FTCs. First of all, the current export composition of China is more suitable to the development of Chinese GTCs. In 1990, the export of primary products took one-third of the export composition, while manufactured products occupied two-thirds of the export composition, 10 percent of which were high-technology products. Such a composition coincides with that of Japan in the high-growth era of the GTCs (Fu 1992: 57).

Second, the Chinese FTCs can follow the example of the Japanese GTCs to forge closer links with manufacturing enterprises and financial institutions. This facilitates diversification of the FTCs and helps promote the integration of manufacturing and trade and consolidates the trade agency system. This is not only very crucial for the survival of the FTCs, but also can help control competition among the Chinese trading firms. The new FTCs' control is not the kind of monopoly that they used to enjoy, as they will have to compete with each other, but will be more like what the GTCs have been doing.

Third, by following the model of the GTCs, the FTCs can help improve the composition of the Chinese export and market structure. With its relatively developed information network, the comparatively easy access to domestic and international funds, and the ability to take risk, a Chinese GTC can help promote the export of Chinese manufactured products and equipment, such as the export of machinery equipment, which normally involves large deals with installment payments.

Finally, the management of Japanese GTCs' overseas investment is also more applicable to that of the FTCs. With relatively limited financial resources and a low technology-level, the FTCs can hardly follow the model of American MNCs in overseas investment. In particular, China's foreign exchange is still very limited; it is unrealistic to channel all of this limited money to overseas investment.

Having said all this, the FTCs cannot simply model themselves after the Japanese GTCs. Owing to historical reasons, the FTCs are much more specialized than the Japanese GTCs in certain products. The FTCs do not have a group attachment, and this serves as the base of their operations. The fragmented and underdeveloped market also poses a major hindrance to the development of Chinese GTCs. Yet, in spite of these incompatibilities, Japanese GTCs are still the best model for the FTCs to follow.

SUMMARY/CONCLUSION

This chapter has traced the historical evolutions of the Japanese GTCs and the Chinese FTCs. A comparative assessment of their functions and roles was made to highlight their differences. On that basis, discussions were made to compare the new trends of development in the 1980s for GTCs and FTCs. Finally, it was concluded that FTCs are rapidly moving toward the model of the GTCs.

As the chapter has shown, the Japanese GTCs and the Chinese FTCs are both trade dinosaurs developed under specific historical circumstances with the support of their respective governments. Operating in different economic systems, both played dominant roles in the development of foreign trade in their respective countries. Into the 1980s, both of them encountered increasing challenges and were under pressure to change. Since the mid-1980s, both have followed the strategies of diversification and internationalization.

Despite the many similarities, they are very different from each other. The Japanese GTCs originated in late 19th century Japan, while the Chinese FTCs started in the mid-20th century. The Japanese GTCs were formed as private businesses and developed their dominant influences through market mechanisms, whereas the Chinese FTCs were created and owned by the state and enjoyed their monopoly through state protection. The Japanese GTCs have been from the very beginning much more diversified than the Chinese FTCs in their business operations. The Japanese GTCs are much larger, financially much more powerful, far more experienced in overseas investment, more advanced in technology, and have a much more sophisticated information network than the Chinese FTCs. Also, the Chinese FTCs are decades behind the Japanese GTCs in diversification and internationalization.

In spite of increasing challenges in the 1990s, neither the Japanese GTCs nor the Chinese FTCs will likely become a passing phenomenon, judging by the readjusting measures they have already undertaken. Moreover, the Japanese GTCs have adapted themselves to the changes in their environment several times throughout history, while the Chinese FTCs have also survived the impact of the radical Chinese trade reforms. It is quite possible that higher levels of diversification and internationalization will continue to keep both of them on the forefront of international trade and investment.

QUESTIONS FOR DISCUSSION

1 How did the GTCs develop their monopolistic influences in Japan's foreign trade?
2 What were the FTCs' structure and function before the 1979 reforms?
3 Why are the FTCs not as dynamic as the GTCs?
4 What changes did the GTCs adopt in the 1980s in order to cope with the expected challenges of the 1990s?

5   Since 1979 how have the FTCs transformed themselves in the context of overall Chinese reform and do you agree that they should follow the model of GTCs?

FURTHER READING

De Mente, Boye (1991) *How to Do Business with the Japanese*, Lincolnwood, Ill.: NTC Books.

Fu, Qiang (1992) "Use the Model of Japanese Conglomerates for Reference, Pursue Globalization Chinese Style," *International Trade Journal*, 10: 54–58.

Hsiao, Gene T. (1977) *The Foreign Trade of China*, Los Angeles: University of California Press.

Jian, Chuan *et al.* (1991) *China's Foreign Trade Develops Rapidly*, Beijing: New Star Publishers.

Kleinberg, Robert (1990) *China's Opening to the Outside World: The Experiment with Foreign Capitalism*, Boulder, Colo.: Westview Press.

Lardy, Nicholas R. (1992) *Foreign Trade and Economic Reform in China 1978–1990*, New York: Cambridge University Press.

Lifson, Thomas (1981) "A Theoretical Model of Japan's *Sogo Shosha* (General Trading Firms)," *Proceedings of the Academy of Management*.

Kleinberg, Robert (1990) *China's Opening to the Outside World*, Boulder, Colo.: Westview Press.

Sarathy, Ravi (1985) "Japanese Trading Companies: Can They Be Copied?," *Journal of International Business Studies*, (Summer): 101–119.

Shenkar, Oded (ed.) (1991) *Organization and Management in China 1979–1990*, Armonk, N.Y.: M.E. Sharpe.

Sun, Wen-xiu (1989) "The Reform of the Foreign Trade System," *Planned Economy Research* 8: 53–59.

Szuprowicz, Bohdan and Maria R. Szuprowicz (1978) *Doing Business with the People's Republic of China*, New York: John Wiley & Sons.

Wik, Philip (1984) *How to Do Business with The People's Republic of China*, Reston, Va.: Reston Publishing Company, Inc.

Yonekawa, Shin'ichi (ed.) (1990) *General Trading Companies*, Tokyo: The United Nations University.

Yoshihara, Kunio (1981) *Sogo Shosha: The Vanguard of the Japanese Economy*, Oxford: Oxford University Press.

Yoshino, M.Y. and Thomas B. Lifson (1986) *The Invisible Link: Japan's Sogo Shosha and the Organization of Trade*, Cambridge, Mass.: The MIT Press.

Zimmerman, Mark (1985) *How to Do Business with the Japanese*, New York: Random House.

Chapter 19

The Japanese distribution system in transition

INTRODUCTION

In the past few years the Japanese distribution system has received much public attention as a point of contention between the United States and Japan. It is often cited as a major barrier to trade, responsible for Japan's relatively low level of manufactured goods imports from the United States and Western Europe. For many Western business people, the Japanese distribution system is extremely complex, hardly transparent, and very costly to penetrate. It is charged as being "archaic," "inefficient," "confusing," "fragmented," and "backward." The multi-layered distribution network and intertwined wholesalers (or *tonya*) have suffocated competition. Japanese business practices, which are largely based on personal relationships and complicated networks, are also often criticized. In spite of some remarkable changes, the Japanese distribution system continues to be perceived by many as what it was two decades ago.

In an attempt to present an up-to-date analysis of the Japanese distribution system, this chapter is designed to achieve four objectives. First, it will describe the historical, social and cultural sources of Japanese distribution, with an emphasis on how these factors have contributed to the uniqueness of the Japanese distribution system. Second, it will analyze the structure of Japanese distribution channels, focusing on characteristics of the structure and process. Third, it will discuss the current changes and trends occurring in the distribution system. Finally, the major channels of export and the related comparative advantages will be briefly explored.

HISTORICAL, SOCIAL AND CULTURAL SOURCES

Generally speaking, a distribution system develops a certain way for a specific logical reason. The existing Japanese system, according to many specialists, has evolved as the most efficient and economical means for serving the market environment of Japan. Therefore, it seems necessary to trace briefly the historical development of the Japanese distribution system before moving into a discussion of the pros and cons of today's situation.

During the feudal era of Japan, the country was divided into many small regions that were basically self-contained. Subsequently, each region developed its own distribution system. Even after the feudal system was abandoned, the uniqueness and separateness of these territories were kept largely intact. Manufacturers who wished to penetrate these separate territories efficiently had to develop proper distribution systems for each territory. As Japan consisted of around 500 regions, many manufacturers were obliged to use wholesalers for each territory. Geographical difficulties characterized by mountainous islands further hampered the movement of both people and merchandise.

As time went by, there emerged a corresponding production system that was characterized by many small manufacturers who relied heavily on the financing, distribution, and storage capabilities of wholesalers for survival. These manufacturers were particularly dependent on wholesalers to market their products in other regions. Only through a multi-layered distribution system could they have their products marketed at a small percentage of direct sales cost. Moreover, indirect sales by manufacturers significantly lessened the logistical complexity, which entailed a large number of contacts and deliveries.

On the other hand, numerous small retailers who serviced the fragmented markets spread throughout Japan also needed the service of wholesalers for survival. They were usually dependent on wholesalers for cheap retail credit and inventory. This heavy dependency on wholesalers led to a very close relationship between retailers and wholesalers in Japan. Therefore, the geographical and historical factors make wholesalers an indispensable link between manufacturers and retailers.

Japanese consumers have developed an unusual preference of choosing from among a nearly unlimited number of types of shops, which can provide a wide-range of personal services in their home neighborhoods. Culturally speaking, this has become an inseparable element to the quality of life Japanese consumers are accustomed to, though this has resulted in much higher costs. Furthermore, the Japanese have a special partiality for fresh foods. The large number of small specialist shops selling fruit, vegetables, meat, and fish in every small residential area throughout the country caters for this particular need of Japanese consumers. Of the more than 1.6 million retail shops in Japan, almost half are food shops (Batzer and Laumer 1989: 50).

Furthermore, large purchases of stock are not common practices in Japanese tradition. This is not only related to the unusual partiality for fresh foods but also due to the relatively small size of Japanese homes. In addition, the frequent but small purchases enable the Japanese consumers to make close personal contacts with their neighbors. Shopping at the corner store offers an important opportunity for socializing for Japanese housewives. Similar functions are also provided by the department stores, which have not only been shopping places but also centers of social life.

Due to this unusually close relationship between consumers and shops, Japanese shops are highly service-orientated and put the needs of their customers as their top priority. Shops usually remain open until late in the evening during the week and are also open at weekends. Moreover, shop assistants are exceptionally polite. Frequently, small quantities of goods are delivered without additional charge – and immediately – to the customer's home upon request. Uniquely, the services provided by small Japanese retailers are wide-ranging, and apart from the free and swift delivery include considerate personal advice, the provision of a reliable maintenance and repair service, the commitment to procure spare parts and a relatively short delivery time for consumer durables.

Like retailing, wholesaling also gives a high priority to customer service. Wholesalers are willing to deliver even the smallest quantities to retailers upon request, accept unsold goods without complaint, grant their long-term clients special discounts, and offer them credit for up to five months. Moreover, they help the retailers with a wide range of matters like, for example, how to advertise and display their goods. They even go as far as to provide their clients with professional training on such topics as book-keeping and customer service. The small retailers, who can afford to keep only a minimum of storage space, have easy access to credit and provide reliable customer service, have developed a heavy dependence on whole-salers and are reluctant to change or terminate this long-tested relationship.

Other cultural norms, such as the concept of *wa* (harmony) and of *giri* (loyalty), further contribute to this unique distribution culture. For many nondurable consumer products, for example, the Japanese try to maintain retail prices at a similar level in all classes of trade. The retailers who venture to break the price line are often regarded by both manufacturers and retailers as untrustworthy, and, consequently, harmony is disrupted. The concept of *giri* contributes to the system of exclusive distributors in which each distributor is a dedicated wholesaler for one manufacturer in each product category. Normally, an exclusive distributor does not or cannot aggressively sell any brand other than the one he is contracted with. As a result, a Japanese consumer often has to visit five shops in order to choose from five different brands (Zimmerman 1985: 136–137).

As far as the social system is concerned, the Japanese government has for decades pursued a policy of protecting small businesses, which is, among other reasons, designed to allow as many Japanese as possible to make a living. Major policy instruments used by the Japanese government include the Department Store Law of 1956 and the Large Retail Store Law of 1974 which replaced it. The former could only restrict the establishment or expansion of department stores with a sales space of over 3,000 m² in the seven largest cities, and over 1,500 m² in all other cities; the latter was broadened to cover all large retail stores that had sales space of over 3,000 m² in the ten largest cities and over 1,500 m² in all other cities. Upon the proposal of local retailers and town planning and trading experts, the Minister of MITI could make decisions on delaying an opening, on placing restrictions on new sales space, on the number of days per annum on which the store had to be closed, and on the number of hours it can be open per day. Under the pressure of small and medium-scale retailers, a powerful lobby in Japan, the Japanese government amended The Large Retail Store Law in 1978 to give local administration even greater control over the development of large retail stores (Czinkota and Woronoff 1986: 111–112).

The Japanese government's concerns for full employment were justified by the labor shortages during the 1960s and the 1970s. One reason for the existence of a large number of small retailers in Japan can be explained by the employment system (Batzer and Laumer 1989: 53–54). For a long time, the practice of lifetime employment among large corporations required employees to retire at the age of 55, though the most recent development has been the postponement of retirement to a later age. Employees retiring under this system often felt too young to live as pensioners. Moreover, the pension they received at this time until they reached 65, when the state pension became available, was often totally insufficient. Many early retirees from large corporations were virtually obliged to try their luck at self-employment in the commercial sector, with the help of a severance payment from their former employers. Thus, the tertiary industries, which were regarded as relatively easy for amateurs to operate, provided a safety net for hidden unemployment.

WHOLESALE STRUCTURE AND PRACTICE

A unique feature of the distribution system in Japan is the dominant position of the wholesalers. This dominance has in recent years been under increasing challenge from the rapidly growing high-turnover supermarket chains and industrial groups, which have been trying to regain some control on the sale of their own products. In spite of the erosion, specifically in the consumer products sector, Japanese wholesalers have maintained substantially more influence in the marketing channel than wholesalers in any other major industrial country.

As discussed earlier, Japanese wholesalers usually assume greater risk by providing financially weak retailers and small manufacturers with long periods of credit, with promissory notes frequently used for 90 to 120 days (Czinkota and Woronoff 1991: 94). The retailers normally purchase goods on a commission basis, i.e. they do not have to pay until they have sold the goods. In case they cannot sell the goods, they can expect to return these unsold goods to the wholesalers. This means that, except for the goods that the wholesalers can pass back to the manufacturers, they bear substantial selling risk.

Moreover, wholesalers participate in a complicated and non-transparent system of rebates. On the one hand, wholesalers, as agents of manufacturers, receive rebates or commissions ranging from 2 to 5 percent for collecting from the channel members. Large wholesalers are frequently granted a rebate on the basis of a cumulative discount, ranging from 1 to 3 percent. Wholesalers are normally offered rebates by manufacturers for their efforts to restrict retailers' aggressive discounting. If wholesalers can make quick payment within 30 days, they often receive a cash payment discount of approximately 3 percent (Czinkota and Woronoff 1991: 95). Moreover, wholesalers may pass part of these rebates to retailers for their cooperation.

In addition, the wholesalers have traditionally assumed the burden for storage, whereas the retailers, who have never had much storage space, have developed a heavy dependency on wholesalers' willingness to deliver constantly, often daily or several times a day. Since storage space is in acute shortage in major urban centers and can only be obtained at fairly high costs, the wholesalers who have control of the limited storage space are in an envious position for guaranteeing rapid delivery to retailers, who in turn are willing to pay slightly higher prices for the service.

Another unique feature of the Japanese distribution system is the existence of a large number of wholesalers, who have formed a complicated and interdependent multi-layered system of their own. A product ends up in the consumer's hands only after it has passed through a distribution chain of at least two and sometimes as many as four or five layers of wholesalers, with each layer adding their own profit margin. As a result, Japan has more wholesalers than the United States, even though the latter has twice the population and 25 times the territory of Japan.

In layer one, there are approximately 230,000 registered primary wholesalers and several thousand unregistered ones (De Mente 1991: 180). Among them are several hundred large corporations, including the giant general trading companies. Together they hold a dominant position and are usually referred to as top-ranking wholesalers. They purchase goods in large quantities directly from manufacturers and then sell them to wholesalers at lower levels. These primary wholesalers have obtained their predominant position through long-formed feudalistic ties between themselves and their sources. They have the financial power to support and control manufacturers, who have traditionally left distribution of their goods to wholesalers and have allowed them to be their exclusive agents.

Immediately below the primary wholesalers is the second layer of distribution made up of numerous wholesalers who purchase from the primary wholesalers. These secondary wholesalers then, sell to a large number of smaller tertiary wholesalers who service the many small and mid-sized stores and neighborhood shops that are spread throughout the country, as well as to the large retail stores. Many of the secondary wholesalers are very large corporations that match, or even exceed, the size of the primary wholesalers from whom they purchase. The main reason that many of them do not purchase directly from manufacturers is that they do not have the exclusive rights of the primary wholesalers.

The tertiary wholesalers make up a very complicated distribution network. The overwhelming majority of them are very small operations, run by anything from one or two people up to five or six shop assistants. They usually use small vehicles such as mini-trucks (some even use bicycles), and cover a small number of retailers. Compared with other leading industrialized nations, Japan has the highest wholesale to retail sales ratio.

Generally speaking, large general wholesalers are the most efficient channels because they normally sell directly to large retailers such as the Daiei and Seiyu Supermarket chains, who in turn sell to consumers at a much lower price than can be found in the corner stores that have to obtain their goods from a secondary wholesaler. By the time goods have passed through the secondary wholesalers and into the small retailers, they have acquired an additional cost of 50 to 60 percent (Zimmerman 1985: 136). In comparison, an additional 30 percent for a non-food product and 10 percent for a food product are more common in the United States.

Although there are several layers of wholesalers, not all of them are involved in the physical distribution of goods. It is not uncommon for intermediate wholesalers to play the role of a purchasing center for local wholesalers further down the line, while manufacturers make their deliveries directly to these local wholesalers. These intermediate wholesalers receive a commission from manufacturers for their services, which include paying and collecting payments from local wholesalers. In terms of pure economic rationality, the service of some of these intermediate wholesalers could be done away with. Nevertheless, the unwritten rules of conduct in the hierarchic relationships of the Japanese distribution system require that each established wholesaler within the network continually enjoy access to the distribution business. Therefore, identical products are often found to be distributed through quite different channels. The following three cases (Czinkota and Woronoff 1991: 95–96) represent the logic of such distribution alternatives (see also Figure 19.1).

Case 1 embodies the most commonly used distribution channel, in which the products are delivered by the manufacturer to a wholesaler who in turn delivers them to retailers. The retailer pays the wholesaler who in turn pays the manufacturer.

Case 2 is another commonly used channel of distribution, in which wholesaler A sells the products to the smaller wholesaler B. The products, however, flow directly from the manufacturer to wholesaler B, who supplies the retailer. The fact that wholesaler B, rather than wholesaler A, supplies the retailer is often the result of a closer business relationship that wholesaler B has developed with the retailer during an extended period. Similarly, owing to their long-established business relationship, wholesaler B prefers doing business with wholesaler A instead of dealing directly with the manufacturer. The payment is made by the retailer to wholesaler B who in turn pays wholesaler A, who then forwards payment to the manufacturer. In spite of the fact that wholesaler A has not participated in physical distribution, he can receive up to 5 percent commission on the sale from the manufacturer.

In Case 3 the distribution chain is extended by the involvement of another wholesaler, the very small wholesaler C. Although he is largely unknown to the manufacturer, he is directly supplied by the latter on the condition that wholesaler A guarantees payment. Wholesaler A owes this unique role to his long-established business ties with wholesaler B, who in turn is closely associated in a relationship of trust with wholesaler C. Very small wholesaler C is in turn able to make deliveries to small retailers who are located in distant corners. In this way, the manufacturer is ensured nationwide product distribution without bearing the risk of nonpayment. Both wholesalers A and B are happy with their roles, as they do not have to incur heavy expenditures since they do not participate in the physical distribution. They are rewarded with a share in the sales profits in return for their credit service.

Many larger Japanese manufacturers have wholly owned separate companies handling the domestic consumer sales of their products. Tokyo Shibaura Electric Company (Toshiba), for instance, leaves the marketing and sales to Toshiba Shoji (Trading) Company, which has nine major branches and 70 subbranches throughout Japan. There are around 600 franchised wholesalers under these 70 branches who deal directly with retailers. In another example, Meiji Seika, Japan's largest manufacturer of confections, has used Meiji Shoji to sell nearly all of its products. Meiji Shoji maintains six branches in the main urban centers of the country and about 80 subbranches in the secondary areas. The products of Meiji Seika flow from these subbranches to both wholesalers and retailers.

RETAIL STRUCTURE AND PROCESS

Generally speaking, Japan's retail network is much denser than those of the United States and Western Europe, with the highest number of stores per capita and per area. The structure of the nonfood retail sector in Japan is quite similar to that of the United States, as Japan's ratio of 7.9 stores per thousand people is close to the ratio of 6.8 in the United States. On the other hand, the structure of the two food retail sectors is considerably different: the U.S. food retail sector is dominated by large stores, which account for only 6.5 percent of the stores but 46 percent of total food sales. In Japan, the

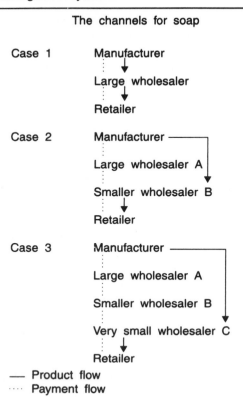

The channels for soap

Case 1   Manufacturer
          ↓
          Large wholesaler
          ↓
          Retailer

Case 2   Manufacturer ———┐
          Large wholesaler A │
          ↓
          Smaller wholesaler B
          ↓
          Retailer

Case 3   Manufacturer ———┐
          Large wholesaler A │
          Smaller wholesaler B │
          Very small wholesaler C
          ↓
          Retailer

—— Product flow
···· Payment flow

Figure 19.1 Variety of distribution alternatives
Source: Czinkota and Woronoff, 1991, p. 96.

food retail sector is dominated by small stores, while the large stores only account for 0.3 percent of the total number of stores and 10 percent of the total food sales (Goldman 1992: 156–157).

Neighborhood shopping areas, or "shopping streets" (*shotengai*) are probably most frequently visited by the Japanese. In major Japanese cities there is one shopping street for every 10,000 people, which normally serves an area within a radius of some 500 meters (De Mente 1991: 157). Each shopping street consists of several dozens of stores selling a wide variety of products, ranging from rice, vegetables, meat, fish, bread, clothing, confections, milk products, electrical appliances, cosmetics, household goods, shoes, drugs, etc. There are also one or two supermarkets, and a number of service shops such as beauty parlors, barbers, tailors and photo shops. Currently, many of these small stores are under growing pressure to amalgamate. In each city there is also a large number of central shopping districts, which are primarily located around major local transportation terminals. Some large shopping districts, such as the Ginza in Tokyo, are like small towns in themselves. The Ginza boasts six top-ranked department stores and several hundred top specialty shops.

Department stores in Japan constitute a very important retail force. In addition to independent department stores, there area round 20 department store chains in Japan, including Mitsukoshi, Daimaru, Takashimaya, Seibu, etc., which offer medium- to high-quality products. The highest volume item in department store sales is clothing, which accounts for about 40 percent of the total sales, followed by foodstuffs, home furnishings, small sundries, etc. Many of them are linked financially to one of the large trading companies, such as Mitsubishi, Mitsui, Marubeni and C. Itoh. Overall, they hold a market share of around 8 percent. Supermarkets and chain stores, such as Daiei, Ito Yokado, Seiyu and Nichii, hold about 18 percent of the total retail market (Batzer and Laumer 1989: 58). Large retailers receive their merchandise mainly from primary wholesalers and sometimes directly from manufacturers. They typically maintain 50 percent retail margins.

For a long time, both small stores and family-run stores have accounted for approximately three-quarters of the total retail sales. During the 1980s, a new type of small retail business – the "convenience store" – has developed from the American model. Such stores are usually small in size and are located in convenient residential district sites. Operating around the clock and offering a limited range of goods (usually no more than 300 articles), they mainly serve young working couples, single working individuals, and students. Their services range from basic food items, ready-cooked food, and daily necessities to dry-cleaning and photocopying (Batzer and Laumer 1989: 61). These convenience stores are usually operated on a franchise basis. Seven Eleven Japan Co., which is 51.4 percent owned by the retail giant Ito-Yokado, is the pioneer of foreign licensing in the Japanese market.

Japanese manufacturers in specific areas, such as confections, fabrics, and home electrical appliances, usually possess large numbers of their own retail outlets which are known as *chokubai-ten*, or literally "direct sales stores." The *chokubai-ten* owned by fabric manufacturers sell material rather than finished products. However, in the areas of confection and electronic appliances, the *chokubai-ten* sell a complete line of finished products. All these manufacturer-owned shops are located in major population centers. Fujiya Confectionery, for instance, has several-hundred stores throughout Japan and operates them on a chain-store basis. Matsushita, Hitachi, Toshiba, and the other large electrical appliance manufacturers also run their own retail outlets.

Besides the *chokubai-ten*, many large Japanese manufacturers of consumer products use what are called *semmon-ten*, or literally "specialty shops." *Semmon-ten* began to spring up as early as the late 1950s and are

privately owned. Normally, these shops purchase directly from their manufacturer–suppliers on 30- to 90-day credit terms. Nevertheless, in order to
push the sales of new products, the manufacturers often give them to the
shops on a consignment basis for a specific period of time. The comparative
advantage of the *semmon-ten* lies in the fact that they have a much larger
variety of styles and sizes of a given product than the department store.
Another advantage is that they can substantially benefit from their
manufacturer–suppliers' advertising campaigns.

As explained earlier, Japanese consumers are among the most demanding in the world. The competition for their sponsorship is mainly
concentrated on service and quality. Perfect quality, complete fitness, absolute freshness of produce, swiftness of delivery, etc. often have a more
decisive influence on consumers than does price alone. One common
Japanese practice in retail business is that retailers organize consumers into
purchasing clubs. Consumers are encouraged to register with the retailer
as members and the retailer monitors and records their purchases. This
practice is designed to achieve full cooperation between retailers and
consumers. With a detailed record, the retailer is able to reward those
customers who have purchased certain quantities of goods each year. Also,
the record can also help the retailer follow the changing patterns and tastes
of their customers. Given the fact that Japanese consumers are among the
most demanding in the world, a good record is almost a necessity for the
retailer to provide good services to their customers.

RECENT DYNAMIC CHANGES

In recent years, there have been some remarkable changes in the Japanese
distribution system (see Figure 19.2). Small-sized retail stores, for example,
have registered a steady decrease in number while small wholesalers have
suffered a corresponding reduction in distribution system share. In contrast, both medium- and large-sized retailers and wholesalers have been
experiencing a steady growth in both numbers and scale. The number of
small retailers with one to two assistants stood at 1.04 million in 1982, but
decreased to 870,000 in 1988 (Shioya 1989: 59). This is a noticeable down-
ward development.

The decrease of small retailers has mainly resulted from either a shift to
other types of business or the closing-down of businesses. From 1982 to
1985, for example, an estimated 220,000 retailers, primarily small stores,
operated by a single person went out of business (Shioya 1989: 59). There
are a number of reasons for the decrease of small retailers, including the
land price hikes in urban centers and other high-growth regions, fierce
competition with other kinds of retail business under the economic slowdown, changes in consumers' lifestyles and needs specifically due to an
increase in the number of working women, the difficulty in locating succes-

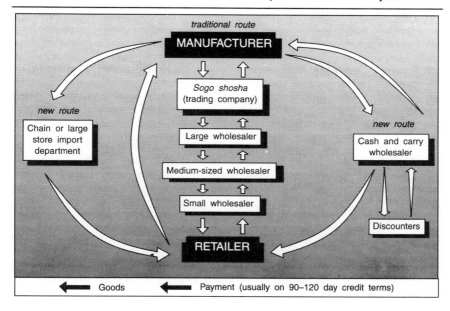

Figure 19.2 Traditional and alternative forms of distribution
Source: Stone, 1992, p. 24. © 1992 *Asian Business*

sors to continue the businesses, changing traffic conditions and the failure to adapt efficiently to rapid changes.

Small retail stores have begun grouping together to emulate the successful chain stores, like Daiei, Ito-Yokado and Seiyu, to increase their clout in purchasing goods. Chain stores have recently become the fastest-growing retailers in Japan. The small size of their outlets has also enabled them to get around the restrictions of the Large Scale Retail Store Law. As the chain stores begin to increase sales, traditional retailers are softening their resistance to changes of laws on large stores. Subsequently, the approval procedure for opening large stores will now take around 18 months, much shorter than the traditional average of seven to 10 years (Stone 1992: 22).

The poor performance in the small-sized retail sector has also unfavorably influenced many small-sized wholesalers. As they have been heavily involved in the financing of channel members and supplying primarily small-sized retail stores, small wholesalers make much thinner margins on investment. In addition, the pressure on smaller manufacturers has also been felt on small wholesalers. Many small manufacturers, which have suffered under the intensified competition from large corporations, are disappearing. Many small wholesalers lose their business, as large corporations do not go through small wholesalers for their financing. As a result, an increasing number of wholesalers are forced to integrate with manufacturers. This is particularly noticeable in the men's and women's apparel industry. Integration is also taking place among various layers of wholesalers. Generally, the power of wholesalers as channel members is on the decline. There are also drastic changes in wholesale structure, such as the emergence of distribution zones and new transportation structures. The wholesaling industry is beginning to get more involved in the importing business.

Most recently, the "cash and carry" wholesalers are rapidly growing in number. A key feature of the new wholesalers is that many of them are excluded from carrying many traditional Japanese brands, which are still controlled by the *keiretsu* groups. Therefore, they have to look for different products, especially imported goods. They also have to channel goods to unconventional but new discount stores. Many of these discount stores, like Yodobashi Camera in Tokyo's Shinjuku district, get cheap imported goods from "the cash and carry" wholesalers. As a rule "the cash and carry" wholesalers do not accept returns from retailers nor do they develop personal relationships. They also tend not to grant rebates or bonuses.

COMPARATIVE IMPORTING CHANNELS

There are a number of major channels available for penetrating the Japanese market. The first is to market through non-Japanese trading companies with subsidiaries or branches in Japan. There are many non-Japanese trading companies that provide their services as marketing partners for trade with Japan and have rich experience doing business in the country. Some companies, such as Hong Kong's Jardine Matheson, have already established sophisticated marketing/service structures, as well as close institutional and personal relationships. The often-quoted problem of using these foreign companies is that they normally sell a large number of directly or indirectly competing products and do not give specific attention to individual foreign manufacturers.

The second is to market through Japanese importers or wholesalers, who normally have sole marketing rights. The Japanese importers include the large Japanese *sogo shoshas* and various import agencies specializing in specific product groups. The chief advantage of marketing through Japanese sole importers is that they are usually responsible for the entire process of importing and distributing, ranging from customer service to advertising and sales. One major problem is that by assigning sole marketing rights, the foreign manufacturer virtually loses any sort of control on marketing promotion and selling prices. Another major problem is that large importers, like *sogo shoshas*, usually sell many similar products, which could hamper the introduction of another manufacturer's products.

The third way is to market directly to large retailers such as department stores and large chain stores. Large retailers are increasingly becoming involved in direct deals with foreign suppliers. By importing directly, they can significantly reduce the cost of distribution. In addition, goods from foreign sources have served as a means of attracting clients to the large department stores, as small retailers can hardly afford to sell foreign goods. Imports by department stores have recently been growing at 20 percent a year, currently accounting for 11 percent of total department store sales (Miura 1991: 75). Most of the large Japanese department stores maintain purchasing offices in Western Europe, North America and in the newly industrializing countries (NICs) in Asia.

The final option is to set up a branch office or sales subsidiary. This is not often used by medium-sized and small-sized foreign manufacturers. The decision to establish a sales office or subsidiary in Japan depends heavily on the size of the market. If the business has achieved a certain volume, such a move is appropriate. In cases where the marketing partner in Japan has proved to be unwilling or unable to develop existing sales potential, a branch office or subsidiary of the manufacturer becomes necessary. One main advantage is that the foreign manufacturer can cultivate product relationships with customers, while establishing an identity, reputation, and credibility in Japan. However, the problem is that of the extended period that a wholly foreign-owned office or subsidiary may need to build its own network of wholesalers and distributors.

In terms of domestic distribution, foreign enterprises in Japan have a number of channels available, such as trading companies, exclusive wholesalers, sales offices, and retailers. Sometimes, several channels are needed for more efficient distribution. The distribution network of Nippon United, for example, can be divided into two. One is via large trading companies and the other is through exclusive wholesalers. Nippon Kaisha, the trading arm of Nippon United, has also been trying to develop direct channels with large retailers. With these three channels, Nippon United not only sells to the urban centers and large retail outlets, but also covers a large number of smaller retail stores all over Japan.

In Japan, the approximate cost of direct import ranges from 35 to 40 percent of product prices, including freight, insurance, customs clearance, inland transportation, and import duties. If the retail margin is figured to be around 50 percent, the imported goods may end up on retailers' shelves at a price of two to three times the free on board (f.o.b.) price. If foreign goods are imported indirectly via trading companies or agents, the price differentials are even higher (Batzer and Laumer 1989: 84). Under such exorbitant price structures for imported goods, many smaller retailers are virtually compelled to give up the idea of selling imported goods or must be prepared to accept a significantly lower profit margin. Partly because of this price hike, there is a trend toward direct importing.

In order to remain profitable for their import sales, larger retailers

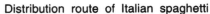

Distribution route of Italian spaghetti

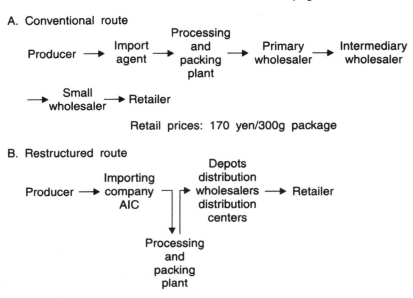

A. Conventional route

Producer → Import agent → Processing and packing plant → Primary wholesaler → Intermediary wholesaler

→ Small wholesaler → Retailer

Retail prices: 170 yen/300g package

B. Restructured route

Producer → Importing company AIC → Depots distribution wholesalers distribution centers → Retailer

Processing and packing plant

Savings: 25%   Retail price: 128 yen/300g package

Figure 19.3 Import distribution alternatives
Source: Czinkota and Woronoff, 1991, p. 104.

increasingly favor buying direct imports, preferably from their own joint importing companies (see Figure 19.3). One such company is called Allied Import Co., which was formed by Jusco, Uny, Izumiya, and Chujitsuya in 1979 for the purpose of joint importation of clothing, foodstuffs, housewares, and leisure goods. Imported goods are mainly located in the supermarket chains and the department stores, accounting for about 10 to 20 percent of the total sales of these two retail categories. Small retailers have a very small share of imports.

SUMMARY/CONCLUSIONS

This chapter has reviewed the key aspects of the Japanese distribution system, which is characterized by multi-layered wholesaling structures and a myriad of small retailers. The interlocking relationships of these wholesalers and retailers, which are based on cultural and historical factors, are complicated and unfriendly to newcomers. In addition, government restrictions on the sales space and business hours of retailing stores have hindered the development of large retail stores. On the whole, the Japanese distribution system can be regarded as a serious barrier to the foreign manufacturer trying to penetrate the Japanese market. Nevertheless, the structural complications and trade practices in the Japanese distribution system have not solely been created to prevent foreign companies from penetrating the Japanese market. They present hurdles to all latecomers from both Japan and foreign countries. The only difference is that newly arrived foreign manufacturers, who are not familiar with the broad cultural and social environment in Japanese society, tend to suffer more setbacks from these structural features and trade practices than do newly emerging Japanese manufacturers.

From this chapter, it should also be noted that the Japanese distribution system has recently been undergoing several significant changes and that the Japanese market is not as complicated as it was ten years ago. On the one hand, the Japanese government has adopted a series of measures to facilitate foreign access to the Japanese market, like the dismantling of tariff barriers, the easing of test standards, the relaxing of the rules of licensing, etc. On the other hand, Japanese consumers and purchasers have developed much more open attitudes toward imports. The introduction of modern marketing has also left its imprint on the distribution system. Nevertheless, while recognizing the progress made by the Japanese government and businesses toward improving the distribution system, one should not expect that the structural barriers inherent in the system will completely vanish overnight. It is also important to keep in mind that there is always room for improvement for foreign firms marketing their products in Japan.

QUESTIONS FOR DISCUSSION

1   What are the major cultural, historical, and social sources of the current Japanese distribution system?
2   What is so unique about the Japanese wholesaling structure and process?
3   Can you name and explain the different categories of Japanese retail stores?
4   What are the recent major changes in the Japanese distribution system and their implications for foreign business?
5   Can you compare several major importing channels in Japan?

FURTHER READING

Ballon, Robert J. (1992) *Foreign Competition in Japan*, London: Routledge.
Batzer, Erich and Helmut Laumer (1989) *Marketing Strategies and Distribution Channels for Foreign Companies in Japan*, Boulder, Colo.: Westview Press.

Christopher, Robert C. (1986) *Second to None: American Companies in Japan,* New York: Crown Publishers, Inc.

Czinkota, Michael and Jon Woronoff (1986) *Japan's Market: The Distribution System,* New York: Praeger.

—— (1991) *Unlocking Japan's Markets: Seizing Marketing and Distribution Opportunities in Today's Japan,* Chicago: Probus Publishing.

De Mente, Boye (1991) *How to Do Business with the Japanese,* Lincolnwood, Ill.: NTC Business Books.

Deutsche, Mitchell F. (1983) *Doing Business with the Japanese,* New York: Nal Books.

Goldman, Arieh (1992) "Evaluating the Performance of the Japanese Distribution System," *Journal of Retailing,* 68 (Summer): 154–183.

Hamada, Tomoko (1991) *American Enterprise in Japan,* Albany, N.Y.: State University of New York Press.

Huddleston Jr., Jackson N. (1990) *Gaijin Kaisha, Running A Foreign Business in Japan,* Armonk, N.Y.: M.E. Sharpe.

Kang, T.W. (1990) *Gaishi: The Foreign Company in Japan,* New York: Basic Books.

Lawrence, Robert Z. (1991) "Keiretsu and Japan's Rigged Distribution System," *The International Economy* (May–June): 64–67.

Maurer, P. Reed (1989) *Competing in Japan,* Tokyo: Japan Times.

Morgan, James C. and J. Jeffrey Morgan (1991) *Cracking the Japanese Market,* New York: The Free Press.

Miura, Manoru (1991) "Department Stores Move Towards Internationalization," *Business Japan* (August): 75.

Shioya, Takafusa (1989) "Japan's Distribution System Is a Result of Economy, Society and Culture – MITI," *Business Japan,* 34 (August): 59–62.

Stone, Eric (1992) *Tricks of the Japan Trade,"* *Asian Business* (February): 20–25.

Woronoff, Jon (1991) *The "No-Nonsense" Guide to Doing Business in Japan,* Tokyo: Yohan.

Zimmerman, Mark (1985) *How to Do Business With the Japanese,* New York: Random House.

Chapter 20

Unlocking joint venture potentials in China

INTRODUCTION

Since China was opened to foreign investment in 1979, it has attracted approximately U.S.$26.7 billion worth of direct foreign investment into the country, with approved enterprises reaching 37,000 in 1991. Equity joint ventures accounted for about one-third of the country's total direct foreign investment, and were favored by foreign investors during the period 1979–1988 (*Beijing Review*, March 1992: 42). In spite of various difficulties, many equity joint ventures have thrived. With a realistic plan and good preparation, one can reasonably expect success in creating and managing a joint venture in China.

Many papers and books have been written on the key factors contributing to joint venture success. General views tend to include longevity, profitability and the ability of the parent company to benefit from its partner in terms of technology, management skills, market shares, etc. (Baird *et al.* 1991: 125–134). Owing to differences in social and cultural backgrounds, ideological concepts and historical developments, many potential conflicts may stand in the way of success. This chapter is written for the benefit of those who are interested in establishing joint ventures in China. It will introduce various fundamental aspects of creating a joint venture in China and briefly analyze some common problems that may constitute major hindrances to success.

FINDING A GOOD PARTNER IN THE RIGHT LOCATION

As in a marriage, the first step toward success is to find a good partner. If a foreign investor prefers an equity joint venture to other forms of investment, he should first lay down the criteria and requirements he wants his potential Chinese partner to meet. This seems to be fairly easy on the surface, as Article One of the Law of the People's Republic of China on Chinese–Foreign Joint Ventures merely requires that the Chinese partner must be an entity enjoying the status of a legal person. Nevertheless, to find a suitable partner is not an easy job.

To begin with, one needs good connections (*guanxi*) to be introduced to the right partner. As explained in Chapter 4, *guanxi* is one of the major dynamics of Chinese society. The term refers to special relationships two people have with each other. It can be best translated as friendship with implications of a continual exchange of favors. On the whole, *guanxi* binds people through the exchange of favors rather than through expressions of sympathy and friendship. However, *guanxi* requires time and patience to cultivate. To establish a good connection network in China is probably the most worthwhile but at the same time the most daunting task to fulfill. Without *guanxi* one often, as the Chinese say, "gets half the result with twice the effort." It is difficult for Western companies to establish a good connection network in China; American companies are especially disadvantaged since they are subject to the Foreign Corrupt Practice Act of 1976.

Guanxi is not the only thing necessary to the success of a joint venture in China. One should have reliable information on the status of the potential Chinese partner. To be more specific, the following questions are fundamental. (1) What is the financial situation of the potential Chinese partner? (2) What ownership does the Chinese partner have? Public, collective or private? (3) Are leading members of the Chinese partner professionally competent and devoted? (4) Does the Chinese partner receive strong backing from its overseeing governmental institution, which has a stake in the prospective joint venture project? (5) How much authority does the partner have in obtaining essential supplies and raw materials? (6) What kind of access does the Chinese side have to China's domestic market? (7) Are competing ventures planned elsewhere or does the Chinese side have the political and economic clout to keep a dominant position in its field? (8) Can the Chinese side successfully assimilate the transferred foreign technology?

There are a number of common pitfalls in locating a suitable Chinese partner. One is that some potential candidates are in serious financial trouble and for them to join forces with a foreign partner may serve to rejuvenate their dying organization. William Mallet of Tianjin Otis Elevator, China, advises that, "foreign investors shouldn't try to resurrect worthless organizations. They should link with ones that were strong financially, because that will provide a good foundation" (Goldenberg 1988: 183–184).

Another pitfall lies in differences among priorities. Generally speaking, foreign partners are interested in market access, cheap labor, and lax rules on pollution control; the Chinese side is interested in capital and technology as well as promoting their exports. When these priorities are at odds, coordination between the joint venture partners becomes very poor. This is the so-called situation of "sleeping in the same bed and having different dreams," as a Chinese phrase goes. Beijing Jeep typified one of these clashes over priorities between foreign and Chinese partners. With a strong interest in absorbing technology, the Chinese felt AMC had reneged on the terms of their contract calling for joint design and production of a new Jeep when AMC suggested postponement of further work when they found that the exhaust system, noise controls, and speed failed to meet international standards (Mann 1989).

Nevertheless, there are many success stories in finding suitable Chinese partners. A good Chinese partner can be very helpful in a number of ways. They can significantly cut the cost of production, help break into the enormous Chinese market, and even enhance the technology of the parent company. The operations of the McDonnell Douglas cooperative venture and the Johnson & Johnson venture in Shanghai are two notable examples of success. In both cases, the Chinese partners played a key role in promoting their products in the Chinese market.

The right location is also very crucial. A recent survey reveals that Shanghai and Shenzhen are home to China's most profitable American joint ventures, with their respective returns on investment at 16.2 percent and 13.6 percent. The inland cities seem to have been the most disappointing locales for American investors. Average return on investment in these locations is only 10.1 percent – lower than the average coastal or SEZ (Special Economic Zone) rate. Moreover, nearly half of the executives reporting on inland investment projects responded that their joint ventures have not met expectations due to less-developed infrastructures, poor transportation networks, and uncertain raw material supplies (Stelzer *et al.* 1991: 54–56).

Nevertheless, being in an inland town or province with a committed municipal or provincial leadership can also have some unusual benefits. There are already many foreign investors in Shenzhen, Shanghai and other coastal cities, but relatively few ventures in many inland cities. Joint ventures located in these regions get more personal attention and support of the provincial governor or mayor. In addition, closer personal interactions with top local decision-makers can be more frequent. These interactions have become increasingly important during the past decade as the Chinese economy has been considerably decentralized, thus shifting substantial power to local governments.

There are many cases where foreign ventures in some small inland cities managed to overcome mounting obstacles due to direct involvement by local governments. This is not normally expected from the municipalities of big cities. Many local officials are zealous supporters of Deng's reform and are eager to attract foreign investment. In order to compete for foreign investment with coastal areas, some of them adopt aggressive policies to offset their disadvantages in terms of geographical location. Many of them go out of their way to be personally involved in supporting joint ventures.

The commitment from local governments is often indispensable to the success of a joint venture.

NEGOTIATING A FEASIBLE CONTRACT

Like any other investment in China, joint ventures must be approved by the local government concerned or by the central government, depending upon the scale of the investment. The most recent rule allows local governments at provincial and municipal levels to authorize joint ventures with less than $30 million in investment. The first step is for the Chinese partner to present a proposal for the joint venture to the foreign investment commission of the local government, or to MOFTEC if the investment involves more than $30 million. The following items should be provided by the foreign side: the name, country of origin and legal address of the foreign firm as well as its scale of operations and business standing; in addition, the foreign investor must provide their proportion of the capital investment (normally no less than 25 percent) and the types of investment, the major products of the joint venture, and the proportions of international sale ("The Law").

This is followed by a feasibility study, which normally includes background of the proposal and economic significance of the investment, market demand, the scale of the proposed product (in terms of necessary resources, raw materials, fuel and public utilities), proposed project location, conditions for putting up the factory, project design scheme, environmental safeguards, organization of production, the number of workers, staff and personnel training, implementation plan for the proposed project, investment estimate and manner of raising funds, estimated product cost, and an assessment of the economic results. This is where problems often arise. One common complaint from foreign partners is that in order to impress them, the overzealous Chinese partners tend to verge on overoptimism, changing the study of feasibility into a sort of study of the "imagination." Therefore, foreign partners are strongly encouraged to get involved in the feasibility study.

Upon approval of the proposal, both sides can begin to draft the contract for the joint venture, which is the key document of the venture and must be in both Chinese and the language of the foreign partner. The contract should also include the duration of the joint venture, the share of roles and power among the executives, the means to resolve disputes, and the way to dissolve the joint venture ("The Regulations").

Negotiations on the contract can be long-winded and complicated, with a tendency to negotiate in a style described by one veteran China trader as "a blend of the Byzantine and evangelical." Chinese negotiators often frustrate Western business people unused to such tactics. Many foreign negotiators leave the table feeling pessimistic about their future partners.

As discussed in Chapter 17, these tactics may include controlling location and schedule, utilizing weaknesses, using shame tactics, pitting competitors against each other, feigning anger, rehashing old issues, and manipulating expectations. Often negotiation continues after the signing of the contract. Therefore, a foreign partner should choose the right negotiators, prepare for time-consuming rounds and develop a sophisticated strategy before starting negotiation.

One major problem at this stage is that foreign suppliers often find themselves in a dilemma when the Chinese demand technology that is "state-of-the-art." Chinese negotiators routinely request the "most advanced" technology from foreign suppliers during initial negotiations, though they may lack sufficient foreign exchange and an adequate infrastructure to utilize complex technology and trained personnel. A McDonnell Douglas Helicopter executive mentioned to the author that after he explained how easily a new-model MD helicopter can be maintained, his Chinese friend became annoyed and privately advised him to describe the maintenance as a complicated process in order to show the "quality" of the technology. To ensure a better chance of success, foreign companies are strongly advised to provide the most appropriate and price-competitive technology.

Another persistent problem is how to decide the contribution made to the venture by each partner. Foreign partners have often found that the Chinese insist that they pay a large sum of foreign cash to the venture. On the other hand, the Chinese side prefers to contribute noncash items – such as land use, existing buildings and construction materials – all of which are easy for the Chinese to overvalue due to the difficulty in assessing prices accurately. One manager that the author interviewed in the summer of 1993 complained that their Chinese partner significantly overvalued their property, causing substantial loss to the foreign side. The value of an out-of-date computer, for example, was estimated at close to its original purchase price, even though the foreign partner had to buy one to replace it. In order to avoid such complications, foreign companies should take advantage of assessments by professional consulting companies.

Once the contract is approved, the Chinese side will need to petition the local office of the Administration of Industry and Commerce for a license for the venture to begin operation. The joint venture is not officially recognized until it receives this license. Upon the granting of this license, the joint venture will need to contact the tax agency, get registered in the customs office, and open accounts in foreign and local currencies. After the completion of all these activities, it can begin its operations and recruit workers.

CREATING A COHESIVE LEADERSHIP

According to the Chinese Joint Venture Law, a joint venture is supposed to be organized and structured to facilitate smooth operation and the partners in the venture should share management and control. The board of directors is the highest authority, and its members are nominated by each side either in equal numbers or in proportion to the shares each owns. The board is empowered to guide the operations, appoint the executive officers and define their duties, make important policies, revise the contract, increase or reduce the total capital and share of each side, cease operations, dissolve the venture, and dispose of assets. In matters concerning the contract and important issues, decisions are generally made by unanimous vote. For all other routine decisions, majority vote is sufficient.

The leadership is exercised by the team of the general manager and the deputy general manager, who make joint decisions on management of operations. One of them is normally selected from the Chinese side while the other is from the foreign side. The general manager and the deputy general manager hold the power of controlling and supervising every aspect of the operations. The office of the general manager is generally assumed in turn by nominees from each side and the term of the office is decided by the board of directors. The cooperation between the general manager and the deputy general manager has proved to be extremely important to the success of a joint venture. In order to form a cohesive team, both sides have to overcome numerous conflicts in culture, personality, political viewpoints and management style. This has not been easy for many joint ventures. It is extremely important that an expatriate study Chinese culture and refrain from showing cultural arrogance.

One persistent problem is that the office of the general manager is constantly subject to the influence of the party branch within the joint venture. Theoretically, the party is not supposed to have a branch in joint ventures, but such organizations exist anyway. Although the directives of the party branch often help promote the goal of the joint venture, the authority of the general manager is seriously undercut. If the Chinese general manager or deputy general manager is the head of the party branch (wearing "two hats" in Chinese political jargon), then there will be no problem. On the other hand, if he is not then his authority will be seriously questioned. In this regard, the foreign partner can do very little.

A joint venture management is supported by various sections dealing with different areas of operations. These sections may include accounting and auditing, personnel, production, maintenance, supplies, transportation, marketing, custodial and security. A chief engineer is appointed to supervise the production section and oversee the facilities. A plant manager will administer engineers, foremen, and workers. Staff members in the upper levels of management come normally from both the Chinese and foreign sides, but the middle and lower levels of managers are mainly Chinese, so that the venture can maximize its benefit from low labor costs (Ho 1990: 23–24).

Although most joint ventures have formal organizational charts show-ing decision-making roles for expatriates and Chinese managers, the connection between the formal structure and actual patterns of decision-making seems to be fairly weak. There has been constant pressure for centralization. Many American and European joint venture managers, for example, have observed that it was difficult to get their Chinese managers actively involved in the decision-making process or to take personal re-sponsibility for their decisions. Owing to the large power distances in the Chinese culture, Chinese managers are reluctant to make decisions and take responsibility. Japanese managers, on the other hand, have tended to complain about their difficulty in practicing the consensus decision process. The traditional dynamics of Japanese-style management, where production efficiency, quality control, and marketing expansion depend heavily on the loyalty of employees, are not easily transferred to the Chinese. One Japanese manager, so frustrated with his attempt to introduce problem-solving meetings when the company was first established, concluded that these were useless practices because "the Chinese offered no suggestions." Later, he simply told the Chinese of his executive decisions (Ireland 1991: 14–17).

STRIVING FOR FOREIGN EXCHANGE BALANCE

The balance of foreign exchange is crucial to the success of a joint venture. According to the Joint Venture Law, foreign exchange inflows and outflows should at least balance over the life of the joint venture. Chinese authorities are very sensitive to the projected foreign exchange balance of a joint venture. According to a recent survey, the high-tech/export producers tend to show the highest return on investment (15.4 percent), with the highest number (58 percent) of respondents indicating that their ventures have generated higher-than-expected returns. Those that produce import sub-stitutes have the lowest return (8.7 percent) and are the least satisfied; 45 percent of those respondents indicated that the results have been below expectation, perhaps reflecting the higher priority the Chinese government has given to export-orientated businesses (Stelzer *et al.* 1991: 56).

Basic principles on foreign exchange are as follows: a joint venture should normally show in its feasibility study a positive foreign exchange balance by the end of the contract's term. Foreign exchange can be used for necessary imports, but a strong preference is given for local substitutes. Foreign employees in the joint venture can be paid in hard currency. The payment of dividends to the foreign partner can be in hard currency. These are some of the general principles that can be applied with varying degrees of flexibility, depending on China's overall reserve of foreign exchange. As a rule, pro forma financial statements that project early foreign exchange surpluses tend to facilitate negotiations and operations. A joint venture must submit periodic reports of its foreign exchange balance to the State General Administration of Exchange Control (SGAEC) ("The Provisional Regulations"). The best strategy to keep a good balance of foreign exchange is to insure an international market for at least 50 percent of the products.

The curtailment of foreign exchange could cause tremendous problems for joint ventures, such as Beijing Jeep, which depend on foreign exchange to pay for imported parts. Beijing Jeep failed to obtain foreign exchange through sales to foreign residents in China as it had originally planned, because they had other priorities for their funds. Most expatriates working in China travel in a company car or use the reasonably priced taxis. Moreover, Beijing Jeeps cost around $8,000 more than their U.S. cousins. The company was virtually stranded until the Chinese government decided to open China's market to the Jeep venture (Goldenberg 1988: 96–97).

Special provisions have been made for customs duties on import and export commodities of joint ventures. Equipment, transportation equipment, office facilities, and other supplies can be imported duty-free as part of the original foreign investment specified in the contract. Additional purchases, approved by the concerned authorities, will also be duty-free. A joint venture can either make these purchases from the Chinese market or from abroad. For domestic purchases, it pays in Chinese currency at prices that are the same as those paid by the Chinese state-owned enterprises. For international purchases, the prices charged to the joint venture should conform to comparable international market prices. Obviously the joint venture that can take advantage of Chinese supplies will enjoy lower material costs. However, sourcing for production in China is no easy task. The quality standards that foreign partners require usually surpass those of Chinese suppliers. When a Chinese supplier's quality is acceptable, its products are in high market demand, causing problems for steady supply or the requirement of payment in foreign currency.

There are now new ways to balance foreign exchange. Income derived from domestic sales, for example, can be converted into foreign currency on the condition that certain production procedures are followed. Income can also be converted into foreign currency through swap markets in accordance with market rates. Some joint ventures, like Johnson & Johnson's venture in Shanghai, mainly sell to the Chinese domestic market for hard currency.

KEEPING UP WITH THE CHANGES IN ACCOUNTING AND TAX SYSTEMS

Another commonly problematic area is in financial management and accounting. A financial and accounting system should be established to comply with the Chinese Law on Income Tax for Joint Ventures and the Regulations on Accounting Systems. The unit of accounting should be the

Chinese currency. Generally speaking, these regulations conform to international accounting practices. One major complexity lies in tax orientation. Usually, there are accounting standards for "book" purposes while the tax legislation is to define the differences for tax purposes. The Chinese accounting regulations provide guidelines for both book and tax purposes. No differences are allowed for book and tax depreciation. Another major complexity lies in currency translation. Foreign exchange accounts should be recorded in foreign currency and the equivalent RMB amount. Any unrealized foreign exchange gains and losses may be recognized in the accounts, but must be amortized over a period of time. The conversion at year-end from foreign currency to RMB is treated in the balance sheet as "currency translation differences" (Price-Waterhouse 1988: 30–31).

There are several other differences: capitalization of research and development is normally not allowed; the direct write-off method must be used for bad debts and accounts receivable; sales are regarded as realized after products have been shipped; once one method of cost accounting (such as product-type, standard-costing, and process-costing) is selected, no change is allowed. Nevertheless, beginning from 1 July 1993, the Chinese Ministry of Finance announced that enterprises in China would strictly follow the standards of the international accounting system. It can be expected that these complexities will gradually be phased out.

According to the Unified Income Tax Law of 1991, joint ventures must pay a flat 30 percent income tax on net income to the central government and another 3 percent to the local government, totaling 33 percent. When the foreign partner of a joint venture remits its share of profit home after tax payment, the joint venture no longer has to pay a further remittance tax of 10 percent. For the joint ventures whose exports exceed 70 percent of their total output, or are located in the special economic zones or in the technology development zones in the open coastal cities, the income tax is cut by half – from 30 percent to 15 percent. For joint ventures with a contract of more than ten years, there will be no tax for the first two profit-making years, and there will be a 50 percent reduction of the income tax for the following three years. Joint ventures that reinvest their profits in China over five consecutive years will have a refund of up to 40 percent of the tax payment for reinvestment ("The United Income Tax Law" and Peck 1991: 12–15). There are already signs that a unified tax system for both foreign and Chinese enterprises will be introduced. Although the preferential tax rates offered in various special economic and development zones will remain, they are applied to both foreign and Chinese enterprises located in these zones. Once the proposed unified tax system is introduced, joint ventures may not enjoy tax advantages over their Chinese competitors.

OVERCOMING DIFFICULTIES IN HUMAN RESOURCES MANAGEMENT

Personnel management is also crucial to the success of a joint venture. One major incentive for foreign companies to invest in China is its relatively low labor cost. If they can manage the workforce well, they can take good advantage of the low cost and have a better chance for success. To attract foreign investment, the Chinese government has authorized a series of prerogatives for joint ventures in hiring, supervising and firing employees and in determining the amount of compensation. China's Labor Laws and Regulations require a labor contract between joint venture management and the union, covering various aspects of personnel management ("The Regulations on Labor Management").

Like their Western counterparts, Chinese trade unions are supposed to protect the welfare of the employees. The unions, for example, have the right to set up a reserve fund for employees' self-improvement in job-related skills, as well as for recreational activities. A joint venture is required by law to pay monthly contributions to the union reserve fund, equivalent to 2 percent of the total wages of the employees who are members of the union. The unions have the right to attend meetings of the board of directors when issues concerning the workers are discussed, and to appeal to the board on behalf of workers with regard to disciplinary action or dismissal. The unions should have the right to supervise the company's operations dealing with employees' insurance and medical care. In a somewhat different vein than Western unions, the unions in China have a distinct responsibility to urge employees to comply with the rules of the joint venture, to complete assignments, and to enhance their efficiency ("The Regulations on Labor Management").

Recently, trade unions have become more aggressive. One interesting phenomenon is that like the unions in the state-owned enterprises, the trade unions in joint ventures usually place the interests of the Party above the interest of the workers. A U.S.–Chinese Business Council survey conducted in 1990 showed that many joint ventures had been pressured to control wages to no more than 150 percent of the wage level of comparable state enterprises, even though the 1986 Provision of the State Council for Encouragement of Foreign Investment stipulates that joint ventures have autonomy in setting wage rates (Pearson 1990: 39).

Employees' wages are usually determined on the basis of the qualification, workload, and contribution to the joint venture. Joint ventures are expected to cover medical costs for the period of an employee's contract. One can either contract with key hospitals or take care of employees through an employer's clinic, in which each employee is subject to a ceiling. Medical insurance is the least-favored system, with its high premiums and relatively low percentage of coverage. Joint ventures are also required by law to contribute 15–20 percent of total wages to a housing fund for Chinese employees or to offer rental subsidies. Joint ventures should provide a retirement allowance, the rate of which ranges from about 20–30 percent depending on the area. Joint ventures are required to make a payment of 1 percent of the average salary of the area each month to the local labor institutions (Casati 1991: 16–22).

A joint venture is required by law to inform the local supervisory agency and the local labor department of the types and numbers of positions open. Any vacancies should be announced publicly. An open test should be held for the candidates to compete on an equal basis. Employees are subject to a probationary period. Those having an unsatisfactory record can be either released or put on a new probationary period. Chinese technical and managerial personnel can also be found through open recruiting both locally and outside the region. Subject to advance notice, a joint venture may lay off employees for either poor performances or serious losses on the part of the venture. On the other hand, employees may also resign with an advance written notice.

In the words of the general manager of one diagnostic reagent-manufacturing joint venture in China, three factors are keys to the success of any venture in China: "people, people, and people" (Epser 1991: 24–30). According to his experiences, several rules should be kept in mind when hiring Chinese staff: (1) avoid taking too many employees from a single source, as this can heighten the risk of hiring a lot of people with similar bad habits who may reinforce each other; (2) practice patience and flexibility when looking for high-quality personnel; (3) resist pressures to overhire by Chinese authorities; (4) find a local confidant among the local management staff who has experience in dealing with the bureaucracy and is trustworthy. Finally, one should not only find the right individuals, but also mold them according to the needs of the company.

It is important to create a corporate culture that contains some aspects of Western management style and is, at the same time, acceptable to the Chinese staff. Expatriate staffs should try to serve as good role models. To help reduce the influence of *guanxi* (connection) and the Chinese reluctance to shoulder responsibility, several rules should be practiced: (1) provide detailed job descriptions, though it is impossible to cover every aspect of employees' responsibilities in a job description; (2) integrate training with daily operations. A corporate culture can be best established through close contact between expatriates and Chinese teams from the very beginning. A good nurturing environment for risk-taking cannot be established without a safety mechanism of checks and balances for major decisions. People should also be allowed to make mistakes, as long as these do not threaten the normal operations and the safety of the staff.

SUMMARY/CONCLUSION

The chapter has discussed various aspects of creating and managing joint ventures in China. The first step toward creating a joint venture has been identified as finding an appropriate partner and a suitable location. It is very important to find a partner with similar rather than conflicting goals. While the coastal areas have better infrastructure, many inland provinces are more eager to get foreign investment, thereby offering various forms of preferential treatment. Negotiating a physical contract is the next important step in which a feasibility study should be conducted and a sustainable contract signed. The third and most important step is to create a cohesive leadership without which it would be difficult to hold the joint venture together. The fourth step, identified as being extremely important by many authors, is to keep a good balance of foreign exchange. In the past many joint ventures have foundered due to a lack of foreign exchange. The fifth one is to keep up with the rapid changes of the accounting tax system in China. Finally, overcoming difficulties in human resources management is discussed, in which good training and clear job descriptions have been identified as being of utmost importance.

With all the "lurid" stories on the hardships of joint venturing in China, a recent survey shows that most joint ventures are making money, with 60 percent reporting a return on investment (ROI) of 10 percent or higher. Nearly a third reported an ROI equal to, or exceeding 18 percent. Although such returns would be considered minimal by venture capitalists in the United States, the average ROI of 11.6 percent is fairly decent for China-based international businesses; only 12 percent of the sampled firms appear to be losing money (Stelzer *et al.* 1991: 54). When more U.S. companies do their homework and prepare themselves for ventures in China, a higher percentage of success can be expected. Since 1990, the Chinese government has considerably enhanced transparency in its investment policies and promulgated a series of laws and regulations. At the same time, attracting foreign investment has become part of its long-term development strategy. Continued improvement in China's investment environment will further boost the chance of success for Sino-foreign joint ventures in the years to come.

QUESTIONS FOR DISCUSSION

1 Describe the meaning of the Chinese phrase "sleeping in the same bed and having different dreams" and discuss its effects on your decisions in finding a Chinese partner.

2 Why is a feasibility study so important to the success of the joint venture?

> 3 What do you think is the best way to form cohesive leadership
> in a joint venture with the Chinese?
> 4 In what ways can you insure that the foreign exchange balance
> is in good shape?
> 5 In your opinion what are the most difficult aspects of human
> resources management in China?

FURTHER READING

Baird, Ingrid S. *et al.* (1991) "Joint Venture Success: A Sino-U.S. Perspective," in Oded Shenkar (ed.), *Organizations and Management in China 1979–1990*, New York: M.E. Sharpe, pp. 125–134.

Beijing Review (1992) March 23–29: 42.

Casati, Christine (1991) "Satisfying Labor Laws – and Needs," *The China Business Review* (July–August): 16–22.

Chen, Min (1993) "Tricks of the China Trade," *The China Business Review* (March–April): 12–16.

Epser, Pavel (1991) "Managing Chinese Employees," *The China Business Review* (July–August): 24–30.

Goldenberg, Susan (1988) *Hands Across the Ocean: Managing Joint Ventures*, Boston: Harvard Business School Press.

Harrigan, K.R. (1986) *Managing for Joint Venture Success*, Lexington, Mass.: Lexington.

Ho, Alfred K. (1990) *Joint Ventures in the People's Republic of China*, New York: Praeger.

The Income Tax Law of the People's Republic of China for Enterprises with Foreign Investment and Foreign Enterprises (1991) "The United Income Tax Law," 9 April.

Ireland, Jill (1991) "Finding the Right Management Approach," *The China Business Review* (January–February): 14–17.

The Law of the People's Republic of China on Joint Ventures Using Chinese and Foreign Investment (1979) "The Law," 1 July, Beijing.

Mann, Jim (1989) *Beijing Jeep*, New York: Simon & Schuster.

Pearson, Margaret (1990) "Party and Politics in Joint Ventures," *The China Business Review* (November–December): 38–40.

Peck, Joyce (1991) "Standardizing Foreign Income Taxes," *The China Business Review* (September–October): 12–15.

Price-Waterhouse (1988) *Doing Business in the People's Republic of China*, Beijing: Price-Waterhouse.

The Provisional Regulations for Exchange Control of the People's Republic of China (1980) "The Provisional Regulations," December, Beijing.

The Regulations for the Implementation of the Law of the People's Republic of China on Joint Ventures Using Chinese and Foreign Investment (1983) "The Regulations," 20 September, Beijing.

The Regulations on Labor Management in Joint Ventures Using Chinese and Foreign Investment (1980) "The Regulations on Labor Management," 26 July, Beijing.

Stelzer, Leigh *et al.* (1991) "Gauging Investor Satisfaction," *The China Business Review* (November–December): 54–56.

Conclusion

The Asian management systems that have been discussed throughout the book indeed have their own unique comparative advantages (with the possible exception of the pre-reform Chinese state enterprises), but at the same time they also have many weaknesses. On the whole, all of them are quite different from Western business management practices, though they have benefitted from Western business techniques. Since the beginning of the 1980s, all of them have experienced rather dramatic changes – not only in organization but also in business operation. While they share some fundamental cultural similarities, they have many differences in both management styles and organizational structures mainly as a result of different historical, political, economic, and social environments.

This last part of the book is divided into three sections. The first section will concentrate on the discussion of general similarities and differences in the Asian management systems. This is basically a summary of the comparative studies from the second and third parts of the book. The second section is a general comparison between the Asian and Western management systems, though unsubstantiated generalizations tend to be avoided. This will help readers better understand the comparative advantages and disadvantages of Asian management systems. The third section will cover such issues as the general trends of these Asian management systems and what can be learned from them.

SIMILARITIES AND DIFFERENCES AMONG THE ASIAN MANAGEMENT SYSTEMS

The four Asian management systems have been studied on the basis of the research model discussed in the first part of the book. The studies have focused on the business operational environments of these Asian management systems, cultural and social influences, and their internal organizational and managerial features, as well as competitive business strategies. The four systems, though developed in the different geographical regions of Asia, have all been subject to Confucian influences. Therefore,

Confucian values have served as a key linkage among them. Since they are the products of their own unique historical and developmental environments, prominent features of each system have been discussed in detail. On this basis, comparisons have been made of the similarities and differences between the Overseas Chinese and mainland Chinese companies and between the Japanese and Korean companies.

As has been shown, most of the similarities are concentrated in the area of cultural traditions in the form of Confucianism, which includes the harmony of interpersonal relationships, the hierarchical structure of the society and organization, the importance of family, the prevalence of authoritarianism, paternalism and personalism, the system of mutual obligation, and the universality of the *guanxi* network. In short, human resources management is heavily influenced by Confucianism and the differences between them are more of degree than substance.

Their differences can be discussed along the lines of organizational structure, management process, and business strategies. To begin with, the nature of ownership varies a great deal among the four systems. The Chinese State Enterprise (CSE) is located at one end of the continuum, with state ownership and long-term direct state participation in management. At the other end of the continuum are the thousands of small Chinese family businesses (CFBs), with the family not only owning the company, but also tightly controlling almost every key aspect of management, giving very limited room for professional managers. In between are the Japanese *keiretsus* and the Korean *chaebols*. For the former, family ownership and business management have long been dissociated, while the latter is in the process of giving professional managers more decision-making power, though most families still hold the key posts in the companies. In addition, the ownership of large Japanese companies has become fairly public while the ownership of Korean business groups remains largely private.

They also differ from each other a great deal in terms of organizational size, ranging from very small CFBs to very large *keiretsus*, with Korean *chaebols* and the Chinese CSEs lying in between. Except for the *keiretsus*, the other three are highly centralized, with small CFBs probably having the highest degree of centralization. The degree of organizational formalization and divisionalization for all of them is relatively low, with the CFBs having the lowest formalization and divisionalization and the highest informal organizational structure. All of them suffer from various degrees of cliquism within their organizations.

In terms of leadership style and decision-making, the degree of authoritarianism is generally high, though the Japanese managers seem to be more interested in collecting information and seeking opinions from their subordinates, as evidenced in the *nemawashi* and *ringi* process. Among the four, the leaders of the CFBs seem to have the most authoritarian style of leadership and intuitive decision-making; the participation of CFB professionals in the decision-making process is generally the lowest. Directors of CSEs who are not also Party secretaries are probably in the most vulnerable position as they do not have the institutional support of ownership and are subject to regular interference from the Party secretaries.

As far as managerial control is concerned, all four Asian organizations have a strong vertical information-sharing and control system. In contrast, Japanese management probably constitutes the only exception to relatively poor horizontal communication. While all of them emphasize the importance of institutional loyalty, the degree to which the companies and their employees feel a common bond varies a great deal. Both the Chinese CFBs and CSEs have probably the lowest degree of institutional loyalty, but for entirely different reasons. The former suffers from the impersonality of state ownership and management while the latter suffers from the differentiated treatment based on the relationship to the owner-family. Korean and Chinese employees, however, have strong loyalty to specific leaders within their organization, while Japanese loyalty goes more to the organizations themselves. In order to maintain harmony, all four Asian organizations have low degrees of open confrontation, though internal strife and manipulation are prevalent, with the possible exception of Japanese organizations.

Market relations and business strategies of the four Asian businesses also vary a great deal. While all four emphasize the importance of *guanxi* in market competition, they use different strategies to control market share. The Japanese have managed to secure their relationships through sophisticated corporate cross-holdings and trade alliances. For Japanese companies, market share has been the top priority in competition. The Koreans have relied on the allocation of the government in specific government-indicated sectors. Many surviving CSEs aim at taking advantage of their special relationship with their governmental institution or form larger enterprise groups to try to achieve a monopolistic situation in their respective industry. The Overseas Chinese have developed various convenient alliances with governments and indigenous businessmen for survival and development. In addition, the Chinese CFBs in Taiwan and Hong Kong have formed various informal alliances to catch millions of opportunities and to expand their influence at the same time.

COMPARISON BETWEEN THE WESTERN AND EASTERN MANAGEMENT SYSTEMS

The co-founder of Honda Motor Corporation, T. Fujisawa, once made the following comment on the differences between American and Japanese management: "Japanese and American management is 95 percent the same, and differs in all important respects" (Adler 1986: 295). His words clearly explain the dialectical relationship between the Western and Eastern management systems, in which the Asian management systems are both linked to and separate from their Western counterparts. Although this book has not specifically discussed Western management systems, attention is drawn here and there throughout the book to some outstanding differences between the Western and Eastern systems when individual Asian management systems and specific topics (such as negotiating with the Chinese and Japanese) are discussed.

In the second chapter of the book, major differences in Western and Eastern religious thinking and ideologies are compared, with a definite conclusion that the West highly cherishes individualism while the East emphasizes communitarianism, while the rest of the world falls somewhere in between these two extremes. There are a number of affiliated features to these two ideologies. Closely associated with individualism is the idea of *equal opportunity* and the notion of the *social contract*, the holiness of *property rights*, the necessity of *limited state* and the emphasis on *scientific specialization*. In contrast to individualism, communitarianism advocates a number of entirely opposite values, such as *equality of result or hierarchy*, the importance of *consensus* and *high duty-consciousness*, the *community need*, the necessity of *powerful state*, and *holism and interdependence* (Lodge and Vogel 1987: 10–22).

While these differences are not absolute, they do clearly outline general differences in Western and Eastern values, which in turn influence Western and Eastern differences in organizational structures and management processes. However, generalizations on differences between Western and Eastern management systems can be very dangerous if not supported by extensive research. In a study on the organizational structures of Japanese and American companies, Chung and Lee (1989: 174–176) found that American companies have a high degree of divisionalization, institutionalization, centralization and formalization. Such features of an organization symbolize a "mechanistic structure." Japanese companies, on the other hand, were found to have a relatively low degree of these four dimensions. Therefore, Japanese companies can be characterized as having an "organic structure." Interestingly, Korean companies were found to be closer to U.S. companies in the areas of institutionalization, centralization and formalization, but share similar features with Japanese companies in the area of divisionalization.

The picture of the managerial process is even more complicated. In some areas there is a clear difference between the East and the West. In terms of conflict resolution, for example, all four Asian management systems encourage the avoidance of direct and open conflict. When open conflict breaks out, Asians either tend to use authority to suppress it or to resort to private coordination. In American companies, on the other hand, managers are used to confronting the problem directly and to bring it out into the open. In another example, the overall institutional loyalty is higher in Asian

organizations than in Western organizations, though Chinese family businesses do have a very high turnover rate among the "outsiders" of the
companies. On the whole, owing to different styles of human resources
management, Asian employees tend to be a bit more emotionally attached
to their organizations than their Western counterparts.

Generalizations on leadership styles, decision-making processes, and
managerial control are again very difficult. Authoritarian leadership styles
and decision-making, for example, are found in both Western and Eastern
systems, but the Eastern system tends to contain both extremes, i.e. the most
authoritarian leadership styles and decision-making and the most democratic group consensus-making. In another example, the control process of
American companies is characterized by information sharing, output-
orientated control, and autonomous control. The Japanese companies focus
more on information sharing and self-control by employees than they do
on output-orientated formal control. Like American companies, the Korean
companies tend to emphasize output-orientated control, but they do not
attach great importance to information sharing nor do they emphasize
self-control (Chung and Lee 1989: 176–177). Thus, the pattern between the
East and the West is blurred.

In his book *21st Century Management: Keeping Ahead of The Japanese and
Chinese*, Dan Waters has offered a very interesting comparison between the
Eastern and Western management systems (see Table C.1). Again, some of
his generalizations are in contradiction with the findings of other scholars
and are open for debate. With regard to planning, for example, both the
Japanese and the Koreans use detailed long-term planning. Since this book
is not written to compare Western and Eastern differences, but rather to
bring out unique features of the four Eastern management systems, broad
generalizations are avoided. The comparisons made in this book have been
made to achieve a better understanding of the Eastern management systems, as most of these comparisons were made among the four systems.

THE TRENDS OF THE ASIAN MANAGEMENT SYSTEMS AND THE CHALLENGES OF THE PACIFIC CENTURY

As Asian economies continue to develop at an average rate higher than that
of the world average, there is a growing consensus that the 21st century will
be the "Pacific century." It is time that Western societies change their
traditional views toward Asian management systems, which have helped
bring about so many economic miracles. On the other hand, Western
management skills, especially those developed in the United States, still
have many good things to offer and will continue to be attractive to Asian
managers (Nimgade 1989: 98–105). Therefore, two approaches are deemed
very harmful in the process of readjusting Western views toward Asian
management systems. Those who hold the first approach tend to blindly

Table C.1 Comparison of Western and East Asian management styles

	Western	East Asian
1.	Hierarchical, egalitarian command, segmented concern	Free-form command, roles loosely defined, holistic concern
2.	Professional managers, position related to function	Social leaders often with high-sounding titles for low-ranking jobs
3.	Particularism, specialized career path possibly with rapid evaluation and promotion, individually orientated	Non-specialized career paths, slow evaluation, regimented promotion, socially orientated
4.	Decentralization of power	Centralization of power
5.	Mobility	Stability
6.	Diversity	Unity
7.	Direct approach	Indirect approach
8.	Systematic analysis, standardization, categorization, classification, conceptualization, precision	Ambiguity, reaction, adaptation
9.	Long-term set planning	Often lack of formal set planning, high flexibility in adjustment
10.	Explicit control mechanisms	Implicit control mechanisms
11.	Organizations and systems adapt to change	Leaders/managers adapt to change

Source: Waters, 1991, p. 106.

worship the advantages of Asian management systems, especially those of the Japanese management system. The second approach is more conservative, categorically attributing Asian advantages to their unfair business practices and summarily rejecting all the Asian elements in management as feasible for Western companies.

A more realistic approach is to conduct a careful and comprehensive study of Asian management systems and the environments in which they were born and continue to grow. One should recognize the fact that Asian management systems have contributed to a continued high growth rate and thus are worthy of special attention. At the same time, one should not ignore the fact that there are many successful Western companies which are among the most competitive in the world. Furthermore, major Asian management systems are significantly different from each other in many aspects, as has already been pointed out, with each having its own unique competitive advantage and critical weakness. It is, therefore, better to borrow the strong points of the others to supplement one's own system than to abandon one's own system and strive for full-scale "Easternization."

As has been analyzed throughout the book, all the Asian management systems are currently undergoing a rapid process of modernization. Samsung Group's intensive drive to modernize its management by grafting Western work practices onto its authoritarian corporate structure serves as a typical example (Paisley 1993: 64–69). For the past few decades it has been learning from the Western system and combining modern management techniques with its own culturally and socially influenced management systems. In a sense, its system is becoming more similar to that of the West in various aspects. Asian management systems have already become more individually motivated, less seniority-based, more interested in management by objectives and less authoritarian. Asian business organizations have also become better structured with the assistance of Western organizational concepts.

What then should a Western business learn from Asian management systems? Unfortunately, there is no one standard answer to this question; many scholars in the West have studied the issue but reached their own conclusions (Makabe 1991). In spite of their differences, many scholars in the West tend to agree on one point: Asian management focuses on people, while Western management focuses on work tasks (Totoki 1990: 2). The most important contribution to organizational efficiency and the business success of Asian companies is probably their long-term investment in people, the development of relationships, and their humanistic approach toward management. Only when an organization is committed to its own employees can they be willingly committed to the organization. When the organization and its employees are strongly identified with and committed to each other, business success is no longer an abstract concept.

As for how to mix the West with the East, the answer is even more complicated, and depends on a wide range of factors such as the changing business operational environment, the types of organizations and management tasks, and proper mix of business culture. In Professor Gordon Redding's words:

> Creating and combining business systems is like cooking: You start with a set of ingredients, put them together at different times under different conditions and through an unfathomable process of trial and error, accident, or great culinary skill, the end results can be so good as to cause admiration and satisfaction to those able to enjoy them, and envy in those who can't.

(Redding 1992: 50)

The world's most inspiring management experiments are taking place in the dynamic Western Pacific Rim, where Japanese, Koreans, Overseas Chinese, mainland Chinese and other Asian managers are working side by side with as well as competing against their Western counterparts. As the overall economy of the Western Pacific Rim continues to grow at an average rate higher than that in other parts of the world, increasing business opportunities will attract more companies from the West to join the market competition there. The Western Pacific Rim is becoming not only a focus of heated business competition but also an international school of business where companies can learn a great deal from each other via business competition and dealings. Through various business alliances, such as joint ventures and trading partnerships, they are learning how to incorporate different management systems and manage people from different management systems. The urban centers of the Western Pacific Rim, ranging from the regional trading centers of Hong Kong and Singapore to the business centers of the various Asian countries such as Shanghai, Jakarta, and Taipei, are indeed, as Professor Gordon Redding has rightly predicted, becoming ever-bustling kitchens, experimenting with new recipes for management in the Pacific century.

QUESTIONS FOR DISCUSSION

1　Discuss the major differences and similarities among the Asian management systems.
2　Do you agree with T. Fujisawa that Japanese and American management is 95 percent the same? If so, why?
3　How do you reflect on Dan Water's comparison of Western and Eastern management styles embodied in Table C.1?
4　Having read the book, do you think East Asian management systems are a passing phenomenon? Why?
5　Do you agree with Professor Redding that East Asia will be the center stage for creating a new management system for the next century?

FURTHER READING

Adler, Nancy J. (1986) "From the Atlantic to the Pacific Century: Cross-Cultural Management Reviewed," *The Journal of Management* 12(2): 295–316.

Brown, Robert M. and Teresa F. Blevins (1989) "Should America Embrace Japanese Management Techniques?," *SAM Advanced Management Journal* 54(1) (Winter): 22–29.

Chung, Kae H. and Hak Chong Lee (1989) "National Differences in Managerial Practices," *Korean Managerial Dynamics*, New York: Praeger, pp. 163–180.

England, George W. (1993) "Japanese and American Management: Theory Z and Beyond," *Journal of International Business Studies* (Fall): 131–140.

Garratt, Bob (1981) "Contrasts in Chinese and Western Management Thinking," *Leadership and Organization Development Journal* 2(1): 17–22.

Hall, Richard H. and Weiman Xu (1990) "Research Note: Run Silent, Run Deep – Cultural Influences on Organizations in the Far East," *Organization Studies* 11(4): 569–576.

Lodge, George C. and Ezra F. Vogel (1987) *Ideology and National Competitiveness*, Boston: Harvard Business School Press.

Makabe, Tomoko (1991) *How Can Japanese Management Make a Positive Contribution?*, Lewiston, N.Y.: The Edwin Mellen Press.

Nadler, Leonard (1984) "What Japan Learned from the U.S. – That We Forgot to Remember," *California Management Review* 26(4) (Summer): 46–61.

Nimgade, Ashok (1989) "American Management as Viewed by International Professionals," *Business Horizons* (November–December): 98–105.

Oh, Tai K. (1991) "Understanding Managerial Values and Behavior Among the Gang of Four: South Korea, Taiwan, Singapore and Hong Kong," *Journal of Management* 10(2): 46–56.

Paisley, Ed (1993) "Innovate, Not Imitate," *Far Eastern Economic Review* (13 May): 64–69.

Redding, Gordon (1992) "Capitalist Cooking Lessons," *Asian Business* (November): 50–52.

Totoki, Akira (1990) "Management Style for Tomorrow's Needs," *Journal of Business Logistics* 11(2): 1–4.

Waters, Dan (1991) *21st Century Management: Keeping Ahead of the Japanese and Chinese*, Singapore: Prentice-Hall.

Index